MW00827311

A CHICKEN IN THE WIND AND HOW HE GREW

STORIES FROM AN ADHD DAD

FRANK SOUTH

A RATTLESNAKE BOOK

PRAISE FOR FRANK SOUTH

For *Pay Attention*
... "hilarious, instructive and poignant, a funny and bittersweet tale of someone who, while not conquering them, has at least been able to keep his demons in check."

- LA Weekly

"Playwright Frank South's engrossing autobiographical solo show explores that unexpectedly shifting border that lies between the twin no man's land of genius and madness."

- Backstage

For *2 by South*
"Mr. South creates folksy, Middle American characters – then squeezes and squeezes them until they start to spurt blood."

- New York Times

These stories are as true as I could make them. Outside of family members, the names and descriptions of some people have been changed and many are composites of different individuals. Some incidents and locations have been changed or compressed. In the end, all stories are products of my fevered imagination in an attempt to understand what the hell was going on.

Grateful acknowledgement is made to ADDitude Magazine (ADDitudemag.com) where, with the exception of *Chicken, Meet Wind*, all stories first appeared over the last eight years, though many with different titles and in different form. Also thanks to the other publications and websites where some of these stories also appeared in whole or in part, including esperanza magazine, US News and World Report, Easy to Love but Hard to Raise (book and website), A Mom's View of ADHD, and Life of Dad.

Cover painting by Annette Bennett
© Annette Bennet annettebennett.com

Excerpt from "My Picture Perfect Family" by Kay Marner used with permission.
© Kay Marner

Excerpt from "For Trey" by Berna Deane South used with permission.
© Berna Deane South

RATTLESNAKE PUBLISHING

GOOD BOOKS WITH A BITE

Copyright © 2018 by Frank South
All rights reserved. Except in the case of short quotations in critical articles or reviews, no part of this publication may be reproduced, distributed, stored in a retrieval system, or transmitted in any form by any means without the prior written permission of the publisher.

Rattlesnake Publishing Inc.
Warner Robins, Georgia
rattlesnakepublishing.com
facebook.com/RattlesnakePublishing

ISBN-13: 978-0-9994878-0-8
ISBN-13: 978-0-9994878-1-5 (Kindle)

First Rattlesnake Edition: January 2018
June 2018 Awards Run
December 2018 Awards Run

Also by Frank South

Aloha Island - The Story of the Stones

Plays

Pay Attention

The Night Talkers

Rattlesnake in a Cooler
Precious Blood
(Produced Off-Broadway as *2 by South*)

For my mother,

Bernadeane South

Poet and guiding light

"But 'twas all of no use. The day seemed to be always just racing ahead of her, and turning a corner before she could catch up to it..."

- Margaret Sidney
"Five Little Peppers and How They Grew"

ACKNOWLEDGEMENTS

I am deeply grateful to everyone at ADDitude magazine for publishing my idiosyncratic stories and articles. To Susan Caughman, Anni Rodgers, who gave me my first assignment, Mary Kearl, Brittany Shoot, and all the editors who've worked on my material, your ideas, encouragement and appreciation have been gifts of incalculable value to me. I am especially grateful to Wayne Kalyn. His belief in my work, his effort to understand and clarify what he didn't, his ideas, and his conviction that there was always one more story I could tell, and one more draft to tell it better.

Thank you to all the mental health professionals I've been fortunate to have on my side over the years, particularly Richard Gibson M.D. back in Honolulu, and now in Georgia, Richard B. Ellis M.D., Christopher Pyle LCSW and everyone at Wellston Behavioral.

To my friends who helped this book along, Mark Travis, and all the Travis Workshop groups, Brian Shaughnessy, Joseph Lowery, and the many others who shared their time and thoughts, thank you. To Annette Bennett, there has never been a more perfect chicken.

I am of course indebted to my entire clan for their love and trust in me, the very definition of an unreliable narrator, to feature them in these stories. So, thank you to my strong, good-hearted brother, Dr. Robert C. South, to my mother, Berna Deane, to whom this book is dedicated, and to my father, Frank, whose unwavering courage in every battle he faced throughout his life was inspiring and humbling.

Thank you to our children Harry and Catherine, both of whom share similar brain wiring with me, for all your impatience, rebellion, and devotion.

Finally, this book would never have been written without my wife Margaret insisting it into existence. The faith, imagination, humor and editorial talent that she devoted to this manuscript are what gave it shape and meaning. She's done the same for me and our life together for over thirty years. Thank you, my love.

CONTENTS

Chicken, Meet Wind

Somewhere in the last third of the eighteen years I worked in television, I was again between jobs, but this time without any prospects. My wife, Margaret said, "So what? We'll sell the big house; find something human-sized, and cut back spending."

And we did. Our two kids seemed fine with it. Well, our oldest, Harry, was acting out some at school, but he was just in third grade and Margaret had it handled. She had it all handled. All I needed to do was get work. And she was confident that I could write and sell a pilot, or find a staff job before things got desperate.

But I wasn't confident or fine with anything. A dam had burst in my head. The lack of focus, tuning-out, and base-level confusion that I had always managed to muscle into submission whenever I needed to work or be responsible, had roared in and drowned all the will power or strength I had. Then the massive anxiety and self-loathing sharks swam in and tore everything left all to pieces, and I scrambled to our bedroom, curled up under the covers and stayed there for a week. A couple of days into week two, Margaret and I talked and figured it was time to scoop up what was left of me into a wheelbarrow and roll it over to the doctors to see what they could do.

After a complete physical, my GP suggested a psychologist. After a session or two the psychologist suggested tests. My dad was a scientist. As a kid I watched when he tested rats in his lab. I'm suspicious.

Doot – doot - doot – doot...

It's a clicker button like they've got on Jeopardy that's plugged into a computer. Simple: Press the button when you hear the atypical sound which is *dunn*. The *doot* is the typical and I heard nothing but *doots* since the psychologist left the testing room.

The chair I'm in tilts to the right just enough to so I have to keep adjusting myself. *Doot - doot...* When I looked down I could see it; two legs are about an eighth of an inch longer than the other two. Ergo, tilt. Fishy, don't you think? *Doot.* Maybe you don't get into little details like this. I do. *Doot.* Or maybe you do, but then you move on. I don't. *Doot.* Think about it. If everything is a setup, a trick, who are you supposed to trust?

Dunn. Wait- wait! *Doo* - click– *oot.* Swing and a miss.

They thought they could scare me with this lame bullshit? They were wrong. I was a Hollywood TV writer. I've got a PhD in lame and a black belt in bullshit. So here's the story line: I finish all the tests and the psychologist has called in the head of the California Psychological Association who says, "Mr. South, we'd like to apologize. You do not have ADHD or any other learning disability. What you *do* have is the most stunning genius level intuitive intellect we have ever seen. Pick up your MacArthur Grant at the door on your way out."

Tests over, I sat across from the psychologist in her office. Didn't look like she'd called in anybody. She's doing something on the computer. I stared at her nameplate, "Dr. Meghan Ott" on top of a wooden base carved into the shape of a playful sea otter. Little porcelain sea otters perch on shelves next to her medical books. Her family picture is framed by plastic sea otters chasing each other's tails.

My teeth ache. I want out of here.

"Mr. South? Mr. South?" Dr. Ott pointed to a bar graph on her computer that featured one bar that's ten times taller than its closest competitor.

"Is that me?" I asked.

"Yes. As I was saying, even after averaging in the norm for hypo-manic learning disabled individuals, what we're looking at with your case is, well, a significant score."

"So, is that good?"

"We don't like to put value judgments on clinical diagnoses." Maybe she doesn't, but come on - look my size on that bar graph.

"Simply put, Mr. South, you have abnormally high ADHD scores along with a number of pronounced comorbid disorders..."

"Comorbid? What's that mean? It sounds well, morbid."

Dr. Ott picks up a ceramic otter. I watch her fiddle with it as she talks. "Comorbidity refers to the presence of one or more disorders in addition to a primary and their combined effect. There's nothing morbid about it."

"Oh, I think there is..."

"Mr. South," she said, irritated now. Everybody gets irritated. But she's a shrink; it's her job to be patient and understanding. She's not cut out for this. "If I could have your attention," she said, "my point is that with the number and severity of your behavioral and cognitive disorders, it's surprising that you're able to function at all."

* * * *

When Harry was four years old we introduced him to the movie "The Wizard of Oz." From the jump he was completely absorbed, especially excited when the tornado hit and the farmhouse and Dorothy and Toto were pulled into the sky. Then when the house landed and Dorothy opened the door to the Technicolor Land of Oz, he lasted a few minutes then lost interest, got up and walked away. He didn't like bright, colorful Oz. "I like the chickens," he said, "The chickens in the wind."

We laughed, turned off the TV and had ice cream in the kitchen. But when I thought about it, I felt the same way. The chickens blown all over the sky in a tornado was like real life. The rest of the movie seemed made up.

FORGET ABOUT IT

It's a Friday afternoon in March 2009. We live in Honolulu. I'm on a deadline, trying to finish an article on procrastination that I've put off even starting for days, and now it's down to the wire.

My wife and twenty-year-old son are both at work and I'm home alone hunched over the computer mumbling stupid-lazy-stupid-stupid-stupid when my thirteen-year-old daughter, Coco slams home from school. She grabs a banana from the kitchen, and followed by Danny Boy, our big dog, walks into my office. With a sigh, Coco plops down in the chair across the desk from me. Danny sits next to her, sniffs her leg, and gives it a lick.

"Hey," she says to me.

"Hey," I say, "Listen, I can't talk -"

"I need you to look at my knee, Dad. It's really killing me."

Coco's knee is always really killing her. Or her shoulder, or her ankle, or her nails that she won't stop biting, last week she thought she might be going blind. I nod and give her a quick smile.

"Honey, I'm swamped right now so..."

She props her foot on my desk and examines her knee. "I swear, the nurse said I should stay off it." She takes a bite of banana. "My shoulder hurts too. But that's 'cause Jay hit me. He got kicked out of class today. But not for that, and coach says I need a new sports bra."

I tell her I'll look at her knee later but I have to get this work done first. She says okay, starts to limp away then turns back and says oh she forgot but could I sign this envelope for her - it's nothing - just field trip stuff

I need to get this article done that I rigorously put off all week so I quick sign so she'll let me work. Thing is, I want to believe that being an ADHD adult should make me a more understanding parent to my two adolescent ADHD children.

It just makes sense that since I bang around in the same kind of brain that my kids do that I'd naturally be more empathetic and patient with them than their mom, who at least is passably normal and doesn't have mind-meld instincts I do with our kids. I know first-hand the misfires in their mental wiring. I know what it feels like to constantly try and constantly fail, and all that rigmarole. Which for sleeves up parenting is like well, not useless, but of only occasional value.

But it was Margaret who found the urgent note from Coco's teacher about homework not turned in and projects not completed that was in that envelope I signed. I forget that my kids know I'm ADHD too, they know what I'm going through and they know how to use it when they need to. So sometimes I get played.

Here's the thing, though. The kids and I are always forgetting everything all the time. So we figure, in our house anyway, we've got a low-consequences zone going on. You forget, then do it now, or say next time, or whatever. The point is to keep the drama down, which keeps the tension down which keeps the frustration temper flare-ups down for all of us.

Both Coco and her older brother Harry, awhile back when I was lecturing Coco after completely losing it over a missing drawing pencil made it clear to me that I yell and go nuts at them, foaming at the mouth like a rabid rabbit jumping and screaming out of nowhere for the tiniest stuff, quite a lot.

And, by the way, Coco loved her big brother sticking up for her, and it didn't matter we all knew that it was an opportunistic family political play to get me to stop yelling at him, too. I granted them the point and we called a truce on frustration-fueled irrational insane flaming outbursts. Hence, the low-consequences zone.

All three of us do snap to, however, when Margaret quietly points out something we should draw a red circle around and put some effort into remembering to do -- whatever that thing is she wants us to keep in the normal- consequences zone.

I just turned sixty. I'm not big on birthdays, don't need presents, and due to the especially nuts time we were all going through this year – I made it clear weeks earlier that I didn't want a party or anything like that. But as the date grew nearer I started obsessing - Hey, this is my sixtieth birthday. You see movies where family members come from miles around to hug and kiss and shower love and presents on the father figure who turns sixty. Aren't there movies like that? It's traditionally a big deal, I think.

So, without any outward signs, I'm freaking out that this big day has been nudged by everyone, including Margaret into the low-consequences zone. I know, I know, I told them that's what I wanted, but still. Since everybody's busy and stressed I go to get the stuff for the birthday dinner myself. At least for my birthday I can go off my diet and indulge the one sin left to a recovering alcoholic non-smoker: Safeway bakery oatmeal raisin walnut cookies.

I roll the cart into Safeway past all the vegetables and stand stunned looking at the empty display kiosk where the boxes of oatmeal cookies should be. Safeway, for the first time in my admittedly poor memory, is out of the only thing that will make it all better.

At the bakery counter they say it'll be a couple of days. A minute or two goes by as this sinks in, the bakery lady and I looking at each other. "Did you really say a couple of days? What? Why the hell is that? Today that's all I want in this whole stupid useless world. You tell me, is that too much to ask? Is it? Is it? Is it?"

All that roars through my head, but not out my mouth. Maybe a little mumble drips out, but not anything intelligible. Hope not, anyway.

"Is there anything else I can help you with?" the bakery lady asks. I shrug, say no thanks and roll my cart back toward carrots.

The weekend goes by with apologies from Margaret and the kids and I keep saying who cares, forget about it, I hate birthdays.

And I do, but I can't get the mushy father-figure movie out of my head and I'm about to roll into some serious self-pity when I overhear my son, Harry tell Coco, "Really, don't worry about it,

Dad's never cared about his own birthday. He's cool that way." That did it. Suddenly it was time to live up to my son's vision of me and let the birthday, soppy movie and all, stay where it belonged in the low-consequences zone. But I was still mad.

Two days later in one of Coco's plop-downs at my desk after school she said, "Here, Happy Birthday, Dad," and hands me a box.

There's nothing inside it. The box is the thing. Folded and cut from two pieces of white cardstock paper she had formed a kind of Chinese food take-out carton. Using acrylic paint, crayon and pencil, she'd decorated it inside and out with carefully whimsical representations of palm trees and islands and rabbits and quilts and masks and flowers, and a skull. Caught again by her power of knowing, and the power in this family, I barely manage to croak out a thank you. She smiles makes the kissing sound and pads out of my office, her bare feet taking her to the kitchen to hunt up some mochi.

That was my only birthday present this year, except for over-hearing my son talking about me with respect and insight. And Margaret and I holding hands, walked down to the beach that night. Laughing at something I said, she kissed me.

DAD SOLO

It was right here a second ago. I had a great idea; I clipped the pen to the back of the pad and put the list down before I went to the carport to check if we still had that rolling duffle. Or maybe I took the list with me. Relax, breathe, visualize. That had to be it.

I turned and started to run to the carport and banged right into my twenty-year-old son, Harry, walking into my office.

"Whoa, sorry, son," I said.

He didn't seem to notice. "Um, Dad, I was wondering about something..."

"Look, I really can't talk now, Harry. Maybe later, okay?"

Harry muses about almost everything in existence and comes up with questions that I usually find interesting and enjoy talking with him about. But right now I'm busy freaking out because the day after tomorrow I'm leaving home for three months to rehearse and then open my solo show, *Pay Attention* in Los Angeles.

One – doing this show in Los Angeles scares me silly. Two – this will be the longest I've been away from my family and Hawaii in years and that scares me more. Not exactly a profile in courage, I know, but I'm trying to be honest here. Maybe I should dial the honesty back when I start looking pathetic; because I'm aware my separation pales in comparison to deployments that troops and their families in the Armed Services deal with. All right, it also pales in comparison to separations sales reps, corporate V.P.'s and airline personnel deal with regularly too. The fact is, my plight pales in comparison to almost any hardship suffered by any parent or spouse or family anywhere.

So what? It's still making me nuts. And that makes me irritable. And puts me way on edge, especially since I have to stop wallowing in self-pity where I'm comfortable and get myself organized for the trip.

Harry follows me out to the carport where I grab my list, and then wanders off when I continue to ignore him and focus on my all-important packing list. But by now I've mucked it up so much with arrows, boxes and underlines that it's illegible. Start over. Change it to three lists – Show / Trip Info & Tickets / Clothes & Toiletries. Does show wardrobe go under show or clothes? Doesn't matter, doesn't matter – just choose. I give each list a sub- heading – Have / Don't Have. Wait, I need to add a fourth list – Stationary & Computer related stuff. All four lists are on one yellow pad each starting a few pages after the previous to give them room – thinking ahead. I make scotch tape tabs on the side of the first page of each list. Looking good.

And suddenly I'm burning through this four-part list – its working great. I'm remembering stuff I forgot I needed – cross-referencing – double-covering in case of error and it's all neat and legible. It shines. It is a thing of beauty. It has almost magical depth and meaning. Over the top, maybe, but still -

It means you can pull it together.

It means you can be prepared, be structured, and be rational.

It means you can end up calm and organized at airport check-in and stroll through security with your shoes off, ID and boarding pass out, and head held high with the bemused attitude of a seasoned traveler in your smile and no trace of suicidal panic in your eyes. You have remembered everything. You have forgotten nothing. With your beautiful list strapped on like bullet-proof vest, you know you can handle whatever curves and confusions life throws at you.

Its three p.m., later than I thought. But that's fine. Packing, getting on the plane and all the rest of that trip stuff is covered in the perfect, beautiful list calmly sitting on my desk, in front of me.

I decide to leave it there and to walk, not rushing, out to the carport to get the rolling duffle. I pass my son, Harry, and our over-sized standard poodle Danny-Boy lying together on the living-room couch watching Family Guy on his iPod, and give them both a calm, fatherly nod.

In the garage, I stop and look at the locked door to the storage closet where the suitcases are kept and realize I need my keys to open it. No problem. Still calm, I walk back inside past my son and poodle who don't look up from the iPod this time, to get my keys from the desk drawer and maybe while I'm there check my beautiful list for any information that might help with the duffle decision.

The list isn't on my desk. Why does this keep happening? I left it right there, before I walked out, I know I did. Idiot idiot idiot. Back to the carport, moving into a trot – list not there, but take a minute look around the carport carefully – check on the art table, on the junk shelves – no and no. I zoom back through the front door to the office. Danny Boy barks as I fly by.

In my office I start tearing through drawers and bookshelves. I feel a panic attack coming on. I stop and activate the coping skill set from my psychiatrist – relax, breathe – slow and steady then visualize. I'm supposed to lie back in a chair or lie down when I'm doing this but this is an emergency and it's not working anyway.

Where is it – where is it – where is it? I swear I'll rip this whole house down to the studs if I have to. I hear Harry behind me, stepping into the office.

"Um, Dad..."

I'm tearing into the back bookshelves. "What, Harry? What!?" "I just..."

I turn to him, my face flushed in frustration. "Can't you leave me alone for a second?"

"Sure," he says, "But out in the driveway? I found this yellow pad of yours on the hood of the Jeep." Harry holds my beautiful list with scotch tape tabs and promise of sanity out to me. As I take it I say, "Harry, I'm sorry. I'm sorry I yelled, and I'm... well, I'm going to miss you."

Harry smiles and pats me on the shoulder. "I'll miss you too, Dad," he says, "But you know, you gotta calm down."

He's right, of course he is. But I've just realized I forgot to confirm the car rental – I didn't even put it on the list. Harry stands there watching me as I sit down behind my desk and start clacking furiously away on the computer.

I want to stop and appreciate my son right here and now – tell him how much he means to me. I know that's the important thing to do. But the overbearing frantic urgency is still running things, so I don't. Instead, I curse and bang away at the keyboard desperate to confirm my rental car right now before all the rental cars in the entire greater Los Angeles area are rented and there's not one car left for me anywhere because I was disorganized and forgot until it was too late. Harry sees the cooked brain look in my eyes.

"It's stuffy in here, Dad," he says, and opens the sliding door to the back yard before he heads back into the living room and gets back to the Family Guy episode that he and our dog were watching on his iPod on the couch.

The computer isn't cooperating – the car website keeps crashing halfway through me filling out the form. And now day-biting mosquitoes are attacking my legs through the door Harry opened because I haven't gotten around to fixing the screen.

I slap at my legs, cursing. I think I'm hyper-ventilating now. Then our dog, Danny-boy comes in, puts his head on my desk and raises an eyebrow at me (I swear, he does this.) He wants to know what's going on with me and when I'll cut it out. I stare back at him, hyperventilating. Well, me too, dog, me too.

He lets out a big disappointed sigh. I've been running around the house upsetting him and my son with my panicky preparations for this stupid trip. Now my wife, Margaret, and my daughter are back from the store and my banging around and cursing in my office is upsetting them. Danny-Boy seems to be a calm, concerned emissary.

Maybe I'm crazier than even the most pessimistic psychiatrists I've had think I am. One once warned my wife that, though I seemed to be stable at the time, she should call him immediately if I woke up in the morning and told her I wanted to buy Japan – he said he wasn't joking. But I don't want to buy Japan, though I do like the shoji screens we have in our house, I don't know what I'd do with a whole country full of them. What I want is to get to Los Angeles without forgetting something important.

Danny-Boy, in cross-species mind-reading communication says, "I'm a dog and I know what's important. And you don't have a clue, ass-wipe."

Right then, Margaret, Coco, and Harry all come into my office. Margaret has picked up some stuff for my trip at the store, and the kids want to know what they can do to help. I look at them. My family. My best friend / wife, my two funny, shining children and a dog who talks to me with his eyebrows. These people and this dog and the love we have for each other are the only really important things in my life. And Danny-Boy's right – in giving in to my frantic brain overload, I'd lost my moorings to what made my life mean something – to me.

No wonder I was hyper-ventilating. And no wonder I'm upset. I don't want to be away from them. I turn off the computer, they refuse my apologies, so I thank them for being in my life, they say yeah, whatever and we all decide to go to Burger King and blow off anything else. On the way out the door Margaret gives me a quick kiss and whispers, "We love you, you lunatic."

* * * *

I land at LAX and head into the unnerving, unbelievable chaos super-focused on the baggage claim signs and arrows, and chanting baggage claim five, baggage claim five, baggage claim five, over and over to myself. This is the point in travel where I tend to get distracted, forget something and then panic and screw things up even worse. Or the fear of getting distracted and screwing up gets so intense that I trigger a panic attack without any outside stimulus at all. So, I'm going down escalators, into blank over-lit tunnels, moved on people-mover strips, pushed through revolving no-backup or alarms-will-sound-you-idiot doors, and dumped out looking for number five, five, don't see five – did I have it right? Breathe. Breathe.

Then I hear my name called, and once again, realize how lucky I am in my life. A family friend of many years is there to pick me up and take me to her home to stay with her and her family for two months in a modest suburb, far enough from Hollywood and what I'm doing there to be sane.

The lurking panic suddenly doesn't even have a crack to find a toe-hold as I sit in the living room and catch up with her and her husband, mom and kids, with pictures of her kids and my kids together back when they really were kids, looking down from the walls. Maybe everything has a chance to work out.

The next day I wake up missing my wife and family and the nagging feeling that I shouldn't be here. But the generosity of our old friends around me pushes it back again, and I drive into Burbank to start rehearsing with my director, Mark Travis. More generosity comes my way - we're rehearsing in his living room so I don't have to rent a space.

We start work and it is rocky. The panic is coming back, rising slowly like that goop in lava lamps. All the ingrained deep fears about exposing my mental, um, weirdness... okay, okay - my ADHD and other pronounced co-morbid disorders - those fears are boiling over and making it hard to concentrate or to even focus at all.

So over and over we try one part or another and I can't remember the words. I can't remember any of my lines – which is problematic, considering that the play is two hours of just me talking and acting out all the parts. My director looks sympathetic as we once more try again and I mess up again. Now he's starting to look worried. The lava lamp in my head is hot, bright red, bubbling faster than it's meant to, and about ready to blow through the glass.

* * * *

What a shitty day. As I left Mark's house he said positive, encouraging things. I'm not buying. Heading down the freeway to impose on my generous friend and her family for another night, a wave of clarity floods the rental car and I see the insane selfishness of my raging over-inflated ego thinking I could take money from my wife and kids so I could waste all these people's time and effort to prop me up on a stage to spew and whine artless crap about me-me-me is wrong and, and, sickening... what the hell is wrong with me? Maybe I'm a sociopathic psycho. That's what they do right? Don't care, only think of themselves? I know intellectually from tons of reading and countless shrink hours that these kinds of messages are echoes from the past and have no real weight, but it doesn't matter. My head is dry and empty, and right now my body has decided to crash the party.

My heart is beating way too fast, my chest burns, can't get my breath. Tires screech and horns honk like mad as I try to cut across lanes to an exit. Heart attack, this is good. Die now, skip the whole sickening act. Just as I make it to the exit, the urge to breathe and the burning chest pain collide in my throat and I throw up, get a small breath, then throw up again, but I keep my head up so I can keep most of the mess of bile and junk on me instead of the rental and so I can see and drive, and use the turn signal at the top of the exit and get myself stopped in the parking lot of a gas station/mini-mart without killing anyone. I lean back against the headrest, trying out the breathing, appreciating everything about it.

So not a heart attack - I can breathe again. Heart rate going down some. Chest still burns, but less. Just a top of the line anxiety attack bringing on a good showing of acid reflux.

I'm trying to breathe slowly with my eyes closed – too little, too late, but it helps anyway and I know I have to do what I'd always rather avoid, and face this ruinous self-destruction of mine head-on.

With the advent of cell phones, the sight of someone alone in a parked car talking out to air doesn't look as weird as it used to. But then again, at this point, I'm yelling at myself and slapping at the dashboard over and over. And I've got vomit on my shirt. I am, if nothing else, dramatic. My luck holds, though, and aside from a couple of odd looks, no one interrupts me hollering, "Stop it!" and "Listen to yourself!" at the top of my lungs. This is not what my psychologist recommends you deal with yourself after you've finally managed to calm down after a particularly ruinous, nearly fatal freeway panic attack. Sometimes a little exorcism does the trick for me in the short run. A little later, a little calmer, I leave the shirt in the car, I go into the mini-mart bathroom in a zipped up jacket and wash up a little. On the way out I get an LA sweat shirt, a little pack of Oreos and a can of double-shot mocha as a reward for 1) putting down the panic attack, 2) regaining enough self-regard to not give up, and 3) not crying too much.

I am lost, however. So I get a freeway map with my rewards, sit back in the car and try to figure out how to get back where I'm staying at my friend's house.

After the snack, putting on the sweatshirt and checking the map, I make it back to my friend's home and have carne asada and homemade salsa with her and her family. We talk and play with the dog, and I find myself getting used to what I will have to do to get the job done here in Los Angeles before I get to go home.

My work starts going a little better in rehearsals – still not great, but I'm resigned to the feeling that there's nothing I can do to keep my ADHD, anxiety, hypomania and other comorbid disorders from sabotaging and destroying this project in the end.

Here's what's weird – well everything seems weird right now – but here's what's most weird: I'm going around cheerfully doing what I'm supposed to do in rehearsals and in the business dealings with the theater, etc. Outwardly, I seem energetic and cheerful and positive. But I know this is all just me going through the motions because it's what's expected, and that in the end I'll at best pull off a mediocre show, which is also what's expected because after all, I'm a stammering brain-scrambled nut-ball.

This kind of self-reduced expectation vortex can suck you down into a kind of safety zone where you feel better because you're all comfy in a lowest common denominator baseline existence. You don't ask much of yourself because you and everyone else know you're not capable. No disappointments when you don't try. And you're smiling and pleasant all the time.

So, this is how I'm operating when I get a call from Coco back home. She says she'd "just like to chat." That's a phrase she picked up from my dad last Christmas. She likes the way her grandfather the professor talks.

Coco tells me that she's trying harder in PE, especially in volleyball. She forgot about a report for English, and so she'll have to do it this weekend and turn it in late which stinks, because that means no sleep-over at Lexi's house. In math, a boy next to her keeps grabbing at her pencil when she's working because he wants her to "totally lose it," which she is famous for, when pushed enough. But she said today she switched seats with a friend. She's still behind in math, but she's thinking the new seat will help, and she's still got that A in art.

Then Coco says, "How are you doing?"

"I'm all right," I say, "I'm just rehearsing. You know, doing the same things over and over. Trying to get it right, and not."

"Sounds boring, when you put it like that, Dad."

She's right. No wonder I was so unhappy. "But your play isn't boring," she says.

I thank my daughter for the compliment, but she's not praising me, she's reminding me that I've always told her not to hide behind your ADHD, dyslexia or any other learning or behavior difference that puts you outside the norm. Don't use it as an excuse when you're tired or scared, I told her. She reminds me what I said to her - don't join up with the crowd that wants to label and defeat you, they don't need any help.

I tell her good night and thanks – I'll quit making excuses and try harder tomorrow. And we'll chat again tomorrow night, our voices going back and forth on the two-way parenting street.

* * * *

Rehearsals for the *Pay Attention* kept going through April and though I'd taken my daughter's words to heart, it was still difficult for me to believe that anything good was going to come out of all the work Margaret (producer & wife), Mark (director & friend), and I (playwright, actor, and chump change loser mental case) had put into the project, because at the core, whatever was going to happen really depended on me - the weak link.

Screwing up and disappointing others is so much a part of the everyday life experience of people with ADHD and other mental health or developmental challenges that I think, by the time we're adults, many of us have fashioned a cushioned protective fail-safe coat around us as one of our principal coping and survival skills. Stitched together out of all the myriad failures that we've catalogued and kept, its insidious message is simple and debilitating: Of course we'll fail. Look at the evidence. What else did we expect?

This protective coat's negative message is warm and comforting because we can step back from ourselves, look at the evidence and stand on the sideline with all the other smart people we imagine judging us and shake our heads and say "See? I told him he should have stayed home and kept his mouth shut."

Imagining success when you know you don't have a prayer is impossible. I was thinking about quitting, it was easy to imagine failure – been there, done that – when one day in the middle of a mid-rehearsal self-questioning stammering fit it hit me: I don't know I don't have a prayer. I don't know anything.

One of the many things ADHD has taught me is that the only thing certain is uncertainty. That's when I started pulling off the fail-safe coat. It hit me that without ADHD I wouldn't be doing this play at all, and no matter how that or my hypomania, alcoholism, anxiety, depression, word-retrieval and short-term memory issues, and a stammer that comes on like a freight train when I get tense might have limited me in the world, they've expanded my world a million times more. These impairments, disabilities, disorders, or whatever they're called, are not anything I'd wish on someone else, but they're mine, and they're me, and that's fine.

And as a dad, if there a couple of things I can pass on to my two kids from my experience they're these:

1) As long as you accept them and use them as an integral part of yourself, any mental health or developmental challenges you have won't stop you from trying to do anything in life you want to do. They'll just make it a lot more interesting.

2) Definitions of "do": Trying and succeeding, trying and failing and learning and trying again, changing your mind and trying something else, never giving up.

COCO'S PERFECT STORM

Kids with ADHD sometimes get so worn down with the immense effort it takes to do what they expect of themselves, that when a perfect storm of missed assignments, overdue work, broken promises, and looming deadlines hits them they call themselves stupid and lazy and worse before anyone else can.

Besides ADHD, my daughter Coco also has to deal with other learning disabilities like pretty severe dyslexia and some memory issues that are similar to mine. Consequently, for years it seemed as though she'd never be able to read or write. In second grade she still couldn't recognize letters. It was a daily frustrating and heartbreaking struggle for her as she worked at it at home with us, in school with her teachers, and after school with tutors. There were days where she'd seem to get it – recognize letters and words and how sentences worked, and then the next day it'd be gone again.

"I can't do this! I can't! I'm too stupid," she'd cry, imprisoned by the constant defeat. Each time we'd continue the patient encouragement, always reassuring her that she wasn't stupid at all. We told her that soon she'd be able to understand, though we too were beginning to lose faith that that day would ever come.

The day did come, though. When she was eleven years-old, Coco somehow put it all together, and seemingly overnight, made a startling breakthrough in reading and writing. Of course it wasn't overnight. Breaking through this barrier was the cumulative result of the years of her hard work combined with the mystery of the growing pre-adolescent brain. Now, at thirteen, she writes for school assignments, and also writes stories about her life. She's able to read at school above her grade level and also reads like crazy for enjoyment - going through books from the whole "Twilight" vampire series to the juvenile delinquent classic, "The Outsiders" to the death and disaster-filled "The History of Shipwrecks." She likes her reading enjoyment with a little edge.

Coco had worked hard and had busted through a huge barrier not only in reading and writing, but also a barrier of defeat that had held her confidence and hope hostage to an unrelenting internal judge constantly denigrating her self-image. She broke that pattern when she accomplished what had for so long seemed impossible, and she reawakened her natural curiosity and openness as well.

But at the end of this spring's semester, everything flipped backward for her. Despite our help and her dedication to checking her planner during the semester, Coco had lost or not completed overdue homework in Math, English, and Science. Somehow she buckled down in the last couple of weeks, went to study hall every day after school and managed to get it all turned in.

Then at the end of the very last week, the night before the last Social Studies class, it hits her that she's completely spaced her final project and class presentation on the history of Norfolk Island that's due tomorrow and she hasn't even started it. And she's supposed to do it as a Power Point presentation in front of the whole class and then it also hits her that, despite what she's told her teacher, she doesn't have the first idea how to make a Power Point presentation. Coco loves her Social Studies teacher, and that only makes things worse.

"She'll hate me!" she yells, tears welling, "I can't do this! I can't! I'm too stupid! Everybody knows I'm stupid. She'll hate me and give me an F!" When my wife, Margaret, tries to help her, Coco lashes out, throwing her planner down, "Leave me alone, you don't know anything. I can't do this – It's impossible!"

Everybody, and certainly every junior high school kid, has faced a similar landscape of possible defeat. But sometimes my daughter and the other kids with ADHD and comorbid LD's face that landscape knowing that no matter what they accomplish there are so many land mines of demoralizing surprises ahead of them that defeat and failure seem preordained. They get worn down with the immense effort it takes to do what they expect of themselves, that when a perfect storm of missed assignments, overdue work, broken promises, and looming deadlines hits them they fall back inside the barriers they've worked so hard to break down, and are once again trapped, but protected, inside their low expectations. These are the times that try kids' souls.

And that's when I, cheerful Dad, call from Los Angeles to see how every body's doing before I head to the theatre to do my show, and I get the whole thing over the phone. The spaced report and PowerPoint presentation on Norfolk Island, that she told her teacher she knew how to make a PowerPoint presentation, when she didn't have the first clue and it was 6pm and the whole mess was due first thing the next morning.

Coco is in despair, frozen by the certainty of the looming failure and in the barriers of expected failure and lashing out in panic when her mom tries to help. I try to say what I can to be encouraging and help keep this from being a defeat that defines the end of this school year for her, but I'm hearing this high drama from Coco and Margaret over the phone from three thousand miles away, and I can hear their frustration with my absence as they tell me they have to hang up now and deal with this themselves. Being a Dad over the phone is nowhere near being a dad who is actually there. I have to put my phone down and wait to hear how it will turn out.

Three hours later I get a call from my wife and daughter. Facing a tidal wave of impossibility, Coco, unaware she was doing it, pulled out an ADHD secret weapon: hyperfocus.

After finally allowing her mom to show her how to make a basic PowerPoint page Coco demanded to be left alone to figure out the rest, do her research, write her report, and make her presentation. Over the next couple of hours she typed and moused away, never leaving the computer in the living room, never taking her eyes off the screen, mumbling and musing to herself over interesting things she'd found or new ideas she'd come up with as she worked. Never once did she get distracted or bored or even notice anything in the world except her Social Studies project. And with self-doubt and second-guessing banished due to some kind of emergency decree in her head, she blazed through it.

Margaret said it was an amazing thing to witness. Coco didn't see what was so amazing, but she was proud and happy that her report was done and the PowerPoint was safely tucked onto a flash drive for school in the morning. The self-hatred and panic banished, she and her mom were now going to have some ice cream and then get some sleep. We'll keep working on the organizational and other skills to deal with the procrastination problems, but this time Coco's ADHD hyper-focus saved the day, and by the way, she got an "A."

With all the sometimes overwhelming challenges that ADHD presents to children and adults, it seems only fair that it also can give you an awesome positive ability to pull out when we need to bust through the barriers and realize we're not stupid, lazy, or crazy after all. We might even have super-powers.

* * * *

There are a couple of cautions about hyperfocus I'll talk about with Coco when I get home. The first, which is easy enough for her due to her nature, is that some psychologists and others doubt the existence of hyperfocus. Even my spell-check doesn't think it exists. So it's not something you want to brag about in middle school, where peer judgement is deadly enough as it is.

The difficult thing to accept is that you can't depend on it. You can't let procrastination run wild and count on hyperfocus to save you. Sometimes it just won't show up.

And in my experience it's a tool that takes time to learn how to use and get some control over. If left to run wild without reins, hyperfocus can hijack an unsuspecting unusually wired brain to all kinds of places it doesn't want to go. You get pulled down one rabbit hole after another following one solid well-lit idea that leads to another idea that's not solid or well-lit, but can be taken apart and interestingly, has light inside, which tumbles down another offshoot hole, where near the bottom there's a whole family of faintly lit related ideas waiting to be taken apart and examined to see if any can shed new light on the original idea.

They won't, but it doesn't matter now. My brain is humming, calm and happy inhabiting some deep twisty place, prying open little unrelated whys and what-nots. Until I lose interest. When my interest snaps off, I look up startled. I don't know what time it is, where I am, what I'm doing, or how to get out of there. Sometimes that triggers a panic attack, but usually just a medium-long confusion spell and embarrassment. One rarely has much to show for a full-anarchy hyperfocus run. It's hard to remember what was so interesting down there when you're brushing off dirt, blinking in the full light of day.

It's a lesson every Marvel comic book preaches: All superpowers have a price.

HARRY'S HORROR STORY

As an ADHD alcoholic adult, I spent years self-medicating with alcohol. And though it turned down the noise in my head, it just about destroyed me and my life in the process. I can never forget the damage cocktails and I did together, so alarm bells rang all over when it looked like my ADHD son, Harry, might head down the same road.

When Harry turned twenty-one he decided to try out drinking - Pina Coladas, Schnapps, and other sweet vodka and rum drinks. He and his friends partied for the whole week of his birthday, and he spent all the birthday money he got from relatives on booze. We did everything we could to make sure he was safe and that nobody was drinking and driving. Margaret, despite the work she was swamped with, even put the whole gang up at our house one of the nights. Par-tee! Woo-hoo! Though I want to be a supportive husband, I am glad I was in Los Angeles rehearsing and not home for that.

The weird thing is this – I've talked to my son and daughter about alcohol and drugs openly. We've talked about ADHD and substance abuse. Plus, Harry especially remembers when I got sober, and he's proud that I am. He brings it up to friends and parents of his friends. But here he is walking to 7-11 to spend the last of his birthday cash on peppermint schnapps, then the other night coming home and throwing up.

Part of me wants to see this as how he'll learn. Part of me wants to laugh and shake my head at his youthful excess. But the largest part of me looks at my son and the challenges he's facing in life and I'm terrified for him. To his credit, he says that now that he's tried it, he's done with getting drunk. I hope that's true. But I remember how many thousands of times I said that before I stopped blowing apart my life and finally got sober. So I'm still terrified, and no matter how confused and stressed I get in my life, if he thinks I'm going to back-off and keep my nose out of his life, he's crazy.

But after talking with Margaret, I decided that Harry was not me and that overreacting to my fears with restrictions and lectures wouldn't help him make the right decisions. Maybe I won't be able to keep my son and daughter from repeating my mistakes, but I'll lighten up, keep talking and listening to them and maybe they'll at least have an idea what's coming. That was the plan.

So, when Margaret flew from our home in Honolulu to Los Angeles for the closing week of my show in June we left Harry at home alone to take care of the dog, Danny-Boy, and look after the house while we were out of town and his sister stayed with friends on the other side of the island.

It was the honor system. He knew the rules. No parties and no drugs, which he promised us he hadn't even tried and had no interest in. We called to check in and he seemed fine. Then three days later we got a phone call from Harry. He had some things he wanted to tell us before we heard it from the neighbors. Apparently as soon as Margaret got on the plane our house turned into Animal House. Only in real life it wasn't funny.

It was a nightmare of loud parties, drinking, pot-smoking, and Harry's drunken friends arguing with furious neighbors at three a.m. - one of whom is a cop – and Danny-Boy gets out and runs off down the street. He knew this was trouble and wanted nothing to do with it.

Now, Harry told us most of the story, but not all. Margaret got the complete scoop when she flew home. My task was to handle Harry over the phone from Delaware where I'm visiting my parents after the close of the play, while Margaret heads back to Hawaii to deal with him and the neighbors face to face,

Okay, I'm freaking out. My head's exploding with the biggest "I told you so" in human history – or my human history, anyway – on top of full tilt fury slamming up against deep love and concern for my kid and hey what about our poor dog – he had to have been scared shitless by all of that insanity - and the other kids' parents – legal issues – and damn it, he <u>promised</u>.

But I knew, I did. I knew he wouldn't be able to resist temptation. I was a twenty-one year-old kid once. But this isn't about being a kid, this is about trust, ADHD, and alcohol, and the damage my boy can do to himself. This could have been even worse – what if someone had gotten seriously hurt? The more I think about it the more freaked and seriously pissed off I get.

God, I'm going to tan that kid's hide.

I pick up the phone, start punching in Harry's number and then snap it closed. I have to do some breathing. A panic attack could undermine the righteously indignant avenging angel rant I'm planning to bring down on his head. But as I breathe I remember the nightmares I poured into my parents' lives when I was in my teens and twenties, and I realize that nothing I've been thinking about saying will help any of us. The truth is I don't really know what to say to Harry at all. But I'm his dad; I have to figure out something. Harry's sitting in Hawaii waiting for my call.

I'm angry and disappointed in my son, but I don't know what to say to him besides that. So since its 5 o'clock here in Delaware, I avoid calling Harry by making martinis for my parents. I bring the drinks to my mom and dad in their matching wingback chairs along with some crackers and sliced cheese. I like waiting on them. Cripes, they should get something after everything I put them through over the years. I tell my mom and dad what's going on as I get them refills. My dad has especially strong opinions about Harry's misdeeds.

As I close the door to the guest room and punch Harry's number on my cell, I'm hit by the weird irony of a recovering alcoholic son serving drinks to his mother and father before calling up his own son to give him hell about getting drunk and screwing up. I stop the call – I dread the draconian restrictions and restitutions I must and will bring down on him, but I still don't know how to get Harry to really learn from this.

Then I remember when I dropped out of college. It was the morning after I'd shown up on my parents' front porch in the middle of the night screaming drunk, waving an empty scotch bottle and blaming them for everything before I threw up in the bushes. And I still remember what my father said to me.

So I punch in Harry's number again, and when he picks up I say, "First, I love you."

When I got back to Hawaii, Margaret and my daughter Coco had already left on a trip to see other relatives. So Harry and I spent a couple of weeks getting the house cleaned up for their return and talking. I was, as I've said, on edge and wanted to get some things talked out with my son. Things like responsibility, honesty, alcohol abuse, and the hard reality of living as an adult with ADHD and other learning disabilities. But I couldn't find a way to bring any of that up that didn't fray my nerves worse than they were and make Harry pull away and shut down.

Then finally, we found something else to talk about instead of talking directly about his growing up, our relationship, his friends, his life goals and like that. The conversational duck-blind we used was "Dexter," a TV show he was passionate about. During our two weeks alone he showed me all the episodes he'd saved, and during this "Dexter" marathon I began to see what attracted my son so strongly to the show.

Harry had been on me for over a year to watch "Dexter" with him, but I'd resisted. My god, the hero of the show is a serial killer. Nearly every week someone gets butchered by this guy. Harry pointed out that I read tons of thrillers and murder mysteries. But I said they don't glorify violence like that, and besides they're books. Books are better than TV, any intellectual snob knows that, and I'm an intellectual snob that used to write TV, so who knows better than me? Well, in this case, he was right and I was wrong. Every once in a while being wrong happens to a parent, with increasing frequency as everyone in the mix gets older. Admitting it is the hardest part.

But as I said, I could see what drew Harry to this series about a guy who feels like he's wearing a disguise so he can pass as being normal in a world where he struggles to find real connections to others. Harry identified with him, and as we watched I identified too.

Dexter definitely is a butchering psychopath with monstrous murder daddy dreams, but the character is struggling constantly with questions of morality, right and wrong, and the responsibilities of love. So, episode after episode, night after night, of this very bloody and frightening TV horror show Harry and I found a way to communicate about him, his life, and the even more frightening horror of growing up.

NEW DANCE PARTNER

I do not like change. I'm not sure exactly when it happened. I used to be bright, open and adventurous. I liked to go to parties. Not anymore.

I've thought that maybe my personality changed when I was forty-nine, had the breakdown and got diagnosed with all the mental junk. Then sometimes I think my personality changed when I got sober. Other times I think it changed in the last year, or I think my personality hasn't changed at all, that I've always been the same and have only recently begun to see that I've spent my whole life inside a slippery clown suit in order to make it through each terrifying day.

If that's the truth, the clown suit is permanently off now and is stuffed in the garbage can at the curb. So who the hell am I?

My core ADHD hypomanic alcoholic self hasn't really changed. It's just more exposed. I'm still easily led by a distracting thought triggered by a random sight, sound, or smell that turns into a shadow of an idea that wheezles down into a tiny notion inside a detail about whatever caught me that's tucked away in an even tinier wrinkle in my brain. If I can just get in there with a toothpick or something to dig it out.

I'm not a big-picture guy. I can't stand brain-storming meetings. I cannot bat ideas around with other people. You can keep your bat. I'll keep my idea and go somewhere else.

You cannot put me in the same room with people who are getting a feel for the larger landscape, finding common ground, and developing big sweeping changes. I refuse to participate in this evil treatment of human thought. And I'm not a fan of change, especially big changes made by other people. Stay the same and leave me alone. That's all I ask these days. So when my therapist of eight years – the only therapist that I could really talk to – decided to close his practice, I was not happy.

Good therapy, I'd discovered with this guy, is a communication dance, rhythm and steps building trust until you trip over unexpected discoveries together. Now my dance partner was closing shop, going into teaching, and passing me off to some young guy. I'm too old for this bullshit; but I need my meds, so I have to go meet my new dance partner tomorrow at one pm. I've never met him and I hate him. This will never work.

I've hitch-hiked across the country not knowing whether I was going to sleep that night on a rock hill outside of Wendover, Utah, or in a vagrant's cell in Vernal. I've done both, and the cell is more comfortable, plus you get free pancakes and eggs for breakfast.

In my twenties, I moved from Missouri to California, to New York, then back to California, all the while changing jobs, life goals, and girlfriends constantly. I'd been married and divorced twice. It didn't seem an unusual or stressful way to live at the time; instead, it seemed like the best way to keep things interesting. ADHD is all change all the time. I dealt with it by embracing and surfing the chaos. Only now do I appreciate how stone scared I really was.

I finally settled down in Los Angeles with my third and real-deal wife, Margaret. For fifteen years I wrote and produced TV in one city. Even with success in my grasp, I still managed to make it feel like our whole family was hitching across Utah not knowing where we are going to be come nightfall. An easily distracted hypomanic drunk isn't the best guy to be driving the bus.

We made another move - to Hawaii, the most remote land mass on earth, a fact I found deeply comforting. I got sober and, a short time later, I started going to a therapist here, Dr. G. He started by seeing my son. Pretty soon he was seeing the whole family. I didn't just go in for the quick med visits; something in my relationship with him helped me to really work at therapy. I haven't ever trusted anyone enough to do that before. Dr. G read my writing as I worked on things. We talked profoundly and stupidly and laughed. Two years in, I was shocked to find myself more honest and unguarded with him than I'd ever been with anyone in my life besides Margaret. This eight-year relationship, this dance of minds, became an integral part of my life. I was finally able to calm down enough to actually see the world around me. I was able to be present enough to actually see the people besides me in my life.

At the end of our last session we shook hands, and Dr. G handed me an appointment slip for the new doc. I sat in my car in the parking lot for a while, afraid to start the car, afraid to drive, afraid to go home. But I did anyway. Made a stop at Safeway on the way home and picked some oatmeal raisin cookies.

A week later, new office, same-old forms to fill out. We shake hands, sit. He puts a pad and pen on his crossed leg. Dr. G never used a pad. And this new doc is way young. I decide to be super careful here. But then he asks an interesting question, and my answer surprises me. All right, maybe I'll take another step. Maybe this can be good, or good enough, if I can get him to stop with the note pad.

ON THE ROCKS, WITH A TWIST

You could call this a Hollywood alcohol and drug story, but it's not. It's not even a cautionary tale about a rube being misguided by hubris and ego, though I am a rube, for sure, and I did pack my head with a bunch of self-inflating lies.

The honest dirt floor of this story has more to do with the difference between facts and excuses, and how much you're willing to lose, and how much pain you're willing to cause before you finally own up.

Starting with what we know. I was diagnosed with ADHD, hypomania, depression, and anxiety after a breakdown I had when I was forty-nine years old. It seemed to me I had pretty good reasons to fall apart even without all the medical jargon. After crawling back from one implosion of my TV career, I had managed to snag another job retooling a show that, after months of work, promptly bombed. After that, I went to meetings for other shows and the more I wanted any job, the less anyone wanted me. My new agent said people weren't "responding" to me. I was too desperate and scattered. The ADHD I didn't know I had was becoming increasingly obvious and irritating to everyone else. The meetings got shorter and more perfunctory. I stopped being desperate and began telling people what I really thought about their shows. Pretty soon, not even my agent returned my calls.

I sat at home pacing by the phone trying to calm the incessant, negative, vicious chattering going on in my head, the same negative chattering that banged around in there when I came home after a day being a serious big shot. And I did the same thing I did back when we still had our big house and all that, I had a few martinis. The distracting ADHD noise in my head was the same whether I was a success or a failure. Every chattering idea started with, "Yeah, but what about this?" And wound off down yet another unexplored, dark wormhole twisting down to the same pit of self-loathing they all did. But the martinis always worked. They muffled the chattering, plugged up the wormholes. That done, I could sit inside my head drinking, singing, and peeking out the window at everyone else: The interior ADHD noise cure. My exterior was droopy eyed, inattentive, and slurred words. But I was inside, so what did I care? For years, Margaret had tried smashing through that window to pry the bottle out of my hand. But I held on. I was smart, persuasive, contrite, and lied my ass off when I had to, because without the gin or vodka I'd smash myself to pieces inside the walls of my head prison.

Finally, it all came unglued in one evening at home trying to help my then ten-year-old son with his homework. Unseen, by me anyway, psychological stress factors had increased to such a level that they had crushed the walls of my gin-soaked cell and busted everything else I'd built around myself to a million pieces, and I ended up curled up on the bedroom floor in a fetal position. By the time I'd managed to finally scramble to the doctors for help, I was flailing around in the deepest, darkest panic in memory. I was a quivering, weepy mess. I told the therapists I didn't know why my whole life had fallen apart so suddenly. Why couldn't I keep it together? I always had before.

"Frank is a capable child, but has not yet found his place in the group. He seems to feel he must be the clown and constantly entertain the class. For a while he was better, but during the last few days, he has become almost impossible." – My Kindergarten Teacher, Nov. 5, 1954

Okay, maybe not. My childhood was happy -- for me, anyway. Teachers pulled out their hair. Boy Scouts kicked me out permanently for stealing a transistor radio on a hike honoring honesty and then lying about it. I accidentally set some small fires that adults had to put out, got stuck in a few construction sites and got lost running away. To this day, I look at cops as nice folks who will get me out of jams and get me home safe.

My adulthood was happy too -- again, for me, and only sort of. Two previous marriages ending in divorce, countless failed relationships, and an early history of too many jobs in too many places all over the country doesn't sound like a joyful noise, even to me. I was flying solo, without a net, wings, or a place to land. Once in my twenties, after saving and planning for months, my best friend and I hitched to New York from Columbia, Missouri, on our way to Europe. In New York, on the way to the airport, I changed my mind, deserted my best friend and went back to Missouri on the bus. I started and quit college twice, then moved from Columbia to Kansas City, and to San Francisco, all the while constantly drinking and smoking pot. Then I moved to New York, where I was pulled over on St. Mark's Place by an NYPD squad car for singing and running drunk down the middle of the street on my thirtieth birthday. They were nice guys, which I told them over and over again, and made sure I got home safe.

None of what I did seemed all that strange to me. When I peeked out at other people from inside my head, I noticed their reactions to my behavior, whether I was drunk or sober. Man, they were so rigid and judgmental. Thing was, when I was drunk, I didn't care what other people thought so much.

So although there was plenty of evidence outside of me to the contrary, up until this recent breakdown, inside my head I was convinced I was fine. This is how I operated: There's out there, and there's in here. Who are you going to trust, the bottle in here that keeps the noise down, or those nasty bozos out there? What do they know?

And I had some experiential evidence on my side. In 1969, I'd had an anxiety driven depression episode while doing my 2-year Conscientious Objector service at a stateside medical center and went to the psychiatric clinic for help. Those docs put me on a ton of Stelazine, an anti-psychotic and gave me a copy of I'm Okay, You're Okay to read. After a couple of weeks, I dropped them and got through it on beer, weed, and John D. McDonald paperbacks.

Okay, but now it's 1998 and having reacquired my trust of any therapist who would listen to me even though I never listened to them, I'm laying exposed in quivering pieces waiting to be put back together. Or at least get a story to use to build a new little room in my head.

So there I am, a mental breakdown putting me in the safe hands of the medical profession who are testing me six ways from Sunday to find out what's wrong so we can change whatever that is and I can be all better. Problem was, I didn't want to change, figure out coping strategies, make a plan, or you know, do any actual work to get better. I wanted to hang out and trade psych jokes with some cool interns and trippy patients -- Middle Aged Man, Interrupted without the Angelina sad part.

But I did seem to listen, I read the materials, and I did show up for appointments, and I did take all my meds. And I got back to gin as soon as possible. I didn't need a story to build that room in my head where everybody agreed with me because there was just me in there. I just needed gin. The more gin, the stronger the walls. Whenever a doc said it wasn't a good idea, I found another doc.

So, after what for anyone else would have been a sobering diagnosis of multiple mental disorders and with no job prospects and a wife and two children to support, my primary objective was to make sure I had a justification to drink. Not very admirable, I know. But hey, I'm a drunk.

I'm also no lightweight. There was no reason to panic. I knew what I was doing. I got a new agent again, sold a pilot; someone was looking at me for a series. Everybody just sit down, shut up and leave me alone. This is my classic mantra from inside my room in my head with its one little window on the world. You probably have two windows, but as I'm functionally blind in my left eye, I've only got the one. But that's fine with me -- less openings to defend.

And that brings us to what for me what all this is really about for me -- excuses. That one-eyed thing is true but so what? I've always built self-pity escape hatches wherever I go.

There's absolutely no doubt that if you're ADHD you might be susceptible to substance abuse. But that was not and is not the problem as it relates to me. I am not susceptible to substance abuse.

I am substance abuse. I don't need an excuse to party. Done them all and would love to keep doing them all forever, but I cannot, because I'll keep doing them forever everyday all day and all night long until I run out and go over to your place and do all of yours and then borrow your car to go get some more. I mean, c'mon -- otherwise what's the point?

What I said to myself for the three years between diagnoses and sobriety was that the only reason I abused alcohol before was because I was self-medicating my ADHD and hypomania. But now that I was in treatment I could drink because I was all better, see?

I kept propping up this pathetically empty lie until finally one morning in April of 2001. I stood in my kitchen in Honolulu, across the kitchen counter from me stood Margaret and our two children. They were through asking. If I didn't get sober, they were gone. I started to say something, but something in all three of those faces shut me right up. I just nodded my head and started to live one day at a time. That's when I finally squeezed out of that room in my head and stepped out into the world. I dropped all the excuses and lies, and free of that, I put my arms around my family and held on tight.

MAN OVERBOARD

"**D**ad, stop already. The microwave is clean enough. I want to make popcorn."

That's my 13 year-old daughter, Coco. And she's wrong. You have to use a scrubby sponge on the inside ceiling of the microwave to get all the little bits of chili and soup that get stuck up there. You don't want one of those bits falling into your coffee when you heat it up, at least I don't. Besides, I've got to take the rotating plate out and put it through the dishwasher to get off the grime. And the bottom corners have some dried up gook that I'll need to dig out with a fork tine. The popcorn will have to wait until I get this job done properly. Just give me a second. Or a half-hour.

Coco rolls her eyes. "OCD much, Dad?" The accepted myth in my family is that I'm obsessive-compulsive. That seems reasonable, considering OCD is well-documented as a possible comorbid condition with ADHD. But I'm not OCD. I am ADHD - of course. Hypomanic – uh huh. Stammer – y-y-yep, word-retrieval incompetent and pathetic short-term memory - that's me. Alcoholic – well, duh.

But in all the testing I've gone through at various times in my life I've never been diagnosed with Obsessive Compulsive Disorder. No matter how clean I keep the house. Then again, there are a bunch of people that worked with me back when I was a TV writer-producer that would definitely agree with my daughter. My passion for organization, folders, binders, production calendars projecting four months into the future, and scripts finished weeks ahead of production, drove a lot of writers on staff right over the edge. I went to work earlier and earlier and stayed later, pushing myself and everyone else, checking and rechecking, petrified of forgetting something or falling behind. Towards the end of one season an exhausted writer stood in the middle of my office and yelled, "You're not a Pharaoh, Frank! You can't keep loading the work on for no reason!" I had a reason. But it was personal.

Honest, I would cop to OCD it if I had it. Kicking and screaming all the way, I've learned one basic rule from my own experience and from the examples of others with all sorts of disabilities; deal with any challenge straight on – accept whatever it is, get the help you need to understand and handle it, and get on with the day. So, if I'm not in denial, then what's going on?

Over-Compensating Disorder, that's what. I made it up, but listen: I think early on I caused such havoc and disappointment that I developed a psycho- level work ethic to try to fix the things I was bound to screw up or forget before they happened. No matter what disaster I caused in school or Boy Scouts, at least my room was clean and my bed made. When everything is so messy and hard to control inside your head, having the kitchen clean can bring a little peace.

Yes, I'm nuts and confused, but as I told Coco, when I pull my hot cup of coffee out of spotless microwave my head and the world both seem a little easier to handle.

* * * *

Due to the sometimes overwhelming presence of ADHD in my family's life, I read a lot of books, blogs, and articles about the subject, always looking for some new insight I can use. But really, I'm hoping to identify with other people's stories of everyday struggles and small victories. The trouble is, each individual's experience with ADHD, whether as the parent, spouse, or the one who's trying to nail their brain down to one spot, is so... individual.

I was reading a very entertaining piece about not fitting in with the regular world that speculated how great it would be to be on an all-ADHD cruise where everybody would accept abrupt changes of subject and being interrupted in conversations. The idea being, I think, is that ADHD folks would understand and be more tolerant of each other.

I wouldn't last a minute on that boat. I deal with my ADHD in a more desperate and well, fascist-like manner. I sit in the cave in my head and desperately hold onto each wiggling, slippery thought and errant, stammering word. I don't want to lose them before I examine and devour them, or put them in little labeled cages for later. And yes, a second later I forget what wall of the cave I put the cage or the label falls off when I knock it over looking for another cage from last week.

But I do not enjoy chaos. It is my everyday world, and I've found ways to use it creatively, but in an existence of constant flashing lights, ringing bells and bumper cars I crave peace and whatever sliver of order and understanding I can find, and when I find it, I give it everything I've got.

So, when I'm writing or reading and someone interrupts me, I tend to jump out of my skin. When I'm interrupted when I'm talking I go blank and immediately search for my train of thought that has immediately zoomed off for parts unknown, never to be heard from again. I've long ago stopped grieving for these orphan trains, but I still feel a twinge every time a fully formed gorgeous thought turns into empty track. My two kids don't act this way themselves and think I'm skittish, which goes with my generally eccentric home persona. My over-achiever wife is more understanding, but that's probably due in part to being married to me for 25 years and that we're bound to each other for the rest of our days.

The ADHD community is filled with individuals who have much in common and much to share with each other. But due to the fact that our shared impairment directly affects the way we see and interpret the world around us and the world inside our heads, our experiences and how we live with them are amazingly diverse. This is most likely a good thing. Just don't put me on that boat.

HANDS WHERE I CAN SEE THEM

I'm driving in downtown Honolulu at 4 a.m. when my rearview mirror is filled with flashing cop car lights. I pull my very junky '83 Jetta to the curb and a Honolulu Police officer walks up and puts a flashlight on me. I hand over the license and registration, and he asks me where I'm coming from.

"I've just finished a video shoot over at a gym; we have to shoot at night when they're closed..." He shines the light in the back seat filled with ratty duffels filled with camera and lens cases, digital sound equipment, lights and stands

"That your video equipment?" he asks.

"Oh, yeah," I said, and as I glance to the back seat I see another cop standing at the front fender of the cruiser, feet spread, in the ready position, her right hand on her weapon in the un-snapped holster on her hip, eyes glued on me through my dirty rear window, watching intently.

" Yeah, yeah, and the shoot, the video shoot, ran long, ten hours, all my fault, didn't schedule the shoot the best way and should have hired an assistant to handle the lights..."

I've clicked into an upper octave chattering hypo-manic ramble but I can't shut myself up. Every detail seems vitally important so that the very nice policeman can understand the context of how I got to be in this situation, even though I don't know the situation is yet but I truly don't want to get shot so the words keep pouring out, the camera problems, the people were so helpful, I love the islands. He snaps the light back to my face in my face, and interrupts again.

"What gym was this?" he asks.

"Um, the uh..."

I left there fifteen minutes ago, but I'm not ready for that question. I can't remember the name of the place. I was just there. There's a huge red and yellow sign over the door of the place. I can see it in my memory but not what it says.

"It's the one, not 24 Hour, smaller...um..."

The name is plastered everywhere, it's eye-level on the door where I walked out. But I can't come up with it. The door to that information is frozen shut and buried in blithering whiney gibberish that keeps coming out of my mouth.

"It's not neon, it's like a big light box with the front painted and a picture or more like an icon, really, of a guy lifting weights

I'm locked solid. There's no way I'm coming up with the name until I've gotten home, put my feet up, and had a vanilla yogurt with Honey Bunches of Oats on top. I sure wish I had a bowl of that right now. But I don't and I'm still chattering, useless words bouncing around inside my nine-hundred dollar junk heap, irritating all three of us. Hopelessly stammering on, I'm now describing the red and yellow sign in detail to the cop.

"Not an icon, a trademark that's what it'd be. They're local, I'm sure it's registered like in city records or somewhere..."

"You know you ran a stop light back there?"

"I did?" I said, honestly shocked. Being prone to mistakes, I drive so carefully that my ninety year old mother loses patience with me. "Oh. Uh, I didn't see it." Well, that's obvious. What isn't obvious is what I was preoccupied with that caused me not to see the light, if that's the intersection I think it might have been. I open my mouth to start to explain that, and the cop hands me back my license and registration, pointing out that the registration needs to be renewed, and says he's letting me off with a warning. I'm grateful, but I think he just figured that if he had to listen to one more minute of my ping-ponging, hyper-detailed chatter, he'd let his partner put a bullet in my head. And then there would be all that paperwork.

The next day, my wife Margaret says he let me go because he was probably looking for drunk drivers. Lucky thing he didn't stop you a few years ago, she says. No doubt, but back when I was drinking I was actually better at keeping my mouth shut when I was in conflict with authority figures. I didn't want them to smell the booze. Also, when I was drinking, I could tell myself my memory lapses were caused by blackouts. Now I have to accept that my unpredictable lack of short-term memory is the wiring in my head I was born with. There are pluses; I can't remember or tell jokes, and I keep confidences, because I forget them. But being wired like this makes for constant surprises. I hate surprises.

Case in point -- two weeks later I'm pulled over by another cop because my registration sticker is out of date. I had completely spaced the last cop's warning. In the course of things, she asks me what my phone number is. I squint into her flashlight. I should be ready for this question -- it's so easy. But no.

"Uh, its...37...no wait, its 932...no..." I'm trying hard here, gritting my teeth, my eyes closed. But no.

I start to explain that numbers on demand are a challenge for me, especially when I'm questioned by authority figures. Even at the Safeway checkout line, I tell her, when you're supposed to type it in to the little pad if you don't have your Safeway Club card, which I lost the minute I got it. She doesn't care. She just hands me a ticket and sends me home.

At home, I put my feet up with a bowl of yogurt and cereal and wait. The lock-box in my head pops open, and my phone number tumbles out, a happy little useless surprise. But I quietly repeat it over and over to myself as I eat. I'll be ready the next time. The numbers know better, they hula around in my head, smile at me, and wink at each other. They know they'll never be caught by this guy. He just doesn't have the skills.

* * * *

Yesterday, just when I was thinking we were making some headway financially and I was feeling a little better about myself in general, the oil sensor, water pump, and starter all went out on the car at the same time. We had plans for those five hundred dollars. If we even still had it. I might have spent most of it on a new camera tripod.

Truth is, I hate money. Or, it hates me. No matter what I do, we just don't get along, we never have. I try to give our family finances the care and attention they require, but if there's anything in the world that triggers a deficit of attention in me, it's a column of figures that never adds up to a positive number.

It's been this way forever. At ten, I only managed to sell three tickets to the Boy Scout Anniversary Jamboree — two to my parents and one to the depressed lady next door who I think thought I was collecting for the paper. This wasn't enough to get the prize — a Motorola Transistor Radio. But what was worse was when I turned in my official Jamboree cardboard box with "Trustworthy" scrolled across the top in big letters; the Scoutmaster discovered I was short six bucks. I'm pretty sure I had planned to replace it with allowance or lawn-mowing money, but I forgot. I even forgot I'd spent the money, so later when I got the lawn-mower money, I forgot to put that in the "Trustworthy" Jamboree box, so now I was standing in front of the Scoutmaster and the whole troop being fingered as a thief. I wasn't, honest. I just forgot to cover the deficit.

Later, after my dad paid the difference, I went on the Jamboree camp-out and since they all thought I was a thief anyway, I stole the Motorola Transistor Radio from the winner's tent, got caught, and was kicked out of Boy Scouts. See, the winner was such a smarmy show-off and kept rubbing it in. One day I'll get even.

But about money. As what passes for an adult, I got credit cards and promptly forgot every amount I charged as soon as I had whatever I bought in my possession. When the bills came, I paid the minimum — when I remembered — and was shocked when, card by card, they were refused when I tried to buy a TV.

Still, I was basically a poor cook/waiter/starving artist type trying to balance my checkbook and pay my rent, so I couldn't get into that much trouble. Then, success reared its ugly head. When the Hollywood cash rolled in, I figured I never had to worry about money again and promptly began throwing it out the window like confetti.

I put up a sort of "together" front in those days, and both my wife Margaret and I were confident that no matter what, my career in the Los Angeles television world was solid, so there wasn't that much to worry about. We were spectacularly wrong.

Now I'm back to being a poor, starving artist type, and I'm more comfortable in that position in life for a lot of reasons. The people I've admired in life were never the wealthy ones. But still, I'll probably be working off old debt until I'm even older and grayer. And when I see my son and daughter, both ADHD, as they impulse buy and treat money with the same absent disregard I did, I worry.

So I tell them stories of my screw-ups and try to give both of them hints on how to not to focus on possessions, and to stay aware of the dollars flowing in and out of their lives, and help them see that even though it's not how we measure the true value of life, we need to give our individual and family finances the attention they require to at least keep us fed, sheltered, and not totally stressed out by harassing debt-service calls at all hours.

I think they're getting it. Although when I told my daughter, "I really was going to put the money back in the Boy Scout box, I forgot, that's all..." she rolled her eyes.

BRIDGE OF SIGHS

"God, you guys — I'll do my homework after I eat, okay? Stop bugging me about every stupid thing every stupid second! You make my life a nightmare!"

With that, my fourteen-year-old ADHD daughter, Coco, storms into her room with her bowl of mac and cheese, and slams her door so hard it sounds like a gunshot, which sets the dog on a barking jag. Between barks, I can hear Coco kicking the wall. I stand in the kitchen still holding the pot and spoon I made her dinner with, close my eyes, and keep my mouth shut. I am not going to respond in kind. I am going to breathe. Slow even breath in, slow even breath out.

I learned this from my last therapist. The therapist, who after years of slowly building mutual trust and rapport, closed up shop, which left me to face the daily emotional pummeling of being a parent all by myself. So this nightmare, as my daughter calls it, is all his fault, the selfish creep. I should hunt him down and beat his head in with this mac and cheese spoon. But he's not a creep or selfish. He set me up with another therapist before he closed his practice. And I'm not facing this parenting stuff alone. My wife, Margaret, is right here, sitting at the kitchen table.

"Your cheese is dripping," she says. Margaret has a less extreme approach to life. She sees the humor in both of our kids' dramas. She watches as I put the spoon in the sink and wipe up the cheese sauce from the floor. Breathe in, breathe out.

"Are you all right?"

"Mm — hmm," I nod, between slow even breaths.

"Your problem is, you take things too much to heart," Margaret says and smiles.

That's a phrase we picked up from Richard Russo's novel, *Bridge of Sighs,* describing Lucy, a man prone to occasional blackout spells who is nearly immobilized by love, family, guilt and obligation and with whom I identified. It's become a gentle joke between us, because I do. I take everything too much to heart. It's not that I get my feelings hurt; it's that I get immobilized by compassion.

When Coco yells and explodes out of frustration, I identify with her, too. In her eyes, I can see the overload crowding into her head pushing all rational thoughts into an airless corner where the only way out is to react and react big or you're sure you'll suffocate.

No matter how gently requests or questions are put to you — and sometimes that's worse because then it sounds like condescending "careful of the mental patient" talk — but however it comes at you in a short amount of time or just the wrong time for you, you lash out to stop it, but you're also lashing out at yourself inside your head looking to break apart this wall holding in the overload and let air in —just one second of quiet air — that's all you want, and in the moment, bright red rage is the only hope for release and you don't give a damn about anyone else. A second later, you apologize and add that new bag of guilt onto the huge pile you carry around your whole life. And of course, the pressure of that guilt adds to the next overload.

So I'm always telling Coco, "No worries, it's all fine," whenever she apologizes over small things, or even medium things. I think we need to forgive others their slights and slips as much as possible. But more importantly, we have to learn to forgive ourselves and, maybe with some help from others, work on adjusting how we handle things.

In that spirit, Coco and I both work on managing our tempers. We're doing pretty well at it. She told me what she does is slow things down and not talk. "It's not that I'm not listening, Dad," she says "I just don't want to lose my temper and mess things up." The more pressured she feels in her head, the slower she takes it — whether it's getting ready for school in the morning, doing homework, or getting ready for bed at night.

I don't know what I can do about taking everything too much to heart, especially when it comes to those I love and value, but I can probably do better at shaking off the anxiety. I'll work on adjusting that. I might try a little of Coco's "go slow" approach myself.

* * * *

These days, my life is pretty much all chores. My wife, Margaret, is working hard out in the world keeping her company, and therefore our family, afloat, so I'm the housekeeper and stay-at-home parent doing the laundry, dishes, and housekeeping chores. This is a very fair arrangement; I've already testified to my cleaning obsession, and we've found a useful way to harness it. And I'm doing some small-scale video shooting and editing, which I can do out of the home. That brings in a little money. And the kids like me around, when they get home, to talk to and make them stuff to eat. I love the kids and my wife. My wife and kids love me.

Considering what most people are dealing with in their lives, I couldn't have it better. By all rights, I should be the prime example of a happy, healthy dad and husband. I certainly shouldn't be yelling "I don't know! I'm sorry! I'm stupid okay? You know I'm stupid!" at Margaret, and then slamming out of our bedroom at night. That happens sometimes when you have a mental condition, I guess. Though losing my mind two days after I write a mature-sounding story about dealing with my daughter's explosive temper is personally embarrassing.

It was a little thing, really. A text message buzzed on my phone while I was video-editing at the computer. I picked it up thinking it might be my son texting me from school needing something. But it was a message from the bank saying to call immediately due to some "activity" on our account. Now, I don't do the money in our household anymore. I've already testified to my ineptitude in that area, but I do know we are perpetually on financial thin ice, so I call the number on the screen.

Turns out it was a phishing scam. And I had keyed all our bank account info into it. Later, I mentioned the bank emergency to Margaret, and she was understandably concerned about what I'd done, and I tried to explain but couldn't because I couldn't remember how it had happened exactly because I was distracted thinking about a video edit as I did it, and then couldn't talk because I was paralyzed by how stupid I'd been to do it, which reminded me of every other unbelievably stupid thing I'd ever done in my long personal history crammed to bursting with countless stupefying mindless mistakes in judgment and lack of common sense. And then, just like my daughter, I lashed out.

Later, after all that was over, and the card was canceled, and our account was safe, Margaret and I talked. "What are you so angry about? And why are you so angry at me?" she asked.

I told her I wasn't angry at her, but angry at myself, disgusted by myself, really, and tried to explain the lashing out again, but it's hard for her to understand when she's the one who's been recently lashed out at. I agreed to talk to the shrink about it at the next visit. And I will. And I'll turn up the vigilance on my temper. But sometimes I'm doing the chores around the house and I feel like my mom, the frustrated writer/housewife in the fifties -- cleaning and criticizing herself for unwritten words and too-clean bathrooms.

And sometimes I don't see the bright side of ADHD, hypomania, stammering or any of the other brain crap. All I see is the constant, every-second struggle to pay attention, remember the word, the name, the appointment, or even find a clean, clear thought. I get tired and want nothing more than to go hide in a book. That helps.

And sometimes, if I'm lucky, when it's late enough that everyone else in the house is asleep, I'll turn on the computer and start typing. And usually if I do that, I realize that writing about our life is how I begin to understand the layers of love and shared purpose in a family give it meaning, and with that, learn to appreciate it. With time, crafting honest writing can cut fear and dread down to nearly human size so you can at least shake hands with them and take their measure instead of giving up and diving under the covers. Maybe if I write more, I'll lash out at others less.

That would be a bonus. Thing is, there are no guarantees when you start pounding out honest words. Honesty, like public nudity, is not for everybody.

* * * *

I'm in the middle of a video project that's like any project any of us do for money -- demanding, nerve-wracking, and hard. I'm aware that's why they call it work, and I know that I'm wildly lucky that this job fell in my lap because we needed the money like yesterday. So this is not ordinary bitching and moaning. This is spinning out in front of my computer freaking. And then bitching and moaning about the freaking, neither of which I think qualify as the kind of ungrateful, selfish attitude that could get me fried by a lightning bolt from God. So that's all right.

Like I said, I'm freaking about the video project, and I'm on edge. Not because it's hard and demanding. I do hard and demanding every day. And the amount of it is starting to piss me off. It takes concentrated effort to remember to rinse the conditioner out of my hair before I step out of the shower and start rubbing a towel into the pink goop -- and yeah, I've tried 2-in-1 shampoos, but they don't work on the Alfalfa cowlick that sticks up from the back of my head. I'm vain about the hair. And that pisses me off.

And forgetting to take my afternoon medication pisses me off. I never remember until about three or four in the afternoon and I'm already an insomniac so I'd like to skip the stimulants by that time. But if I do, dinner will be a mess for the whole family with me forgetting the salad or burning the chicken, and getting so tense I yell at everybody for nothing, if I even remember to cook anything at all.

Of course, my skipped-meds consequences don't hold a candle burning at both ends to my bi-polar friend's skipped-meds consequences. After a four hour phone conversation convincing someone you care about that the only way to keep the black hole behind his headboard from sucking him into oblivion is to get his prescription out of the backpack in the hall no matter how impossibly far away the backpack or any possibility hope and meaning in life is, my worries seem trivial. "They're in the backpack, all right? Meaning and hope are right under those child-proof caps waiting for you."

And the video project is an exercise video with a real good trainer, a smart, thoughtful woman. It's not her. It's me. I direct, light, and shoot the footage. Then, I get home and capture it into the editing program. Now, as the editor who's got to make the end product out of whatever was shot, I look at the footage and I can't believe what I see. I forgot to match lighting on consecutive scenes, I forgot insert shots, I didn't see the huge lighting instrument reflected in the mirror right behind her while she's talking to camera, and look at this! -- A whole scene shot without sound because I forgot to turn on the lavaliere microphone.

It's hard enough banging around through life with a blown-out brain leaving little piles of burnt disasters in your wake without having to watch video evidence of your disasters repeating in front of you in digitally corrected color. But I'll fix it in editing somehow. Maybe do a reshoot for that sound glitch. I'm bitching about this because the client's coming over to look at a cut, my hair looks stupid and I need to take my meds.

Next time, I'll be more together. I will. Or maybe I just think I will, which will get me to put my guard down and I'll be knocked flat on my ass.

* * * *

In late rounds this week, ADHD led with a distracting jab and then hit Dad with a surprise comorbid roundhouse right to the head, knocking him flat with panic, despair, and a hopelessly dark world-view. Petrified that his therapist will want to put him on anti-depressants again, Dad takes a self-imposed sick-week and hides in bedroom. Family says Dad took a dive.

"Now he gets to lie around all day, eat cookies, and read books," family says. "Who's going to do the laundry, clean the kitchen and change the light bulbs?"

"Not I," Dad says from under covers, "My head hurts. Leave me alone. I need quiet."

A couple of days go by. The house is peaceful, not a sound. Dad gets out of bed to get a sandwich and maybe a few more Safeway oatmeal-raisin cookies. The kitchen is empty. The whole house is deserted. Dashing around the place in a growing panic, it hits him that there's no dishes, no clothes, no furniture, no people. His family, seeing he's no longer useful, has packed up and moved away.

Okay, my family didn't run off. But late this week, I did get laid out by that mental punch to the head and heart. And a good-sized part of me is convinced that the only reason my family didn't pack up and leave is because I stayed on my feet and kept up with the household chores, part-time jobs, and all the other people-pleasing behaviors that cover the dark, frustrated fury and self-loathing burning at my rotten core.

My crusty old corner-man in the ring sits me on the stool -- squirts water in my face. "How many times I gotta tell you to keep your head down. No wonder ADHD caught you with that right. Now, he's got you throwing around wild-ass mixed metaphors. Stay focused, kid. Fight your fight."

I get it. But see, it's not that I think that my family is mean and shallow or really treats me like a slave. It's that I know how difficult it can be to be around me when I get overwhelmed, frantic, and short-tempered. I can barely tolerate myself when some combination of ADHD, anxiety, and down-slide hypomania hit me with a wave of burning synapses that gets so huge that I'm sure I'll tumble over and over, and stay lost in confusion and uncertainty forever. And then, trying to keep from drowning, I lash out, desperate to grab anything that makes sense and say or do something scary or hurtful to someone who will probably remember it much longer than I will.

So why on earth would my family stay around for this lunacy? Before, it was probably because I was a mammoth provider. Today, more mouse sized. So I become a mammoth homemaker. And in a snap, I turn into my mother, the 50's housewife putting aside her desires, her writing, and her whole sense of self to take care of her spouse and kids. You have to be seriously tough to pull that off.

My corner-man towels me off, shaking his head. "You're not hard enough for that, kid. I seen some of the toughest ladies in the universe fight that fight and get flattened by a bitter madness that's meaner than anything you can handle," he says. "If you can't stay focused, stay honest. Fight with what you got."

I tell him I don't know what I've got to fight with. ADHD is dancing around in the ring looking bigger and stronger all the time. He can't wait to pound me into screaming mush.

My corner-man slaps me. "It's love, kid. That's what you got -- a whole family full of it. You fight with that, you can't lose. Now get out there and show that bum who you are."

So I do. And the old corner-man is right. The fight may never end, but it's the love we have for each other that gives all of us the reason and power to stay in the ring. And keep an eye out for that roundhouse right.

INVINCIBLE

It's Halloween in Villa Park, Illinois, 1959. I'm ten years old and incredibly dashing in my homemade Zorro costume. My shadow on the moonlit sidewalk looks just like Guy Williams' shadow in the TV show. I am Zorro - "A fox so cunning and free."

My friend David says it's late; we have to get home with our treats before the teenagers came out to do their Halloween tricks. He's worried that we've gone too far to get home in time with our sacks full of Milky Ways and popcorn balls.

But I'm not paying attention. I'm in my own world as I leave David behind, cross the four-lane avenue into Elmhurst, and gallop down an unfamiliar residential street. I am Zorro -- I am invincible – your treats are mine. Except when I'm faced with three Elmhurst teenagers in leather jackets. They surround me at a street lamp. I am suddenly very very vincible. Two of them smoke cigarettes; the guy who picks me up by my cape chews a toothpick. They bounce me around, take my hat, mask, cape, and all my candy and send me scampering back to Villa Park. My shadow on the moonlit sidewalk looks like a scared 10 year-old running home, where I know I'll be safe.

I'm always shocked by a change in the weather or by hard reality exploding apart my day-dreamed life. Just this last September, it seemed to me that we were all doing pretty well, in our house. Coco was transitioning out of Special Ed. Her reading and writing were both above grade level and she wowed them with her project presentations in social studies. And at home, not only was her temper pretty much under control, her compassion and sense of humor were re-flowering.

Harry passed his midterms and actually seemed to like his classmates and some of his teachers. Margaret was working harder than ever at her education company, as well as with her private clients. She had a great response as a presenter and teacher at The Hawaii Writers Conference. It seemed like maybe she'd be able to pull off the first year of her company being in the black. And one of the teachers working for her sold us his car at a unbelievably great price.

And I'd finished a pretty successful tryout run of my solo show in Los Angeles in the summer, and was back in Honolulu in the middle of shooting and editing a local video job that would give us some extra cash. Despite a hiccup or two due to bouts between me and my brain, I was reasonably happy. Plus, the new therapist was working out for the whole family. And we found a way to gate the front door so that our huge dog didn't bound out into the street terrorizing mail carriers, joggers, and the nice lady tending her papaya tree next door.

I was the one that sold our family on the dream of living in Hawaii in the first place, and after ten years of struggling with the reality of making your way in paradise, it seemed the sun was shining for us, a light breeze blowing across the calm tropical sea.

Then in October, Margaret's sister called from Georgia. Their mom was in the hospital. Even though she was out in a couple of days, it jolted us. We saw how far apart we were from family who needed us. My parents on the east coast were even older and my dad was going in for surgery, but we couldn't afford to keep flying back and forth. Also, unrelated to these realities, the Hawaii school system discovered they were out of money, and the upheaval was not good for Margaret's work or my daughter's school. Next, the car we bought developed an unsolvable overheating problem. Then, worried that my progress on my video project was suffering, I buckled down on that and missed my therapist appointment twice. And the dog busted through the screen door again, scared the crap out of the mailman and ran off down the street. Margaret went after the dog while I went to Home Depot to get our third new screen door.

Had things changed that much? Suddenly everything that seemed strong and solid about our life on an island in the middle of the Pacific seemed weak-kneed and wrong-headed. Had I insisted on dragging my family into my ADHD fantasy life only to have it blow up in their faces? Had the Elmhurst teenagers busted through my daydream to give all of us a candy-stealing dose of reality?

In the middle of this spin, Margaret and I sit down. She says, "I think we should move to Georgia."

I said I didn't think that we should. We lived in freaking Hawaii, who gets to do that? But her mom was sick, so it took maybe another couple of minutes before I capitulated. And she was right. Our parents and siblings needed us back there, and our kids needed to be reconnected with their extended family, as well. I told Margaret that it seemed to me like we'd been nurturing our children in clay plots in the greenhouse, and now it was time to transplant them back to their home turf. Maybe not the best analogy, but I was floundering -- trying to find the justification for uprooting everybody in the first place.

Ten years ago, I convinced my wife and kids to move out here, into the middle of the Pacific, to the most remote land mass on earth positive that living away from everything and everybody we knew was the best thing that could happen to us. Hawaii has a different culture, less people, and far less distractions, which is important when you're re-inventing yourself.

Looking back, it was a pretty selfish decision to push on my wife and kids, but I wanted out of Los Angeles and the pull of the business, though truthfully the business was pushing me out and I was pissed off about it even though I knew I didn't belong there anymore. If I was ever going to get a handle on my head problems, get sober and reconnect with my family, it wasn't going to be there.

Anyway, we struggled making a living, but we took the advice of a friend on the island and did our best to give whatever we could to the community and we grew into a deep and rewarding life here. In spite of -- or because of -- our precarious finances, our two kids flourished in paradise, and Margaret jumped into teaching literacy and story structure to children and adults. And I, I think, became a more thoughtful and honest man. In many ways, my life in Hawaii helped heal me and my relationship with my family.

So, maybe I can avoid being crushed by a twenty-ton wet bag of guilt that would send me into a month-long bout of self-hating craziness. That would be good. But the changes keep coming, my mental wobbling commences, and my ADHD brain grabs each new change as positive evidence of the truth -- even though it completely contradicts the truth I was desperately holding onto two minutes ago. Today in March of 2010 back on the east coast, my father is in surgery and I'm sitting by the phone, waiting to hear, powerless to be there to help -- moving back is a good decision.

Margaret is suddenly being recruited for an important job here -- maybe the decision was too hasty.

My daughter swears that if we change our mind, she'll move back to be with her grandparents, aunts, uncles, and cousins by herself -- moving back is a good decision.

My client likes the video project I made and wants me to do more in partnership -- maybe the decision was too hasty. It's way cheaper to live in Georgia than Hawaii and we're all cracking under the constant money pressure -- moving back is a good decision.

We've developed deep friendships and meaningful community connections in Hawaii and I really like it here, damn it -- maybe the decision was too hasty.

In the end, whether I can personally make up my mind or not -- and I never can about anything, ever -- the decision is simple for two reasons.

1) Hawaii reaffirmed in us the value of giving, and now it's time to give to our extended family -- the people who have always, without question, given to us.

2) If Margaret wants to move back, that's good enough for me.

So, as usual, love clears the path. And come the end of the school year in June, we're pulling ourselves out of our lovely clay pots here and planting ourselves in the rich family dirt back home.

SHUT IT

It's last week -- no, the week before, and it had been building since the week before that, and I have a therapist appointment the next day which is good timing because thick dark water is swirling around me getting higher, darker, and thicker by the minute.

It's right up under my chin, licking at my lips, slipping up and up and I can't get away from it. It's inside and out, sucking me down, my own personal Drowning Pool of certain failure. But I'm holding on because I'm doing well with the new shrink, and I see him tomorrow. Wait...no, I missed it. The appointment was yesterday.

I'm sure you've all seen the ads popping up announcing simple and/or instant ADHD cures. This gets on my nerves after a while. Do these people really think we haven't educated ourselves about what's actually, chemically and neurologically, going on in our brains? We know that there's no fixing this to make us "normal." Because we're reasonably bright and industrious we've found that there's work, acceptance, knowledge, medicine, love and faith, but no cure for ADHD. We don't want to cure who we are, for god's sake. We want to be able to handle it better. And maybe try to see the humor in it.

Then, there are the articles arguing that ADHD doesn't exist at all. That attention deficit disorder was made up to trick parents to drug their spoiled kids or as a way for sneaky teens and adults to cop speed scrips. These folks are out there telling us that we're making this stuff up. According to this pack of dingbats, we're hiding behind med-happy pharmaceutical companies and complicit doctors because we don't have the will to enforce old-fashioned hard work values on our kids or ourselves. They're saying we call our kids or ourselves ADHD because we're undisciplined, unmotivated, or just plain lazy.

This really pisses me the hell off. I don't know how it is for you, but oh yeah, sure, I'm just scrambling with everything I've got not to be sucked under this wet foaming mass of raging indecision, self-loathing, shameful fear, guilt, and at least a week of residual elevated stammering if I ever even get out of this idiotic mess, because I'm lazy.

When my brain goes down here, and it's sneaky, slippery quick, my life, which objectively is just fine, disintegrates into a foul soup of problems I'll never be able to solve because I can't sort any of them out. The soup swirls around making it impossible to figure out which problem I should try to fix because I can't figure which one is the important one and if it is, I'm sure I'm not the one to fix it, and if I try anyway, I'll be ignoring the one problem I can fix, but I can't do anything if I keep hyperventilating and yelling at people to shut up so I can think.

That kind of behavior puts a little stress on the family unit. So I try to do less of that. And crying? That gives everybody, including me, the heebie-jeebies. I don't do that anymore.

I'm working hard here -- giving it everything I've got -- but what the hell do I do? Which do I choose? Is it my looming work deadline, or my dad's health, or the pile of undone laundry growing by the washing machine? There's Coco's school problems (she's transitioning out of Special Ed and needs support), or Harry's school problems (he quit), or the dirty kitchen (including the floor), or Margaret's company problems, which goes to cash flow which goes back to work deadline.

But what about Margaret's mother's health? And speaking of cash flow –- where's ours? I'm behind on proofing the galleys for my mother's book, but the dirty kitchen floor is nothing compared to the filth hiding in the living room carpet which I can't fix because of the stupid broken overpriced freaking French vacuum cleaner, which I'd take in to get repaired except for the Pontiac's cooling system. And besides, we're moving and I'm getting fat because I never exercise even though I promise myself I will tomorrow morning. Moving? We can't move, I can't move, it's too big, but I better move; I better get off the island quick before everybody finally sees what an immense incompetent putz I really am. Hey, I'm kind of crazy, but I'm no slacker. I'm working here.

So here's the truth:

1. ADHD people are not stupid. So keep your snake-oil.

2. ADHD is real and we are not lazy, spoiled or weak-willed. So shut up with that stuff. It's ignorant and insulting.

I made it out of that particular panic pool without embarrassing myself, too much, anyway. My daughter did see me sort of bonking my forehead on my desk when she came home from school, but she just said, "You all right?" I said, "Yeah" between bonks, and she went to the kitchen, with its just-cleaned floor, and got herself a snack.

I got it together enough to solve another problem that day. I rescheduled with my therapist, and tomorrow we'll do some work on this, and maybe have a few laughs. But I was always wired like this for good or ill. Before diagnoses, acceptance, and help, I just held on and rode the sucker, drinking to cool the jets, knowing somewhere in the back of all that screwy wiring that one day I'd have to take my real self seriously.

* * * *

This was Thanksgiving 1997, in our beautiful big house in Pasadena. It's a great day, our home filled with friends, relatives and kids of all sizes. Everybody's happy, and I'm trying to be as well, but even though I'm in the kitchen cooking, which is what I want and love to do on Thanksgiving, my happy is caught up in fried brain wiring and escalating confusion. I'm holding a full hot pot and there are laughing obstructions between me and the sink and I yell. "Kids! Get away from the goddamn pie. I told you already!"

Margaret swoops in and shoos out the little dressed-up mob of our kids and guest kids through the swinging kitchen door as I tumble a pot of hot, boiled Yukon Gold potatoes into a mixing bowl, turning my head away from the steam.

"You all right?" she asks.

"I'm fine, fine...but where's the butter and milk?" "Next to the mixer" she says.

"My martini?"

"Behind you, next to the sink," Margaret says, and takes the potato pot from me as I take a slug of gin. "How many is that?" she asks.

"This is only my second, hon, and no more today."

There's a beat as she looks at me. Has she been counting? She turns to the stove. "I'll start taking things out," she says.

"Everything but the gravy," I say, "that'll go out with the potatoes."

Margaret heads into the dining room with string beans and sausage stuffing as I start the mixer, and pour the butter and milk in with the potatoes. As soon as the kitchen door swings closed behind Margaret, I pour more gin into my glass. Maybe it was more like three. Anyway, this only makes it three and a half, or four and a half. I'm not sure. I thought I'd stopped lying. I have, except about drinking.

It's Thanksgiving and drunk or sober, I'm acutely aware that I've got a huge undeserved mountain of luck to be thankful for. I'm still a couple of years from getting my diagnosis, and anyone can see I'm on a roll. I'm a show-runner on a hit TV series. My wife and I have two gorgeous kids. We've just moved into this sprawling classic Pasadena house with a circular drive where we park our German cars. Friends and family are gathering around the dining room table to toast us and each other, everyone will be honestly grateful for the blessings life has bestowed on each of us.

But in the kitchen, as I spoon the mashed potatoes into a serving bowl, I know that there's no amount of thanks I can give to any higher power that can make it right that this life I'm living here is mine.

Other people might be fooled for a little while, but I know what a screw-up I am, and soon they will, too. I wasn't just having trouble multi-tasking; I could barely task half the time. I'm always back-filling for important things I forgot and mistakes I made, even though I get to the office hours before anyone else to organize and nail down each day before it happens and practice looking like a calm, articulate show-runner in the bathroom mirror down the hall from my office. There is no way that I've earned the fairy-tale life I'm living. And when that comes out, boy it'll be a mess.

As it turns out, I did end up losing that particular job on the hit series, and after a couple of other show-runner jobs, I ended up leaving the business. But it wasn't because I was discovered to be a scatterbrained, worthless fraud. Well, I did go through a period of calling myself that in the shower, but that wasn't really the truth.

I wasn't an idiot. I just wasn't interested.

Getting diagnosed, getting on meds, getting sober, and getting into therapy have all helped me become infinitely more honest and comfortable with myself, but for just an instant, a glimmer of truth shone through on that Thanksgiving in 1997.

I brought out the mashed potatoes and gravy; we all said grace and toasted our thanks. Then, as another scatterbrained-worthless-fraud tape-loop started playing in my head, I realized the dinner I'd made was perfect. Every dish, the gigantic beer-basted turkey, the sausage stuffing, the acorn squash, the sautéed green beans, the mashed Yukon golds, and the made-from-scratch gravy all had wildly different cooking times and prep, but they all hit the table perfectly done, hot, and all at the same exact time. If you don't know, this takes skills like multi-tasking, concentration, and my old bugaboo, time management.

But I think the most basic skill, and most difficult to pull off because it may not be how you make your living at first or ever, is to find what excites and fulfills you and go do it. At that Thanksgiving table, I got the first inkling that whether we have mental or physical disabilities or not, our life keeps coming ever faster with deep joy and tragedy and shallow distractions tumbling over us with equal confounding force that can knock us flat. The strength and clarity to stand and ignore the distractions is ours when we are true to ourselves and bound to those we love.

That glimmer of truth went away for a couple of years, but I remembered it in time. And though distractions will always be a challenge and I wasn't going to go back to working in kitchens like I did in my twenties, I was going to go back to doing work that interested me, and only work that interested me.

So this Thanksgiving, in our tiny house in Hawaii near Waimanalo beach, I'll give thanks to that 1997 Thanksgiving and promise to remind my two kids of that glimmer of truth I saw back then. Because I want them to remember that when they are doing what captivates them, they can grow into their true selves, and show the world some serious skills.

* * * *

So that's settled. I can make things better right here right now. I'll go to Safeway do the shopping for the week, and reward myself for my brilliant insights with some bakery oatmeal cookies. This is me using positive reinforcement to help me help my family. Psychological self-help pro, that's me. I know what I am and I know what to do about it. I make a list, I yell out to Coco to let her know where I'm going, and I'm off.

At the front of the store I get the cart, then stop and do a check. Wallet back pocket, car keys front pocket, not left in the car, reading glasses in shirt pocket, and I have my list right here in my hand. Good to go. Not that it does any good. I always forget something important, no matter how many circles or boxes I draw around it, because eventually, somewhere in the supermarket, the list goes in my pocket, and then it might as well be on Mars. I won't see it again until I discover its remnants in the bottom of the clothes dryer. But that's not the problem, right now. Right now, it's the cookies. Should I get some?

If I do get them, should I get two of the 18-count boxes? That seems extreme since the kids don't like raisins or walnuts in their cookies, so there's no disguising the fact that this purchase is just for fat, old me. But my wife, Margaret, also likes them, but not nearly with the intensity that I like them. Though she's been known to plow through a bunch, given the right DVD on the tube. So if I don't get the extra box, it's possible that not enough cookies will survive after I get them home for me to get the deep satisfaction of an even dozen fresh Safeway oatmeal raisin cookies sitting next to me late at night in the white china mixing bowl on the end table along with my iced tea and detective novel. So maybe the cookies aren't the whole problem.

Maybe since I no longer drink, smoke, do drugs, or stay out late catting around with those that do, I've made these particular cookies my addiction of choice. These innocent snacks are my last living sin. And I treat them with the same addictive obsession that I used to bring to booze, cigarettes, drugs, and haunting after-hours clubs.

I never grab and dump the cookies into the cart. I always carefully pull a package from the back of the display, checking the date stamps to get the freshest, and then put them gently in the little shopping cart baby seat. Now, I've told myself to stop with this, already. I don't need these cookies to be happy. (Yes I do, I do!) And I certainly don't need any more sugar in my diet. (Who cares? So what?) Why deny yourself? To see if you can. Is that a reason? It should be. Why? Oh, shut up. No, you shut up.

I'm putting the cookies back on the display kiosk for the third time, determined to kick the habit and get to the broccoli just fifteen feet on the other side, when I hear my name called.

There's a familiar-looking woman trying to get her cart around where I've blocked the aisle for anywhere from five minutes to a year, I have no way of knowing. She shakes her head and smiles as I rejoin what's called reality by everyone else. I wonder if I've been talking out loud. That would not be a good sign.

"Frank, I thought that was you. You seemed so preoccupied. I didn't want to disturb you, but you're kind of holding up traffic here."

Then I remember her. It turns out she used to work on a show with me. She's good at her job and we always got along well. We get out of the way of other carts and do a quick catch-up and she says she saw my attention deficit disorder show when I did it here in town. Whew, she says, you really are crazy, and she twirls her finger by her temple in the universal nutso sign. We both laugh. "Are you okay?" she asks.

I assure her I am, was just you know... thinking for a second. No, she says, she means in the larger sense, are you handling life okay? Yes, fine, really. Super. Thanks.

She heads off and I wince to myself. Hawaii is a small place and I fear pretty soon folks we know will hear about me standing in the middle of Safeway playing with cookies and mumbling to myself.

Maybe so, but I can't worry about that. I need to get broccoli, bananas, and where's the list? I get a little frantic checking my pockets, looking in the empty cart over and over, it's nowhere. But there are little tiny pieces of white paper sprinkled on the floor around my feet.

NORMAL EYES

*I have one final fallback strategy for those times when my
brain fails me, when I can't come up with a parenting strategy
effective enough, fair enough, creative enough.*

It's love.

*I simply hold (read: restrain) Natalie, make sure my hands,
cheek, or lips are touching skin, close my eyes, and concentrate as
hard as I can on filling her with love. Does it help? Not a bit. It does
absolutely nothing. But as the last resort of a slow-thinker, I could
do worse.*

- Kay Marner, from "My Picture-Perfect Family"

Because I want to broaden my outlook and explore new
information, perspectives, and ideas, I try to carefully read as much
about ADHD and other mental health issues from as many and as
varied sources as I can.

Oh, bullshit. I don't do anything of the kind.

I tear into articles and blogs about attention deficit disorder
and the rest of it when my stress level reaches some internal red-line
and starts shaking the crap out of the foundations. Then, I attack the
reading in a big rushed, scramble-search for a psychological life
preserver before my ADHD's comorbid pals -- hypomania and
depression -- blow things to pieces and let in the darkness.

I'm not looking for new ideas. I want tried-and-true, and I
want it quick. I'm scanning through material like a human Google
looking for keywords that signal ideas I already agree with. When it
comes to ADHD (and probably a lot of other things, too), I prefer
reading stuff that supports what I already believe, and that's written

from a perspective I can identify with. If pressed, I'd blame my brain for this. My wiring needs the familiar to concentrate. Or, I struggle with this crap every day, so who knows more about it than I do?

Well, a number of people, as it turns out. In the past few weeks, I've been trying to escape an approaching, large-looking depression that's gathering on the horizon. I see my therapist on Monday and we'll hash it out, but I really don't want to go on anti-depressants again. So I'm dashing around trying to ignore the darkening clouds, hoping that keeping active will diffuse them. But they keep growing and getting darker and begin to take over the sky like a Midwestern summer storm -- with tornado warnings. But this storm comes from within, and two of its sustaining fuels are isolation (feeling like you're utterly alone and friendless as you desperately try to find some way out from the closing darkness), and the relentless self-pity that grows from the hopeless muck of this belief.

So I'm zip-scrolling through blogs looking for keywords that agree with me, when I find myself slowing down and carefully reading a post in Kay Marner's blog, "My Picture-Perfect Family." Kay's young daughter has ADHD, but Kay doesn't; she's a "normal," and is primarily, as she describes herself, "a glass half-full person." Then why am I stopping here? This is no place to find a tried-and-true life preserver to get me through my ugly, dark storm...

Yeah, I'm mangling my metaphors here, but bear with me because I can't do anything about it now, and besides, the point is Kay Marner has gotten me to forget about my own ADHD drama for a second. I'm reading about attention deficit disorder from the other side of the experience. This is the side I always dismissed as not knowing, at a gut level, what it's like to live with this kind of ADHD brain, day in and day out. But now, as I read Kay describe pulling out of her despair after a particularly tough day trying to help and understand her daughter, I realize on a whole different level how hard the "normal" loved ones work to help us. And, more to the point: how much they really do know about us and how we think and behave and why, and how much, despite all we put them through, they care.

This may be no big insight to folks less self-obsessed than I am. But for me, reading Kay's spare, honest words about her life has given me a wider perspective. Best of all, it has helped me re-appreciate my amazing wife and family, my friends, and what they've all done for me over the years.

Later in the day, in the middle of checking production proofs of my mother's book of poetry and stories –- pencil tracking back and forth across the page, nosing out errors in spelling, spacing, and punctuation –- I'm brought up short by a poem she had written for me decades ago. I'd read those words many times over the years, but now -- on that different level -- I get a glimpse of my mother as the young woman struggling to understand and discover what she could do to help her mysteriously difficult child.

Stories Mom Never Told

But no escape, my darling, No turning place to hide.
I offer you no amulet,
No stone to fell Goliaths.
These mortal hands protect you
Only as my shadow halts the moving sun. Believe the trust
you give, I will not Betray you. A shadow is a shield.
                    -Berna Deane South from "For Trey"

My mother wrote the poem the above stanza is taken from years ago, when I was a kid. She told me when, but I don't remember exactly. "Trey" is my family nickname.

When I read her poem now, I imagine her as a young mother and poet sitting down at the kitchen table after everybody in the house is finally asleep, and trying to work through the frustration and fear of raising the mysteriously difficult child I was. This last summer, I also found a letter to Dr. Spock from that time folded up in a picture album. In it, she desperately pleads for some answer, some way to wrangle their daydreaming, unfocused, and willful son. She was hoping for at least a hint of how to help Trey get through childhood and adolescence without her and my dad going completely crazy in the process. As I was finishing fifth grade, I think my father was becoming more concerned with the damage I might inflict on the rest of the world.

I went to elementary school in Villa Park, a working class suburb of Chicago in the 1950s. Nobody knew what ADHD was. The term didn't exist. But everybody knew what a JD was, a juvenile delinquent, the buzzword for unruly teens. It was biggest threat to the young and society at large, after polio. But when we got the sugar cube with the Salk vaccine, the JD threat shot to the top of the charts.

We younger kids were constantly warned by teachers, scoutmasters, and policemen that it'd be better to be dead than to turn into one of those sneering, gum-chewing punks on the corner cleaning their fingernails with their switchblades. But look back at *Rebel without a Cause* now. James Dean's got all the ADHD symptoms , especially in that over-the-top, rambling speech to his dad, Jim Backus. Nobody to this day knows what James Dean was screaming about. And Sal Mineo is just a complete unfocused mess. Everybody in that movie could have used some goal-oriented therapy, ADHD meds, and hand-fidgets that weren't as pointy and lethal as the switchblades. The exception was Natalie Wood; she was the normal one who tried to keep everybody together, but she was in way over her head.

And that brings me back to my mom. I was in no danger of becoming a JD no matter how much I'd have liked to. I was a doofus ten-year-old with thick glasses and a tendency to breathe through my mouth and walk into things. Dad was gone at the university lab in Chicago all day during the week, and he worked at home a lot on the weekends.

So it was primarily Mom who dealt with things. Like a cop who brought me home completely covered in mud after he'd saved me from drowning in a deep, fenced-off slough surrounded by warning signs at a construction site where I was playing. Or the other cop who showed up at our front door after he saw me running away from a brush fire I'd accidentally started by the community center and he put out with some help from some firemen. Or the expensive bicycle I borrowed from a friend and then turned around and loaned to a stranger who promptly stole it. Or walking out of the classroom for recess and erasing the lesson the teacher had just finished putting on the board, and then telling the teacher I was acting out because my mean Grandma was visiting -- but my Grandma wasn't mean, I liked her a lot, and she wasn't visiting, which my teacher found out when she called my mother.

I explained every time that I didn't know how whatever happened ended up happening. I didn't mean to say or do whatever it was. I just wasn't paying attention. I could see the frustration and concern in her eyes. But she never lost it with me. She stayed as calm as she could, let me know about whatever consequences I had to face, and still left no doubt that she and dad loved me no matter what inexplicable thing I did next.

This amazes me to this day. My kids have ADHD. They have their challenges and sometimes act out, but they are dyed in the wool saints in comparison to me at any comparable age of their lives.

Back in the fifties and sixties, there wasn't any of the understanding and help available to parents of kids like me that we have now. But when I look back at my childhood, I remember the main thing that my parents provided for me and my brother that got us into adulthood in one piece: unquestioning, constant love that doesn't go away, no matter what. Then or now, or in the future, I think it's always the main ingredient for any kid to succeed on their own terms, or any adult, for that matter.

Not to say that parents, spouses, and friends of kids like me should never give voice to their frustrations. Sometimes it's necessary for your own survival, if nothing else. My favorite reaction from my father came on a Saturday about a month after I'd been drummed out of Boy Scouts for stealing from another Scout and lying to everybody about it for weeks. He looks out the window and sees me across the street playing with matches and accidentally starting yet another fire and then panicking and running off. After running across the street and stomping it out, he tracks me down, drags me home, and on our front lawn, howls, "My god, you're a thief, you're an arsonist, what's next? Murder?"

That made an impression. At ten years old, I honestly felt sorry for my mom and dad. So I promised I'd try harder to change my behavior, and to pay attention. And I did. I tried.

* * * *

The clear glass angel shines and sparkles. It's in the perfect place, with a blue light right behind it. It's not hanging straight though. It's caught up on a lower branch of the Christmas tree. If it was hanging free it would look a lot better, more like an angel is supposed to look. I can't reach it yet. If I scoot back under and get back behind the tree I can fix it. Just a little farther, I've got it, but I need to break that little piece of the lower branch off I think – almost got it, if I get up on my knees... And then it's moving away from me, the whole tree is moving away, falling, oh no... with a whoosh and a crash, the family Christmas tree falls to the living room floor. The water from the stand spreads on the rug, soaking through the wrapping on the presents.

My mom and dad rush in from the kitchen to find me standing over the lovingly decorated family tree like a seven-year-old Paul Bunyan. A blubbering, wailing Paul Bunyan terrified that he's going to be punished horribly. His presents thrown into a pile and burned in the front yard, and he'd throw himself on top, a Christmas funeral pyre. This Paul Bunyan has an over-dramatic and morbid imagination.

"What happened? Are you all right?" My parents hug me, and tell me not to worry about it, accidents happen, "but what were you doing behind the tree?"

I try to explain, but being me, I get side-tracked into the soaked wrapping falling off the bottom of the presents and getting a peek at what's hidden, and besides they'd never understand about the angel. I'm a normal, curious kid, maybe a little strange; but hey, lesson learned right? You would think.

Next year, on Christmas Eve, I'm scooting under the tree to drape tinsel behind the crèche scene so it'd look like icicles hanging over the barn to make it more dramatic for baby Jesus and maybe pull the one tree light down to be the star... whoosh, crash the tree goes over. This time Paul Bunyan doesn't get much sympathy at all – my dad's face is flushed with bottled up fury, "For God's sake stay out from behind the Christmas Tree!" No front-yard funeral pyre, but the look he gives me is scary.

Now that should finally burn the connection between action and consequences into my brain for the rest of my life. That assumes that I will sometime before I die ever give a shit about consequences.

The next year, I'm nine, old enough to understand the value of message repetition in advertising, politics, and family dynamics.

Since Halloween I've been working the whole family with my mature young gentleman act. There is no need to worry about the coming Yuletide; all the holiday decorations will remain upright and intact. This is my guarantee. And please, let me help you with that. After weeks of this over breakfasts, dinners and weekends my parents finally buckle and assure me that this coming year's gift-giving, in quantity or quality will not be affected by the last two years' tree incidents.

But as soon as my dad lugs the twine bound tree through the front door my good-hearted, liberal, understanding parents go Twilight Zone and turn into cold-eyed, flat voiced aliens.

They sit me down on a dining room chair and warn me that no tree tipping will be tolerated at all this year. No excuses no bullshit, this is serious. Great Aunt Jean will be visiting from New York. Tree falls, you die. My five year old little brother, Rob is deeply delighted that I'm not allowed anywhere near the back, or even the side, or within a foot of the front of the tree after decorating.

I'm only to decorate the front. Eye-level only. We're not fooling around here. This year the tree stays standing up until it's time to toss its tinsel-covered carcass in the gutter after New Year's Eve. The day after Christmas, Dad's upstairs at his desk, Great Aunt Jean is taking a nap and Mom is in the kitchen with Rob. I am in the living room, alone with the tree.

For days now I've been aching with the knowledge that I have to make one little adjustment. The red and gold antique Santa ornament should be higher and closer to the window. It just has to be that way; otherwise the whole display is out of balance. I'm the only one that sees this, so I'm the only one who can fix it. So damn the torpedoes, I move it, very carefully. I stand back and everything looks one hundred percent better. I wonder if Mom and Dad will notice when they come in. But then antique Santa slips from his branch. I dash over try to grab him before he breaks and my foot slips on the tree skirt. Over it goes. I don't remember exactly what my parents did or what consequences I suffered. My memory is blank after Great Aunt Jean's crystal angel tree-topper shattered against the wall. I think that year I was lucky to get out alive.

I don't know if this is symptomatic of any disorder, but sometimes, it's like my alarm system for even the most important relationship, career, or life-saving warnings can be completely ignored and over-ridden by the smallest impulse. Don't go behind the tree. Got it. I won't, I promise. Really. Yes, I know I promised, but the tinsel...

These incidents crossed my mind last night as my wife and I once again try to talk to my 21 year-old ADHD son about buying Christmas presents for others this year before spending what little money he has on other stuff. He says he'll get the presents if he has enough money left after he gets the "other stuff." Around and around we go, until finally he seems to understand and promises to get presents, just small tokens even, for other people before the other stuff.

That's when I hear, "For God's sake stay out from behind the Christmas tree," echoing in my head. We'll keep reminding him, and maybe this year or the next the alarm in his head won't get over-ridden by impulse at Game Stop. I decide not to count on it. The tree looks good.

Night Blows Up

It's New Year's Eve, 2003 and I'm curled up in our bed in a fetal position, eyes closed, hands over my ears. I'm working on calm, deep breathing – trying hard to not hyperventilate.

I've been in this position before when I had some panic attacks, and completely cracked up and had to put in some serious time with the doctors. Cracking up feels exactly like this – the world around me is pounding and exploding, getting louder and more insistent, like a rising climax of insane fireworks. Our dog, zonked out on veterinary Valium, has joined me on the bed, both of us trembling.

In Hawaii, especially in the local kind of neighborhood we lived in at the time, New Year's Eve is all about fireworks. Big fireworks at home, in the driveway, lanai, backyard, front yard, and roof – all going off at once and building to a smoke-clogged midnight crescendo.

The explosions shake the walls of our little house. It's LOUD - howitzer, carpet-bombing, end of civilization as we know it LOUD. Then again, maybe I'm a little over-sensitive to the gunpowder blasting away all around us. I've never liked fireworks.

It's not lost on me that cowering in the bedroom spooned with my petrified dog, while the rest of my family oohs and aahs at star bursts and pinwheels on the lanai isn't a very manly way to act.

Pa doesn't hide from danger in "The Little House on the Prairie." He protected his family. But, how do you protect your family from something that only freaks you out? How to you convince them that the prudent move during any noisy community celebration is to huddle under the covers with your drugged-up dog, who now has begun a panting, drooling action that's making things messy?

Not a good example to set when you go around preaching to your kids to face their fears. I stand up on wobbly knees, and step out to the lanai. I casually lean against the porch rail, a picture of easy confident calm. "So, howzit goin' guys?" All that manly effort and nobody even notices me. They're all watching the neighbors' rocket-spouting Freedom Fountain explode terrifying burning embers all over dry leaves and roofs, while it lets out an ear-piercing whistle that sounds like a screaming Kamikaze plummeting out of the sky to kill us all.

Smoke from all the exploding gunpowder hangs thick in the air as our other neighbor sets off the longest string of firecrackers in all of Polynesia. In the beach picnic grounds across the way, cheers fill the air as dozens of M-80s boom, blowing apart Parks and Recreation trash cans. People call this fun? This is horrible. The family notices me now. I must have said that last bit out loud. "What are you doing out here? You hate this stuff."

"Whoa Dad, really, you should go back inside. You don't look so good."

I guess my macho act needs a little work. I stumble back to join the dog in the bedroom. Later, as the noise finally begins to die down, Margaret curls up next to me and the dog. "I never knew that junk got to you so much."

"I shrug. "I never let on I guess. Maybe I didn't know." And that's the truth of it, in a way. I'd been working with a new therapist and new meds. I was in my second year of sobriety and feeling out who the hell I was. I was discovering that the more I stopped covering up who I really was to myself, the more that real-self was exposed to others. Apparently my real-self doesn't like things exploding around him. Sounds reasonable to me.

Besides, if I remember correctly, Pa in "Little House on the Prairie" didn't protect his family by shooting and blowing up the prairie. He just worked hard for them, stayed honest and picked up and moved the whole family whenever he thought he should.

So, call me Pa.

FATHER IN THE WILD

"Harry?"

"Yeah?"

"Are you going to do the kitchen or not?" There's no answer. At least I think there's no answer. It's hard to tell because I'm talking to a closed door. "Harry!"

My son, now twenty-one years old is in his room on the other side of the door. We're trying to break him of this rude habit of communicating to the family from behind a locked barrier. I've taken the door off the hinges and carted it out to the garage a couple of times, but then we're all subject to the sight of his incredibly messy room. When he promised to be a more responsive member of the household, we let him put it back up. Once I took it down and put it back up before he even came back from school because I couldn't take even walking by the open entrance of the nuclear waste dump where he sleeps, plays video games, practices guitar, and eats Ramen noodles.

My son will tell you he's not ADHD. He thinks terms like ADHD non-hyperactive type are stupid. He'll cop to being maybe a little ADD, but he refuses to take his meds, and since he did pretty well this semester at community college, we're not fighting him on it. But cripes, the kid's legally a full-fledged adult for God's sake, and I can't get him to clean the kitchen when I ask him to, or even open the door to his room when he's talking, or in this case, not talking to me. We've always been a engaged full-service parenting operation, equipped with the standard arsenal of love, respect, rules, manners, discipline, expectations, rewards, consequences, and blah-blah-blah.

We get tired and space out sometimes; but most of the time we're there pushing for the best for our kids, I think. These days it seems that's all I do with my son – push. I'm tired of always being the cop in this relationship. I'm tired of always being on his ass. Yes, he's got learning disabilities; but so did I growing up.

Just before I go into a "When I was your age..." self-righteous rage, Harry opens his door and says, "Chill, Dad... I was just getting my iPod." Then he walks past me with headphones on and starts cleaning the kitchen – slowly, with one hand. His other hand is occupied with IPod adjustments. I've told him a kazillion times that cleaning is a two-handed job. I was a professional dishwasher at his age before moving up to grill cook and you have to grab work with both hands, the same way you have to grab life if you expect to get anything from it... anyway, you get the idea. Harry does too. That's why he's got Eminem pounding in his ears.

My son Harry's brain wiring and mine are very different in a lot of ways. I'm an on-edge, jumpy, combined ADHD type with comorbid emotional and psychological doo-dads lurking in my head like unexploded bombs that go off with the smallest nudge, who has learned to use meds, power tools, or whatever it takes to bolt down my concentration to what's in front of me. Harry's ADHD, combined with his co-morbid auditory processing delay, which he also doesn't cop to, has him buried down in a cavern, looking at the stuff that he's gathered around him and not all that interested in venturing out into the sunlight to experience anything new.

For a while it seemed like no matter what either Harry or I did, we were going to be stuck forever in this boring dance of hyperactive discipline and passive-aggressive rebellion. Then I noticed that when we talked to each other we barely looked each other in the eyes. We'd start with eye contact, and then we'd both slide off as our attention was drawn to other things while we were talking. It's a small ADHD habit we share.

So, I'm trying something new. I keep my eyes on his when we talk, through the whole conversation. And, yes, I also try to talk about other stuff than what chores he should be doing. But, the eye-contact really seems to make a difference. He looks back. Yesterday we shared a smile. That might happen again in a week or so. Or maybe he'll start wearing a blindfold around to keep me at bay. As long as I don't begin obsessing about something else and forget, I'll keep at it and find out.

MUDDLE SCHOOL

Coco, now 14, brought her report card home last night, and it's fine – one A, the rest B's, and two C's. If I'd had a report card like that at her age I would have strutted home with banners flying in front of a brass band.

But Coco's not proud at all. She's miserable. She buries her head in a pillow crying hard, then hugs it to her chest, doing her best to hold her tears and sobs under control.

Coco is embarrassed by the raging sorrow breaking out all over in front of people, especially her parents. Especially me, because she says I get too "emotional". Tonight she's invited me into this intense mother-daughter talk. Coco's cross-legged on our bed next to her mom with me planted at the foot under strict instructions not to interrupt, or get all gooey, hug her and tell her how brilliant and talented she is.

All she wants me to do is to listen to her. Margaret already knows how to listen so she gets a pass on the instructions.

As Coco starts telling us what's going on, I'm not even tempted to interrupt or get gooey, because I discover, as I have repeatedly in the last year or so, that my daughter's not a kid anymore. I'm listening to a smart, perceptive young woman with a clear idea of what's making her so deeply unhappy. And what she wants - more than us trying to jump in and make it all better - is for her mom and dad to sit here, be patient, and hear her out completely.

No matter what we say, she knows her grades should be better. "I'm trying hard, and then just as I start to get it, somebody says something, or something happens in the classroom, and everything gets nuts and then I forget what the teacher was saying and I have to start all over but then it's too late. A lot of the other kids in Special Ed... mostly the boys... just don't care about learning anything – they swear all the time, talk sex junk, call their moms bitches. The teacher can't really control them. I can't take it anymore."

It turns out that today one of the boys in study hall kept taunting and goading her and she hauled off and punched him in the arm. She accepts that she was wrong. She understands that you can't hit people no matter how aggravating they are – a lesson I finally got through my own thick skull sometime in my twenties. But the fact remains that she's desperately unhappy and frustrated in school, and she's come up with a solution.

"I want to be home-schooled for the rest of the semester," she says.

Now, her middle school has a bunch of dedicated teachers in Special Ed, and our meetings with her teachers about starting to slowly mainstream Coco have been great. But, she wants to be able to get away from all the social pressure and craziness at school and study at home until she starts high school when we move to Georgia.

I remember Middle School being a nightmare when I was in eighth grade, but I don't remember thinking as clearly about solutions. I just brooded in my room working out revenge scenarios where I was the wise-cracking TV gambler Maverick and the other kids were dimwit losers.

Coco looks at us from behind her hugged pillow, waiting to hear our response. She doesn't look too hopeful. I can imagine what she'd think we'd say to her idea – something along the line of, "Are you out of your mind, sweetheart?"

But Margaret and I look at each other for a second, and then turn back to Coco and say, "Okay."

"Okay?"

"Yep, we'll call the school tomorrow."

Coco smiles. "Thanks," she says. Then she looks down at the pillow in her arms, "I guess I better wash this. It's soaked."

Margaret and I scoot together and hold hands, watching Coco as she walks out of our bedroom. Crosby, Stills, and Nash had it wrong, I think. It's not "Teach your children well." It's "Shut up and listen."

THE MIND SCHEMES

"If you want to know where your heart is, look where your mind wanders."

> – Unknown, scrolled in the middle of a
> fluffy cloud on the side of a coffee mug

One, I know where my heart is. Two, my mind doesn't wander. At night, using the distracting cover of dreams, my mind makes plans and plots quietly in secret.

Then, sometime during the day when my guard is down, and when it can do the most damage, my mind breaks out of prison and flies into the high grass laughing like mad, the blood hounds braying in pursuit far behind.

I'm in a meeting with a principal at a private school where I'm being hired to do my solo show, *Pay Attention*. The principal, a thoughtful woman in her thirties, has seen me do the show and thinks it'd be good for the teachers to experience ADHD "from the inside."

All the teachers have a few students diagnosed with the disorder, and many are having a hard time dealing with those kids' inattention and class disruption that seems to have no solution. A few in the faculty think these kids are simply challenging their authority in the classroom and that ADHD is just an excuse, or even believe it doesn't exist at all. Consequently the entire faculty will be required to attend.

Not only am I supposed to do the show, I'm supposed to do a Q&A afterward for an hour or so, to let them see that though I too was a problem kid, I grew up to be at least a moderately, sort-of solid citizen.

In a pre-show meeting she and I are reviewing a few aspects that as the principal she feels are vital for the presentation. "In the Q&A afterward, I think it's important that the faculty doesn't feel they're being lectured to. We want them to be as receptive as possible to the insights you're providing."

I nod to her, and just as I begin to respond in a thoughtful, adult manner, my eyes glaze over as I fixate on the L-shape and small size of the principal's office.

Is this a purposeful slight to her? Does she suffer everyday under cruel disapproval communicated to her only by the configuration of the walls surrounding her while she works -- a dark, constant reminder wearing her down? Well, that depends on the relative size of the headmaster's office, doesn't it? He seemed like a nice guy when we were introduced, not the type to play punishing cubicle politics, but I was focused on him and his story about his ... was it his brother? Somebody in his family with clinical depression, but the point is I didn't take in his office.

When did I become the guy everybody tells their family mental illness stories to? I guess I don't mind. I obsess on my own craziness and advertise publicly for sympathy. My new shrink says no. Not my pattern. He says I'm an honest person. But I lie to him. But not about important stuff, just little lies to keep the sessions interesting, and he's a straight shooter –- last week he cleared up some new psychiatric classifications I got concerned about.

"Do you know that hypomania is now classified as bipolar 2"? I ask her.

"Um, no..." the principal says.

My eyes, unglazed, are now locked right on hers. "I'm comorbid hypomanic. I like the term 'hypomanic.' It sounds easy-going, nothing to worry about, right? But 'bipolar 2' sounds kind of dangerous. But not dangerous enough for people to give you that step-back crazy space that straight-up 'bipolar' gets. 'Bipolar 2' just sounds second-rate, like you're trying to be scary but you don't have the stones to pull it off. My shrink says it's just the medical profession trying to reflect the truth as they discover it, and that everything's on a spectrum. If I'm on the bipolar spectrum I want to be scary. But then, like my therapist says, ADHD is on the autism spectrum, but I'm not autistic. Well, maybe compared to some people I am, but my therapist says not to focus on the labels, focus on the day in front of you. And I listen to him about that stuff, because mostly he makes sense. Don't you think?"

There's a beat as she stares at me. I better try to explain, tell her I was daydreaming before I lose this gig before I even get it. Then she bursts out laughing. "That's exactly what I'm talking about, Frank. Like you and your therapist, it's not a lecture if you listen."

Whoa. That was a lucky landing after that prison-break in my head. We talk more, and later I find out that she's got family with some mental health issues so she has practice making metaphors out of mud-pies. Sometimes it takes a talented listener to understand what you didn't even know you meant.

We finish up, make plans and I'm set for my presentation and Q&A next month. As I'm leaving, she leans back against her office door, smiles and says, "By the way Frank, don't worry. You're plenty scary."

FAKER

"**I** am concerned that you are possibly misrepresenting yourself, or at the least exaggerating some small problem for dramatic effect."

It's the end of an exhausting three days of passionate self-expression and concentrated listening at an autobiographical writing and critique group, where I just read my story about living with ADHD earlier in the afternoon, when this perfectly nice, soft-spoken middle aged woman, who didn't say anything after my reading, pulls me aside and accuses me of lying about who I am.

"I mean you obviously don't have any mental disability so pretending you do, even with the best intentions, could be seen as disrespectful of those unfortunate people that really do suffer from mental problems," she continues.

I've seen that "worried mom" look on my mother's face every day growing up so I know what's going on here, no matter how much psycho-babble code this well-meaning lady is tossing at my face like wet confetti.

Thing is, growing up when I got caught lying, and I lied a whole lot, most of the time I confessed, took the punishment and moved on to lie another day. Except that time with my dad when I got kicked out of the Boy Scouts, but that's not important now. What is important now is that I pretty much gave up lying around seventh grade because day to day it was becoming way too hard to remember what was real, never mind a bunch of junk I made up.

Of course there are always exceptions. On our second date I told Margaret, my wife-to-be, that a mule kicked out my front teeth when I was working on a dude ranch in Colorado. That sounded a lot more impressive than getting bridgework after a swimming pool accident. But the point is, these days as much as humanly possible I'm all truth, all the time. So I don't know how to respond to this woman who's keeping me from getting in my car and going home.

Her eyes are wide with concern as she touches my arm. "Frank, I listened carefully to your comments on other writers' work including mine, and everything you said was so well thought out and succinct," the woman says.

"Oh, well, thanks..."

"But that isn't a compliment," she says. "During this weekend I've noticed that when you're not acting out your ADHD material, you are very normal, calm, and perceptive."

At this point I admit I am staring at her open-mouthed. I dig my car keys out of my pocket and immediately drop them on the gravel driveway. I pick them up, unlock my car door, and throw my bag and bedding in the back seat. I don't want to talk to this person. Her assumptions about me and mental illness, learning disabilities, and basic human nature are so skewed and push so many buttons that I think I may short out and scream at her at the top of my lungs to get the hell away from me before I rip her head off and suck the blood from her corpse.

But I'll be damned if I'm going to play to that stereotype. I like stereotypes with more soul and romance. As I may have mentioned, I have "Middle-aged Man Interrupted" fantasies, but without Angelina Jolie going completely bat-shit. So, I don't scream, I take a five count in through my nose and a fifteen count out through my mouth. Then, I explain as best I can that, yes, I do listen carefully, but if you notice, I almost always give my comment last in a group conversation so that I can organize my thoughts and rehearse my comment in my head a couple of times. Then when I have to speak in public I go right through it, calm and collected.

But if the conversation starts going back and forth I back off and stay quiet, unless I'm around folks who know me and are used to my impromptu mangled sentences, malapropos, lost thoughts, names, and ideas, stammering, and back-flip subject-jumps.

Over the years I've worked hard at developing coping skills that help me keep that part of me hidden when I have to, like the careful construction and rehearsal before speaking gambit. It's something I figured out after realizing that when I was acting on stage with a script I'd memorized, I didn't lose my train of thought or stammer. So in certain situations I can write little plays in my head, rehearse, and then act like what's considered a normal person.

I could tell that a third of the way through my explanation she had decided that it was bullshit and stopped listening. I thanked her for her concern, and she left, shaking her head in disgust.

In the end I don't care what my acquaintance from the writing group thinks. Whatever her trite preconceptions of people with mental health issues are, she did buy into my normal act. Score one for my mad skills.

Those of us with any sort of mental or physical disability have developed myriad coping skills to deal with daily life in ways that help us get by as just people. After all, despite whatever challenges each of us face, that's what we are and in the end, that's how we want to be seen. As people.

Play Doctor for Me

I'm in the doctor's office for my yearly physical which with I manage to get every three or four years, or sometimes five. I don't trust most doctors, at least when they're in their offices or the hospital.

They just seem like detached bearers of bad news and pain. Lucky for me I'm a pretty healthy guy, if you put aside the rabid greyhound in my brain straining to break free and run around howling in tighter and tighter circles chasing nothing and yapping incessantly about everything and everybody everywhere, except for who or what is right in front of us. I had a therapist a while back who impressed on me the importance of not referring to myself and my brain as "us." He felt it was a dissociative pattern that kept me from dealing with my problems constructively. But we never trusted that guy either.

But this GP in front of me right now seems like a pleasant guy. I've seen maybe once or twice before, but I still keep my guard up and have to work at keeping eye contact and actually listening to him as he goes over my history with me. No recent illnesses or injuries, which I've accomplished by staying locked inside my house in front of my computer avoiding other people and exercise. I promise him I'll get outside and lose weight, and this time I think I might mean it.

I know it won't be easy. I'll have to remember to write "Go Walk" on my calendar every day ahead of time in order to remember to do it. Maybe I should fill up every day in the whole calendar at one sitting. But that'd be stupid. How far ahead do you write reminders in calendars? I realize I've been mumbling all this out loud as the doctor nods and glances down at my chart.

"So," he asks, "How long ago were you diagnosed with ADHD?"

"Eleven years ago," I tell him.

He nods some more as I elaborate on the comorbid conditions -- be careful what you ask an out-of-the-closet mental patient, they'll never shut up about all the interesting junk going on in their heads, and whatever they read about that junk online this morning. I mention that this spring I'm eight years sober and he says that's good and then asks, "Do you think the ADHD and the drinking were connected?"

I tell him yeah, in a way, but it's not an excuse. I'm an alcoholic, and as any recovering alcoholic will tell you, the drinking is really just connected to you and the drink and whether you drink it or not.

"You take Adderall for the ADHD. Are there any addiction problems with that?"

Whoa, wait a minute. This guy isn't one of those anti-med, ADHD deniers is he? Usually you don't find them in doctor's offices, but I'm sure it's happened before.

"No," I say, "That's not an issue. Sometimes I even forget to take it, and only remember when my day starts going off the rails. Honestly, if you have ADHD, this is in no way a recreational drug. It's a life-saver."

"Uh-huh... And both of your children have ADHD?"

"Yeah..."

"And they take medication as well?"

"Yes, and they're both doing well with it." I realize I'm sitting up very straight on the exam table and my voice has gotten definite and authoritative, and a little defensive. And the truth is, my 21-year-old son refuses to take his meds these days and I don't think he's doing that well without them. But so what? This is not this GP's area. I have a psychiatrist, the doc I trust with my brain, and he's the one in charge of us.

"Do you or your children experience any oppositional behavior problems?

Okay, what's with the third degree? All my alarm bells go off. It's like exam tables give these guys the idea they can ask or say any damn thing they want. Doctors are dangerous on their home turf, power corrupts and all that. I'm not even sure I trust my psychiatrist poking around in my brain every month, and I've been with him a while and my scrambled neurons and misfiring synapses are his area of expertise. They're not this GP's area, and my kids are especially none of his damn business, so I clam up. I take a couple of slow deep breaths.

Then the GP leans back against the wall, his features soften and he says, "I'm sorry I've been asking you so much about you and your family's ADHD. I'm only curious because..." He takes a breath himself and smiles. "It's my son," he says, "I'm concerned about my son. I wanted to get an idea what helped you handle things, as a patient and with your kids, too."

"Have you had your son diagnosed?" I ask.

"Not officially," he says, "No. You'd think I would have, but he just seemed like a really energetic boy growing up. Things really didn't get difficult for him until high school. Now he can't focus, he dropped out of college, and he's not interested in getting any help. Was that your experience at all?"

I tell him that it's difficult to find any real norm for ADHD. I was a basket-case from kindergarten on through to the present, while my son started similarly, but grew less so as he got older. My daughter and I are almost symptom twins, but that doesn't mean I understand her any better than my neuro-typical wife does.

The doctor and I trade stories about the unrelenting stress ADHD can put on a family and he asks how we handle it. I shrug. Sometimes well, sometimes not so well. "But, we've found as parents, and I've found as a patient," I tell him, "that when things get tense, that something as uncomplicated as going with the ADHD individual's flow, but helping them simplify it and slow it down to reduce overloading, can help."

He listens as I tell him that there are all kinds of practical info available at ADDitude as well as other sources including Children and Adults with Attention Deficit/Hyperactivity Disorder (CHADD). I also give him my therapist's name, because he should really get his son to talk to a specialist.

"Cripes," I say, "You're a doctor, you know that."

"Yeah," he says, "But he's my son. I wasn't looking at him as a patient."

One of my favorite surprises is when someone who is playing a normal role in your day breaks the accepted rhythm and then, in front of your eyes, changes into a completely different and fleshed-out human being. Now, as I talk with the doctor I'd been so wary of a few minutes earlier, the exam room ceases to be anybody's home turf. Because he's just another dad like me, just looking for a way to help his kid.

DON'T MAKE A MOVE

Lately I've spent some time with my therapist working on my aversion to change. We've talked about ways to handle the sense of being suddenly overwhelmed by a world that won't stay still long enough for me to see what's going on.

We've also talked through dealing with the rage I experience toward people and things that present problems and disappear while I slowly work through the bazillion facets of the issue at hand -- the solution to which usually no longer applies by the time I come up with it.

We talk about acceptance. The theory being that if you accept the constantly changing nature of life, you are less likely to want to try to freeze events as they happen in order to understand them and always be a step behind. Or to overcompensate by jumping ahead to possible outcomes and worry about those even if they never happen.

Basically, my therapist's suggestion is to try to just be here now and stay aware and flexible enough to not get rattled and pulled off course. Later, you can examine changing events at your leisure, and get a better understanding of what made you anxious about them and what you can do to adjust.

That makes sense in theory, but in the moment when the rhythm of life starts to beat faster and shift around you, how the heck can you possibly "be here now?" Before you know it, the here and the now start flying around all over the place connecting to all sorts of emotions, facts, and thoughts from the past, present and future, all demanding equal time. So a lot of times, I just have to pretend I've got it handled.

It seems to me that the popular notion that ADHD folks are scattered, confused, and can't pay attention, is completely backward. It's the world that's confused and scattered and our problem is that we do pay attention to what is really going on around all of us. Everybody else keeps their head down, eye on the track, chugging along the straight line, ignoring any other part of life that doesn't apply to the goal. Sure, you adjust to change that way, because the track makes it simple. Keep your head down and keep moving. Sounds a little judgmental, I know. And for the most part, I try to just be here and now, too, but lately it's been a real pain.

There's big change looming for our family.

In May we're packing up all four of us and our great big dog and leaving Hawaii. After 10 years of living in paradise we're moving to Georgia. My mother-in-law is moving in with us, which is great -- everybody gets along fine. But there's a brand-new house, a completely new life and I sometimes honestly can't remember why or when we decided to do this.

That's not the problem either, because it's something Margaret wants, and that's good enough for me. Her sisters, my parents, and my brother and his family will be much closer as well. I'll miss my friends here, but I've moved lots of times. It always works out. There's no reason to be freaking out.

Even though I know all of the benefits, and even though I tell Margaret I'm getting things organized, "Look, I've hung a big calendar on the wall and marked the date, see?" Quietly and in private, so as to not freak anyone else out, I am completely freaking, hyperventilating, panicking, the whole bit.

So, being a mature and together man who's working through his difficulties with his therapist, I take one of his suggestions and lie down on my bed in the middle of the day to take a break, get my breathing under control and look calmly at what's making me react like this. And it's working; I think this therapist might turn out to be a great one for me. I've had my doubts, it's taken us nearly a year to get over some trust things, but he's a good guy...

Wait -- we're moving. That means I'll have to get a new therapist. There's no way I can go through that again. This is a disaster. I'm not ready for this and it's all because of that "be here now" garbage he stuffed in my head. If I ever get out of bed and make it to my appointment tomorrow, we'll see what my therapist says about this. Because, honestly, I'm getting real tired of pretending I've got any of this under control.

* * * *

Outwardly I'm doing fine -- got the calendar marked, packing, throwing stuff out, and putting things aside for a garage sale. Inside, though, on a day I'm supposed to sort through a huge bin of VHS tapes of old TV shows I wrote or directed, I'm a full-panic, freak-out disaster. But I'm learning to use calming techniques to keep the panic-fire in my forehead and chest from exploding into a three-alarm inferno -- during which I have been known to get so agitated my hyperventilating free-associating literally comes out of my mouth backwards.

So before I get that far, I dump all the VHS tapes into the garbage. I don't like living in the past; the image of me sitting around misty-eyed with future grandkids watching old episodes of "Melrose Place" and "Baywatch Hawaii" flat-out scares me to death. But dumping the tapes only helps temporarily. Because right now I see this move, my future, and the future of my family, as an uncharted thick forest filled with threat.

I can handle it, though. I lie down, work on my breathing, and calmly let what's bothering me float away, just like my psychiatrist has suggested. But what floats up, and won't go away, is the fact that when we move to Georgia, I have to find a new psychiatrist.

The next day is my therapy appointment. I usually show up a little apprehensive because I have no idea what I'll say after we get settled and he asks the usual, "So, how are you doing?" Not this time. This time I have a definite problem to discuss. But when my psychiatrist -- let's call him Mike (not his name, but he reminds me of my football coach friend Mike, so it fits) -- asks that start-off question, I'm not paying attention. I'm staring at a nature print on his wall. I always thought the two monochrome, contrasting images in the print were of a dead leaf on the left side and a tree branch against a gray sky on the right. But now I'm not sure. That isn't a tree branch on the right. Is it a stream, splitting up over pebbles? And the leaf, is that a hand? No, it's a leaf. I think. Maybe a maple leaf. But that's definitely a stream over pebbles, not a branch.

When I catch myself weighing the odds of the print being an intentional Rorschach/Escher mess-with-your-mind test/trick, I close my eyes, shake it off, and turn to Mike. He's sitting in his chair, smiling, at ease, waiting for me to answer the seemingly simple "How are you doing?" question in whatever time it takes me, and in whatever way I will.

Okay look, here's a sketch or two of some of the worst shrinks I've had, just in case you're feeling a little off one day and you don't want to risk going to get help from someone who'll set you back a decade.

I've had therapists in the past who would have been calling out little verbal slaps, "Frank? Frank?" - trying to force me to focus. That's the hall-monitor type, who let you know that if you'd do just this, just so, you'd be all better -- I never lasted long with that type. I've had worse, though.

In my early twenties after having a mild breakdown, I had a psychiatric intern treating me who prescribed large doses of Stelazine, an anti-psychotic. Week after week I sobbed that the meds didn't help, and worse, that they turned the whole world into incomprehensible pudding. He just nodded and hmm-hmmed and made notes on his stupid little pad. I finally managed to quit him and the meds, and pull myself together on my own, but you can probably tell I still hold a tiny grudge.

In my thirties I saw a psychologist who told me I didn't have a drinking problem and said everything was my wife's fault. This one was my all-time fave for a while. Then I got tired of blaming everyone else for everything and bored with acting out pretend fights with my father by punching a couch cushion. (My father, to my mind, has never been anything but supportive and kind to me. No matter what I tried. The therapist might have had some father issues though.)

In terms of therapists, I've had the dream dissector, the distant judge, the clinical diagnostic, the homey guy with an afghan over his lap, and the nervous Nellie who seemed ready to jump out the window in fright every time I showed up. As a matter of fact, until the therapist I had for seven years before Mike, I was convinced I'd never connect with any of these people. I kept on saying whatever it took to make the therapist happy so he'd write the prescription for my meds and that would be that.

But Mike and his predecessor Dr. G (whom I wrote about when he retired) changed all that. Both these guys have listened intently, but more than that -- when it comes to talking, the language and subject matter have always helped me find the way to deal with my problems from my perspective. Like frontier scouts, they've helped me cut through the forest to find a route that takes me where I want to go. As a bonus, both Dr. G and Mike have dropped a bunch of bright, sparkling insights in the path for us to discover together.

So when Mike asks me how I'm doing, I try to answer as honestly as I can. "I'm getting by, I guess... It's just that prism thing you know? Things are fine if you look at it from one way, but turn it just a little and it's obvious your life is an empty, pointless sham. Maybe it's not that bad, but lately it seems like I've been fighting off the darkness more than usual. But maybe it's just how I'm looking at things. Like that leaf print on your wall -- one minute it's a tree, the next minute it's a roaring river with a man's desperate hand reaching out for help before he drowns or is dashed against the rocks. Is that print supposed to do that? I mean did you get it to help people think about their perceptions?"

Mike glances at the print. "Actually, I got it at Pottery Barn. I thought it seemed peaceful."

He smiles. I shrug. And we spend the next forty minutes cutting through the forest of darkness and confusion I constantly fight, hunting for different ways to calm down and bring in some light. Right at the end I remember what I wanted to talk to him about – there's only two months before my move. What am I going to do? After finally finding Dr. G and then Mike, I would feel too lucky for it to happen to me again. Besides, Dr. G recommended Mike, and Mike doesn't know any psychiatrists in Georgia does he?

Mike says no, he doesn't. But then his eyes light up. "I've got an idea, a project for you. Why don't you start looking for your new therapist now? Call some psychiatrists up; tell them what you're looking for."

"What, you mean like... shopping?"

"Yeah," Mike says, "Why not? It could help you put into words what you want from a therapist. You could even write about it."

It's not shopping, I think later in the car. It's psycho-phone-therapist-speed-dating, with witnesses.

* * * *

Margaret, Coco, and I have just finished dinner, and I'm halfway out of the kitchen when Coco grabs my arm and stops me. "Dad, you shouldn't worry so much," she says.

My daughter's right, but since I worry like most people breathe, that's not so easy to do. Coco should know; she worries and obsesses about everything near, far, past, present, and future so much that Margaret and I are sure we can smell her synapses smoking -- even when she's asleep. As a matter of fact, right now Coco's burning up brain cells worrying about me worrying. And from the look on Margaret's face, she's worried, too. But let's face it even my sorta-normal wife is no stranger to staying up all night, driving yourself crazy, and agonizing over every unsolvable thing in the universe. Given the right circumstances the three of us together could work up a Category 5 hurricane of neuroses.

Harry often regards the rest of us in the family with a look of such complete incomprehension that I'm convinced he thinks we're an alien species. Then again, he keeps whatever insecurities and worries he has so close to the vest that sometimes I think that he doesn't care about anything except whether I remember to get pot stickers at Safeway. Then I'll overhear him talking quietly to Margaret in his room and realize that he may act like a post-hip-hop John Wayne, but with his learning disabilities, his feelings are probably rawer than most kids stumbling into adulthood.

But just as I'm trying to look, listen, and see Harry as the complex, whole human he is, he'll lash out at his little Coco sister over something completely petty, and I get so furious I have to leave the room before I lose my temper and make things worse. I don't see his side. I'm so consumed with the unfairness (he's bigger, older) that I don't see that Coco can handle herself perfectly well in any argument with her brother and sometimes instigates them just to entertain herself. Over and over Margaret tells me, "Don't take it so much to heart. Let them work it out between themselves." I find not taking it to heart nearly impossible when I'm in the same room, so I've learned to grab a book and make tracks to a peaceful corner of the house when the storm clouds gather.

This is what I was doing in the kitchen when Coco grabbed my arm to stop me. But Harry wasn't even home. Coco was lashing out at her mother. She shouldn't do that; Margaret loves her beyond measure, and has sacrificed so much for her. But Margaret instigated the fight this time, pushing a homework issue way too hard. I don't know who will feel the wrath of my temper first, or the most, but it's time to grab that book before I explode. And that's when Coco says, "Dad you worry too much." She and Margaret laugh, and I join in, understanding once again, that they'll work it out between themselves. Good thing I like to read.

Later, while doing dishes and worrying about worrying; I mention my concern to Coco about changing psychiatrists when we move to Georgia. I tell her I'm starting to look for a new one and since it's worked out previously that she, Margaret and I end up sharing the same one, I wonder if she has any preferences.

"He should be young, like our guy now. He's cool. Not someone your age," she says.

I ask her if it matters if it's a man or a woman.

"Considering how I don't get along with women, it should definitely be a guy."

Coco doesn't get along with women? And she's self-aware enough at 14 to see this as an impediment to effective therapy? You know, my wife's right. When you stop worrying so much and start listening more, you learn all kinds of interesting things. Tomorrow I think I'll try it with Harry.

* * * *

Moving day is fast approaching and everyone in my family is handling the increasing tension differently. Margaret and Coco are in the living room packing. After a kind of short shift of packing and cleaning, I'm in the back bedroom reading, trying to avoid a brewing panic attack and trying to ignore the voices, rising in intensity.

"That's just stupid, Mom," Coco says.

"Coco, I'm warning you, don't talk that way to me."

"Why? I'm not calling you stupid," Coco says, "I said what you said was stupid."

"Enough. That's it," Margaret says.

"No! Don't take my laptop!"

Sounds like a scuffle out there. Oh, no, footsteps coming this way. I concentrate harder on the Nevada Barr mystery I'm reading, wedge my head right into the book.

"No! Stop! You can't!" Coco screams from the living room.

Margaret storms into the bedroom, drops Coco's laptop on the dresser, plows onto the bed next to me, and crosses her arms.

"Your daughter's lost her mind," she says.

"Oh..." I say.

More screaming rage in the living room and then more footsteps come this way. It's an invasion. Coco, livid, stomps up to the bed next to me and yells at her mother lying on my other side.

"You don't even listen to me, you just get mad and mean!"

"Coco, I'm not talking to you," Margaret says, "Go to bed."

"No, I won't! It's not fair!"

I jump out of bed. Now, I've always tried to model myself after never-say-die type characters like Scott Glenn as Emmett in *Silverado*, or Vivien Leigh as Scarlet O'Hara in *Gone with the Wind*. I never wanted to be the one who quit under pressure. I never thought I'd one day find myself throwing my hands up in defeat, yelling, "This is too much. Stop. I can't handle this!" But right now, standing between my wife and daughter, I'm doing exactly that.

Coco bursts into tears and runs into the living room, and I follow. Between sobs, she says she didn't mean to yell at mom, she's just feeling bad because now she's decided she doesn't want to move to Georgia after all. She hates change. I can't help it -- I burst out laughing. "Me too," I say, "Change makes me want to throw up."

A crooked smile cracks through Coco's sobs, and, as she turns over, I think she mumbles "You are so weird," into her pillow. I realize Coco's right -- I am weird.

When she and Margaret started to argue, I was in the bedroom fighting off a panic attack that I had manufactured myself. With procrastination and avoidance, I'd wound myself so tightly with fear that I could barely move. The pressures were really there -- the move, writing deadlines -- (What about calling all those therapists like I promised I was going to do? But that would mean really admitting I am leaving my present one -- something I'm not yet willing to do.), a speaking engagement, and a TV-pilot rewrite that I have to do in record time before we move, which, if I do a good job, might actually get shot, but probably won't.

But I deal with these kinds of pressures most often by putting off doing anything about them. It's an old procrastination habit that keeps creeping back -- waiting until the deadline pressure builds up to such a degree that either I am forced to take care of business or crack up. It's a fifty-fifty shot. Thing is, if you keep playing chicken with your sanity, you're likely to end up in a secure hospital wing playing with your food. Maybe not that bad. But for me, it's at least not healthy. I've started on beta-blockers for the panic attack physical symptoms, and more importantly started breaking down tasks into smaller, more manageable monsters that can hopefully be corralled one at a time.

Later that night, after the dust settles, Margaret and Coco decide to sleep together out in the living room in the middle of all the boxes and bubble wrap. From behind my book in the bedroom I can hear them talking in whispers in the dark.

In the morning, they both apologize for putting me into the middle of their fight. But, as it turns out, I'm glad they did. Sometimes it takes a little drama to realize you need to make some alterations in your world. And there's no place better for that than in the middle of some people you trust.

LIFE IN TRANSITION

"**D**ad's had an accident, and it's, um, pretty bad." It's my brother Rob calling from Delaware where he lives with his family near our parents' house.

I'm in Georgia with Coco, in the middle of our move. In a matter of days my wife, son, mother-in-law, and huge dog will arrive, loaded down with luggage, exhaustion, and expectations.

Maybe I'm projecting. Maybe they don't expect the new pans, plates, bowls, and flatware stacked and organized; the lawn mower put together; the Clorox toilet tank tablets freshly sunk, with backups under the sink; and services for our phones, electricity, cable, Internet, garbage pickup, and water all signed up and paid for when they get here. They for sure don't expect or care that I get my Georgia driver's license -- proof of my new existence, laminated with my picture next to our new address -- right now, tomorrow at the latest, but I do.

Consequently, Coco and I are busy. She had a tough last few months in Hawaii, but I've noticed her self-confidence growing since we've taken off together to be the advance team. We help each other stay focused on the endless minutiae of setting up our family's new house, no matter what's on the to-do list: stores and bureaucracy in the morning, house chores in the afternoon, *Gilmore Girls* DVDs at night. The two of us seem to share a deeper understanding, and she's been more open and happier than I've seen her in a while. She relishes this father-daughter time and the routines we've invented together. This afternoon Coco's organizing the kitchen and I'm breaking down boxes in the garage when I get my brother's call and slowly sit down on the floor.

My parents are in their mid-80s, and after raising two sons and finishing their careers, they've remained fiercely committed to living out their lives alone together in their own house. And despite some other accidents and medical emergencies, they've seemed resilient to the point of indestructibility. But from the sound of Rob's voice I know this time is different.

"Dad fell," he says. "He went from standing to landing on his head...fractured his skull. They think he had a stroke first, but anyway, they had to go into his brain to stop the bleeding..."

"Dad!" Coco's yelling at me from the kitchen.

"Hold on a sec," I tell Rob, and hold the cell phone to my chest. "I'm on the phone!" I yell to Coco, and then I'm back to Rob, "Go ahead."

He continues, his normally confident, booming voice subdued and strained, "So, yeah, the docs said the brain surgery went pretty well, but he's on a ventilator and they induced a coma, so we can't see him, not even Mom."

Rob pauses, strapping his emotions down with the gruff, silent steel bands of manhood that he and my father have used throughout their lives. Growing up, it drove me nuts that I was closer in temperament to my mother (though she's always had better control of herself), a Chicken Little freaking out while my dad and younger brother stayed calm inside their John Wayne armor.

But Chicken Little can control his hyperventilating long enough to smell when John Wayne has another bomb to drop. Just as Rob takes a breath to tell me whatever bad news he has yet to reveal, Coco bolts into the garage.

"Dad!" she hollers.

"Not now, damn it!"

"But Dad, a cockroach..."

I explode. "Christ, Coco! Shut up!" I'm anxious, raw, and harsh. I can see my daughter's shock. My words have hurt, but I don't care. I look away from her, stare at the flattened boxes on the garage floor, and focus on my brother's phone call.

Rob's cracked-voiced litany goes on: "Dad will be kept in this coma for days, no telling how damaged his brain is until he wakes, but, all in all, it doesn't look good. Mom's holding it together, went home to sleep, she'll call you tomorrow. Nothing's going to change for a few days -- no need to come now, we know you're in the middle of a move."

I feel a flush of shame. I was just thinking how inconvenient the timing of all this is. Rob read my mind. I don't even have to speak to play out my role in the family as the self-absorbed older brother. Our voices echoing each other's sense of loss, we ask after each other's wives and children, promise to talk tomorrow, and disconnect.

I take a deep breath and look around the garage. My wife, Margaret, will want to know about this, but I don't want to go through it all again, right this second, even though talking to her always makes me feel better. Maybe after Coco and I have dinner and watch some Gilmore Girls. Coco -- I'll have to tell her something; she's 14, but sensitive, and has a finely-tuned radar for picking up emotional signals.

I call out but don't get an answer. She's not in the kitchen or living room. I find her upstairs, sitting on the middle of the carpet in the master bedroom. She's holding herself, her arms tight around her knees. Her head is buried, and she's sobbing quietly.

In a flash, I remember my explosion at her in the garage.

"Coco, I'm sorry I yelled at you. I lost it, and I'm really sorry."

"I know," she says.

I put my arms around her, but she can't stop crying.

"It's not what you said, Dad. I was... It's just..." Coco wipes the tears from her eyes and pulls out of my comforting arms. We're sitting cross-legged on the carpet of a nearly empty bedroom. Coco and I are the vanguard for the move from Hawaii to Georgia -- setting up our new house for the rest of the family who arrive the day after tomorrow.

"Sweetheart, I..."

She stops me with a level look. "Just listen, okay?"

I sit back and shut up.

"I was reaching under the kitchen sink," Coco says. "And, I don't know, I felt this thing, like maybe just a piece of paper fall on my hand? But then ... then I saw it was this huge cockroach. Like super huge, as big as a mouse, wiggling its antenna, and bugs don't bother me all that much really. They didn't in Hawaii -- but I don't know this house or this place. Anyway, I froze -- and it started crawling up my arm. I freaked out... It was on my arm, crawling on me. That's all I was yelling about." Tears well in her eyes again, and she looks away. "I know it's stupid, but you're my dad. I wanted you to make it all better."

When I was twelve, Dad, Mom, Rob, and I moved from Chicago to Colorado. Dad said he hoped the move would be a chance for me to grow up some. (He's never stopped hoping for that.) When we moved in to our new house on a hill near a farm, our parents warned us about going too near the deep, wide, fast-running irrigation ditch that we could see flowing on the other side of a neighboring alfalfa field.

The next day, followed by my brother Rob and our dog Sam, I snuck across the field to see what could be so dangerous about a stupid little ditch. As soon as we got there, Sam slipped off the muddy edge into the ditch and couldn't get out of the rushing water pulling him fast downstream. I'd have rather died than tell my dad that I'd drowned our dog, so I jumped in to get Sam, and Rob ran to get help. The walls of the ditch were too slippery and high to hold, and the rushing muddy water kept pulling me and the dog under.

But Dad came running and pulled me and our dog out and took us home to safety. I was terrified beyond reason. But it was the moment when my father looked down from the edge of the ditch that I remember most. He wasn't angry. He smiled and threw down a rope. "Don't worry; you'll be okay," he said, "Just hold on." I believed him. And that made it all better.

I tell Coco there's nothing stupid in wanting help from your dad. That's what dads are for. I tell her that I love her and I promise I'll always try to make things better for her in any way that I can.

She nods. "You know, Dad, your temper is as bad as mine is."

"Yep, we're a lot alike," I say.

"Of course," she says, "I'm still a kid. Someone your age should be way more mature."

We help each other to our feet and I notice the strength of her hands in mine. The evening sunlight through the window catches her smile, and I promise myself I'll remember this day with my daughter for the rest of my life. This day when she forgave me without saying it, when she flipped from being a young woman to a little girl and back again and took my breath away without knowing it. No matter where she goes in life, I'll have this gift tucked away, safe.

"Come on, time for pizza and *Gilmore Girls*," Coco says, and bounds down the stairs. Not wanting to confuse the issue, I'd avoided saying anything before, but now I have to tell her what that phone call she interrupted in the garage was about. While we wait for the pizza delivery guy, I tell Coco that my dad had a bad accident. He fell and hit his head. He'd had a stroke first, but in the fall, he'd fractured his skull and so they had to operate on his brain.

"Grandpa? Oh no, is he going to be all right?"

I tell her it's pretty bad, but nothing's certain, and if anyone can pull out of this kind of mess, it's her grandpa. Later, I pause a Gilmore episode and I tell her that the day after tomorrow, when her mom gets here, I'm going to leave for a while to help my dad and mom through this.

"You have to go," she says. "They need you."

I don't know what my parents could possibly need from this son who can't focus, remember anything, or ever grow up. Coco's strong young hand squeezes my uncertain fingers. With my other hand I push play.

THE GAPE-MOUTHED MAN

Crammed into an airport van on the way from my new home in Warner Robins, Georgia, to the Atlanta airport, I stare out at the summer-green fields and trees blurring by.

With Beethoven turned way up on my iPod, I plan to bury the ache of missing my family move in and adjust to our new home I left barely an hour ago and drown out the nightmare of my dad's brain injury I am heading toward now. But I can't figure out how to get my earbuds to stay in place. Every bump on the road pops one or the other out, replacing furious classical music with the irritated drawl of the driver moaning about airport traffic. The ache and the nightmare rush back in, and I'm transformed into a selfish 2-year-old holding my breath and squeezing my eyes shut: I don't want to go -- you can't make me. No! No! No!

At the airport, I try calming myself with deep-breathing exercises while I wait at the gate, because on top of all my other neurotic self-obsessions, I detest flying. The waiting, herding, and lack of control, combined with having to jam all six feet and two hundred pounds of myself into an airline seat sucks my soul down into a dark, hot, and angry place. By the third time the drink cart clipped my elbow during last month's marathon flight from Honolulu to Atlanta, my daughter was convinced my head would explode.

"Grow up," I tell myself as I seven-eight-nine-ten exhale. "The flight from Atlanta to Baltimore is only an hour and 45 minutes." Full disclosure: Philadelphia International Airport is actually closer to my parents' house, but the flight is a full two hours and never lands on time, requiring me to sit still a half hour longer in the air. So I opt for the shorter flight and longer drive, following my motto: Take care of your neurotic self-obsessions and they will take care of you.

On the plane, I'm squeezed between two teenagers even bigger than I am, who, despite being friends -- a wild guess I make as they pass chips and cookies back and forth, their crumbs raining down on me -- won't switch seats with me. Neither one likes sitting in the middle.

Keeping my elbows tucked in, I breathe, turn up the Beethoven playing on my iPod, and read. I shake my head "No" to the flight attendant offering drinks, the plane hits an air pocket and both ear buds fall out, the aisle teen spills root beer on my lap, and the window teen knocks over my water bottle. Arms, napkins, and apologies fly around my face. Pringles drop between the pages of my open book.

I took my meds right before the flight, as well as the new beta-blocker for my panic attacks, so, jaw-clenched, my exterior remains peaceful and quiet. Inside my dark, hot head, however, I scream like a banshee and beat everyone within reach into a senseless, bloody pulp. No peace for the crazy, but I try.

I close my eyes and flash back to last year's visit with my parents. Once academics, they're now in their mid-eighties, living in retirement.

I'm in the backyard helping Dad light the charcoal on the grill. He leans on his rolling walker with one hand and drinks a martini with the other. Unlike me, my dad could always handle his liquor. But lately, his crippling disk pain has him popping Percocet and drinking much more than he used to. Dad sips his gin as I finish readying the "chimney charcoal starter" we're using to get the grill going: Crumpled newspaper gets put at the bottom of the starter's aluminum tube and I add briquettes on top, per my dad's careful instructions.

"The back's bad these days, huh?" I ask as I light the paper.

Dad squints at me. "Yes, it is," he says. "And how much I drink is none of your business." He puts down his martini on his walker's built-in seat and picks up the can of liquid charcoal lighter next to his cane lying on the seat's edge.

"Um, I don't think you're supposed to use charcoal lighter with the charcoal chimney starter, Dad..."

"Shit, that thing never works." He squirts the charcoal lighter on the grill and whomp -- the charcoal chimney's engulfed in a tower of flame. He puts down the charcoal lighter and picks up his martini. "Go see if your mother needs help in the kitchen."

Inside, the water's boiling on the stove for potatoes but Mom's not in the kitchen or the living room. I call out, "Mom?"

Her reply is faint and quavering, "In here... I could use some help..."

I find her on the floor in their bedroom, where she's fallen. She laughs as I help her up and sit her on the bed. "I was getting dizzy so I came in for a pill but I dropped them and I bent over to pick them up and kept going down. Now all the pills are hiding under the bed behind the dust bunnies." I get her a pill and some water. "I'm fine," she says, "but you better not leave your father out there by himself too long. He'll burn the house down."

In the backyard, the charcoal grill smolders near the walker, but Dad's not there. Now I'm calling out for him, "Dad?" It's like who let the dogs out or something. Getting no reply, I run to the side yard. I find him lying on the lawn, the martini glass spilled on the coiled hose. "Dad! Are you all right?" Using all his energy trying to grab his cane that's fallen in his pepper patch, out of reach, he doesn't answer. I grab the cane and help him up. "What are you doing over here?"

"Weeding, as if it's any of your business," he says. Then he laughs and shakes his head. "The damn hose gave me a start. Looked like a snake for a second." He pulls free from me and leaning on his cane, heads back to the grill, flicking grass off his shorts with his free hand. "If you really want to help, you can get me another martini."

I pick up the cocktail glass. My father leans on his walker and squirts more charcoal lighter on grill. The flames brighten his face.

When I land in Baltimore, my brother Rob, a kind, non-neurotic, nondrinker who lives with his wife and two kids near my parents and also prefers flying in and out of Baltimore, picks me up and takes me to Mom and Dad's house.

The mood in the car during the hour-and-a-half drive to Delaware is subdued as Rob fills me in on the medical news. Dad's at a rehab place, but he's not recovered enough from the brain surgery to start therapy. He recognizes family but is also convinced his mother is alive, playing cards, and mixing drinks in the room next to his.

"I bet he wants to go over there for cocktails," I say.

"You got it," Rob hoots.

We laugh like our parents do, deflecting the pain, trying to keep our family alive.

Mom, who's been awaiting my arrival with Rob's wife and kids, greets me with pizza and ice cream. Tonight we'll eat. Tomorrow, I'll see my dad.

* * * *

"God, this is a miserable June," my mother says as we make our way across the muggy, hot parking lot to the entrance of the rehab center where my father is recovering. "It wasn't supposed to get like this so early." The rehab center's automatic doors slide open and we walk into the foyer. The blast of air conditioning is a shock. Mom stops to catch her breath.

"You mean the heat?" I ask.

Mom nods. "Mm-hmm ... that and the rest of it, I suppose." She gives my arm a squeeze. "I'm so glad you came to help," she says.

I'm happy that it makes such a difference to my mom that I'm here. But I'm preoccupied with the realization that this will be the first time I've seen my dad since he had a stroke, fell, fractured his skull, and had brain surgery. I want to believe that I can be a help to both him and my mom during this health crisis but I really don't know how, and if I figure it out, I'm not at all confident I'll be up to the task. Our history is clear: My father, the real Frank, is practical, wise, and invincible. I'm Frank the third, Trey to the family, the scattered, self-centered, dreamer son. How can I possibly help him? In my attempts, I can at least hide all this doubt and confusion behind a calm, grown-up front. If I don't panic, there's a chance I won't make this situation worse.

Back home with my wife and children, even though I'm sometimes a scattered, stuttering mess, I know my job and what I need to do to be competent and useful. I don't know my job with my parents now. This is new territory, and I don't think they know their roles yet either.

In the foyer of the rehab center, a man wearing a cardigan over a T-shirt rolls up in a wheelchair next to us and stares. Mom smiles at him. "Hello," she says. "How are you doing today?"

The man frowns at her, turns around, and wheels away. Mom shrugs, releases my arm, and takes back her purse from my shoulder. "Better to walk using my own steam," she says. "Don't want to be mistaken for an inmate."

I follow her down the corridor toward the nurse's station. Cane in one hand, purse in the other, my mother walks with resolve, her brave, look-the-world-in-the-eyes face pushing past a gauntlet of injured and aged patients resigned to their wheelchairs. We're headed toward the nurse station when my mother turns away and approaches a shrunken, white-haired patient who's folded into a wheeled recliner, covered with a blanket, and tucked next to the wall.

We're here to see my dad, what's Mom doing over there talking to that unconscious, gape-mouthed ancient person? Just as she was with that guy who wheeled up to us in the foyer, Mom, a happy Iowa farm girl who became a gritty Great Depression kid on the road with her family, has always been unfailingly courteous to others, going out of her way to befriend the lonely and lost. Even the inanimate have benefited from her hospitality. When no one else would claim them, the ashes of Mrs. Yancy, an elderly widow my mother had become friends with before her death, sat in a gift-wrapped box on a bookcase in my parents' house for years. Mrs. Yancy was toasted on every holiday she spent with the family until one Fourth of July when my mom felt the time was right to bury her in the backyard.

I admire this quality of kindness in my mother, but right now keeping my own panic and fear tied down has frayed my patience thin to breaking and the selfish son in me is breaking through. I want to see my father now. I leave my mother with her new friend and step up to the counter.

"We're here to see Frank South," I begin. The head nurse tilts her head toward my mother who is brushing aside a wisp of the ancient patient's hair. She kisses his forehead. He smiles out of his drugged haze. Opening his eyes, he looks up at my mother and his smile breaks into a crooked grin -- my father's crooked grin.

As I join them, my mother says, "Frank, darling, look who has come to see you. It's Trey."

My father's eyes find mine. He blinks back tears. "Ah, good," he says. "Good." He raises an arm and I step into my father's embrace.

Don't Let Me Down

I've always been the more distracted, self-absorbed, and impractical of their two sons. My younger brother, who lives close to their home, is the steady, competent one.

With him away on a well-deserved vacation with his family, I'm here to do what I can. I'll cook and clean, two things I'm good at, and hope I don't step on any emotional landmines in the process. I tell myself to follow a kind of ADHD Hippocratic oath: "First, pay attention, and then do no harm." If I keep all my personal junk clamped down and stay focused on my parents' needs, I should be able to, at the very least, not make either of them feel any worse. It's a reasonable goal, but considering the gravity of the situation, it's one I'm not sure I have the concentration and understanding to pull off.

This morning I told my mother, who's exhausted from the emotional pummeling of the last month, to stay in bed and rest and that I'd go out to the rehab center to see dad by myself today. She was so tired; she didn't even mind that I took their Lincoln Town Car out of the garage by myself.

My mom and dad are particular about their Lincoln and their garage. Yesterday was the first time in my life I was allowed to back it out. My mother sat beside me, watching me and the mirrors, coaching the whole way, her warning hand raised just in case I got too close to either edge. Inch by inch, swiveling my head back and forth checking the rear-view mirrors, I backed the fat car out of their narrow garage, paying close attention so as not to let the car come within scraping distance of the white wood trim of the garage entrance. All clear, I put the car in park, pushed the button on the visor to lower the garage door, and we both finally took a breath. You'd think my mother and I wouldn't worry that I could pull off something as simple as this. I've been driving for forty-five years, for god's sake.

That said, a couple of months earlier on my last trip up, in a simple attempt to provide her with some much-needed joy and stress relief, I drove my mother to Baltimore in the Lincoln to see the symphony. We left in plenty of time; I'd used Google Maps, called, and planned well. After first dropping my mom off with a friend we were meeting at a restaurant close to the concert hall, I parked the Lincoln on a pretty, tree-lined side street, made sure it was locked, and joined them.

During dinner and Mahler, the Town Car was towed and impounded. I had parked in a pretty, tree-lined tow-away zone. My friend saved us a gazillion dollar cab fare by driving my mother and me all the way back home to Delaware that night, but the point remains I didn't pay attention and that left my mother and me stranded in the middle of the night a hundred miles away from her home. As my friend drove, I stared out the window at the I-95 rushing past, thinking once again that it's when I try the hardest to get things right, that I bring on the biggest disasters.

Back in the present day, I drive to the rehab center without incident and walk in looking for my dad. I'm toting one bag full of laundered warm-up pants, polo shirts, pajamas, sandwiches, and cookies, and another carryall holding an electric razor, barber clippers, scissors, aftershave, and a couple of old sheets. I'm on a mission to make today better than yesterday.

Yesterday was hard. Recently removed head bandages reveal the physical and emotional pain has been coping with. His head and face are badly bruised; the left side of his head, which has been completely shaved, is covered with a huge scar; there are stitches above his right eye from an even more recent fall; and his skin is flaking off his neck, ears, and scalp. My mother and I were sitting with him yesterday when an aide came into the room with his meds, and he introduced us to her. "This is Berna Deane and Frank," he said smiling, "my mother and father." At first we thought he was joking around, but then the more we tried to correct him, the more adamant and agitated he became. He lurched up, suddenly wanting to go to the bathroom. As the aide and I slowly helped him in, he looked in the bathroom mirror and saw himself for the first time since the accident. "Oh my god," he said, "I look like a mental patient."

"No, no you don't," we said, but at the moment, he actually did. I could tell from the look on the aide's face she thought so too. That wasn't right. This is Dr. Frank E. South, Ph.D., an internationally known scientist and WWII Ranger who cherishes his dignity. Of course, everybody in these places is somebody, no matter what their situation is now, but this is my father, damn it. I'm going to make sure he can at least recognize who he really is.

Today, I've come prepared. I've got one old sheet on the floor of his room and one around Dad's neck. Though my intensity of purpose startles my dad at first, he's cooperating, sitting up in his wheelchair, while I clip away, giving him a crew cut.

"Have you seen my mother?" he asks. Locks of white hair fall to his shoulders.

Grandma's been buried in Nebraska for years, but right now, that doesn't matter.

"I think I saw her around somewhere," I say.

"She's probably at the bar," he says.

"Probably so," I say. Then, like a barber and customer in a small town, we both start to relax to the buzz of the clippers and snip of scissors. He picks up a strand of his hair and looks at it.

"It's hard for me to remember things exactly," he says. "I try so hard..."

"Uh huh," I say, "Me too."

"Huh. Really?" he says, and puts the strand of white hair carefully on his sheet-covered knee.

"Yeah," I say, "People's names, places, objects -- the words sometimes just won't come."

"They hide," he says.

"We've got to be patient, wait for one to peek its head around the corner, and then grab it," I say, thinking of how I struggle with language, even as a writer.

My dad nods and smiles. "Right, that's it. You gotta grab quick," he says. I brush dead skin and hair off his shoulders and start clipping the fine hair at the base of his neck.

* * * *

A week later at the rehab center, I notice my dad seems anxious. I show him a notice I'd typed up to let potential caregivers know his family and relationship particulars, as well as the fact that he is a WWII Ranger veteran, has a Ph.D., and was a prominent physiology professor. I'd also asked the doctors and aides to please call him "Dr. South," as he was addressed throughout his professional life, to help him remember who he is.

My dad brushes the document away with a disinterested grunt and turns away in his wheelchair, his shoulders scrunched up tight. I tape the notice above his bed and decide to play barber again, this time shaving my dad's face with his electric razor. This offer of help he accepts. As his shoulders drop some of their tension, he closes his eyes, smiles, and tilts his head back as I buzz his neck and chin.

"I brought some new polo shirts today that Mom got for you," I say. "We'll put one on before we go to lunch."

"It makes me nervous, Trey," he says, using my family nickname. It reassures me to hear that he knows who I am, that I'm his son.

"What does?" I ask.

"What do you think? All this fuss, my wedding," he says.

"Dad, you're already married..."

"Balls," he says, irritated. "My mother bought me a shirt."

If I can remind him gently that by mom, I mean my mother, not his; he might calm down and remember. "Your wife is Berna Deane, my mother..." My father pulls my hand with the razor away from his face and fixes me with a fierce look that burned into me every time he caught me lying as a kid.

"Stop it," he hisses at me. "No more lies. I have to trust you, understand?"

I put the razor down, touching his face. "Yes, I understand. I do. You can trust me. I promise."

"A man can't marry his mother. It's not right." His point made, he relaxes and laughs. "And the Army would have one hell of a fit."

Now, I lose track of time -- all the time, always have -- and I'm never sure what day it is. Words, numbers, and names of people and things vanish and reappear at will. My brain is unruly and uninterested in the day-to-day world, but even so, I know who and where I am when I wake up in the morning.

With Dad smiling at me as I put away the razor and help him into his new polo shirt, I realize that that's no longer the case for my father. For him, confusion has grown in his brain like a hungry jungle choking off every thought he has and everything he sees and feels with a terrifying and unrelenting uncertainty. It has taken complete control and distorts and breaks the past and present into unglued bits that fall away, then reform, shift, and fall away again, just out of sight.

Dad's mood shifts again as we roll toward the dining room. "You need to get me out of here, Trey," he says. "This is a mental hospital."

"It's only until you're better," I say. "A little while longer."

"Let's go home now," he says. "I don't belong with these people."

"Soon..."

"Now," Dad says in his most commanding voice. "Get my things and take me home."

I step around to the front of the wheelchair and get on one knee to face him. "I'm sorry, Dad, I can't. Not yet." He looks at me. His fierce, angry eyes soften with understanding. He pats my hand.

"Don't worry," he says. "I understand." I smile, relieved. He smiles back and says, "We need passports."

The doctors and therapists tell us that recovery takes time and that with help; Dad has a chance to come back to the rest of us in the real world. But as I see him exhaust himself, chopping through shadows until he finds a clearing where he can rest, where his life finally holds still and makes sense for a minute, whether it's 1943, 1963, or 1983 -- I don't think I should explain to him that he must be confused. Not every time. It's just not right.

Dad leans forward, energized. "This piss-ant ship sails on the tide and if we don't have passports, we're stuck. You need to get on this right away. We have to get back home. I'm good and sick of Europe. How about you?"

"I never liked it that much in the first place," I say.

"Right, too many Europeans," he says. "Nothing they say makes sense. You better get a move on and see what can be done about our papers."

I stand to leave. An aide approaches to roll him the rest of the way to the dining room. "Will do," I say. "Don't worry, though. We'll get back home soon."

The aide is just a few steps away as Dad turns to her and says in an odd French accent, "Mademoiselle, un petit moment." She stops and he looks back at me with a conspiratorial wink. "I know we will, son," he says. "I trust you."

Even though my ADHD-related problems are insignificant compared to his, we develop a father-son confusion connection as the days roll on, bewildered buddies rolling our eyes at the clearly unhinged world around us. There is trust between us that we both treasure. I believe it gives my dad some strength for his constant struggle to regain mental footing. But it's a trust that's fleeting in our imaginary world, and just by keeping one foot in the real world as his advocate, a trust that I will likely soon betray.

* * * *

"Danny Boy threw up in my room and it stinks like hell." Coco is calling from home in Georgia. I'm in the guest room at my parents' house, after a long day at the rehab with Dad. "Danny Boy's a dog," I tell Coco. "Sometimes you have to clean up after him."

"I did," she says, "but it still stinks like hell. I can't sleep. But what stinks like hell even worse is that Mom says when Aunt Maureen, Mark, and the baby visit, I have to give up my room and sleep on the floor in your room. When are you coming home?"

"As soon as you stop swearing," I say.

"Uh-huh," she says. "But then again, if you don't get home in time for Aunt Maureen's visit, then I could sleep in bed with Mom, and that'd be better. So why don't you go ahead and stay with Grandma and Grandpa for a couple more weeks?"

"Uh-huh," I say. "I'll see you in a couple of days, Coco. Does your mom know you're up?"

"Dunno. She's asleep," she says.

"You should be too," I say. "It's late."

"Don't you think McGee on NCIS is getting too skinny?" she asks. "He looks weird to me now."

"You just don't like change."

"You should talk," she says, "so shut up."

"You first. I love you. Go to sleep, Coco."

"I refuse. I love you too, Dad, but you can't make me. You're not here."

Our quick-tempered, subject-changing patter goes on a little longer until I hear her winding down, and after phone kisses back and forth, I hang up. I get up from the foldout couch and look around. My wife Margaret and I slept here the weekend I introduced her to my parents. What was that, twenty-six years ago? Then our kids stayed in here, too, on our visits to Grandma and Grandpa's. Is this the same foldout couch that's always been here? I sit back down and bounce a little. It could be -- it's definitely old. But it's still sturdy. I go back into the living room where my mom and I were talking before Coco's call.

"How's my beautiful granddaughter?" she asks.

"Good," I say. "She's good."

"Did you tell her you're coming home Saturday?"

"I said I'd be home soon. I didn't say exactly when."

"Your father and I have kept you away from your wife and kids too long," my mother says. "You belong with your family in Georgia. They need you."

I nod. She's more right than she knows. Margaret is overwhelmed with a super tight budget, new town, new house, our two kids, and Margaret's 81-year-old mother moving into our downstairs bedroom. We talk on the phone every night and she's been totally supportive and hasn't complained once. Maybe once. Last week she moaned about discovering how our son had taken half of the three grand his late great aunt left him for a car and spent it on Internet porn, rap videos, and junk food. Then we bickered back and forth about what to do and decided to take away his laptop until he gets a job and pays it all back.

I can feel the pressure building back home, but I'm terrified of leaving my mom alone with my father and his untethered mind. Lately Dad's been calling Mom at all hours demanding to be "set free" and going off on jagged, time-traveling, paranoid rants filled with old enemies and dead relatives. Mom sees my hesitation and leans forward in her chair and points at me.

"You're worrying about me," she says. "Now stop it. Thanks to you, I've been feeling much more rested and less stressed in the last few days. I'm sure I can handle things myself now."

She points out that despite the phone calls, Dad seems to be slowly improving at the rehab center, and over the last few days we've talked to insurance agents, bank people, and doctors. We've rearranged some furniture and routines around the house to make her more comfortable living by herself. Over dinners that I make sure she eats, we've talked about the shock and sense of loss she's going through since Dad's fall. The big, strong, take-charge man she married went down hard, but there's no reason to give up hope. He'll get better. He'll be able to come home soon.

"Now you have to go home too," she says.

"I guess so," I say. "Are you sure you'll be all right?"

"Of course I will," she says. "You've taken care of everything for me. What could go wrong now?"

Right on cue, the phone rings. I glance at the clock as I get up to answer it. "11:30. I bet its Margaret," I say. "Coco probably woke her up instead of going to bed." My mom thinks that Dad talked an aide into dialing for him again. "Tell your father I spoke to him an hour ago. We'll see him tomorrow."

I pick up and Mom's right, the call is from the rehab center. But it's not Dad on the phone. It's Thomas, the charge nurse on Dad's floor. "I need you to get down here as soon as you can, Mr.

South," Thomas says. "Your father's become violent. He's injured people."

I hop in the car, leaving my mother at home in her robe and slippers doing her best to stay calm. I promise to call from the center as soon as I know what's going on. Cutting through town by the university where my dad had been the head of Life and Health Sciences, I try to keep myself calm and try to imagine what could possibly have happened. My dad, violent? It can't be true. But James had always been one of the most compassionate and unflappable nurses I'd ever met and he sounded pretty damn flustered on the phone tonight. I've seen Dad angry a few times and he could scare me silly as a kid -- but violent? No. He spanked me only once growing up. I was eight and when it was over, he cried more than I did.

Then again, there's Dad the Ranger. There aren't any Nazis at the rehab center. But maybe he thinks there are. He's just lost hold of the only mind he's ever known. Oh come on, he's eighty-six years-old. He couldn't relive D-Day on Rehab Floor 2E if he wanted to. He can't even walk. But those Rangers crawled under bullets and bombs all the way across Europe. He's tough and out of his normal state of mind. What if he got his hands on something sharp?

I push the night button of the rehab center and rush in through the double doors. When I round the corner of his floor, I see Dad parked in his wheelchair in front of the nurse's station. He seems alert, but his head is down and he's looking at the floor. He looks up as I approach and shoots me a sly smile. He doesn't look so much like a soldier as much as me; a defiant and scared kid he caught setting that fire across the street.

He raises his head and watches me with a mixture of guilt and suspicion as Thomas steps up and pulls me aside. "Your father struck and kicked three aides today, hurting all of them," he says. "We sent one woman he kicked in the stomach to the emergency room. She's home now and going to be all right, but this is a serious situation."

I nod, dumbstruck, and tell Thomas my dad has never been violent before. Thomas says that many brain injury and dementia patients go through personality changes. They can get progressively agitated over time, especially in the evening hours when they become obsessed with getting out and going home. The condition is called sundown syndrome, and Dad is one of the most extreme cases Thomas has ever seen.

I tell Thomas that I understand that it's serious and ask what we should do about it. He says tomorrow I'm to meet with the nursing director to discuss finding other accommodations that can handle my father, like a psychiatric institution. "Right now," Thomas says, "We need to get him tranquilized with Ativan. He's refused to take the pills, so we want you to help calm him, holding him if necessary, so we can give him a strong enough injection to turn this behavior off for tonight." I nod and try to absorb what the nurse is saying without looking as horror-stricken and terrified as I actually am.

When I was a kid growing up in the fifties and sixties, ADHD wasn't known, but my parents knew that I was a little odd. Reports from school and neighbors confirmed that when I wasn't distracted and lost in daydreams, I was given to unpredictable spells of energetic acting out, sometimes resulting in fights, stealing stuff, and accidentally setting fires.

Over and over again during those years, my dad told me -- when everybody outside called me a crazy weirdo -- that what the rest of the world thought about me didn't matter. What mattered was my family. Crazy weirdo or not, they loved me. In the end, he said, the people in your home were the only people you could trust. As I finish talking to Thomas and step toward my dad, I think about all those times he'd stood up and took my side against school principals, bullies, cops, and local store owners.

Like he's reading my mind, he winks at me and gestures for me to get down close to him. "I need you to bring me a knife," my dad hisses in an urgent whisper. "An eight-inch knife, no shorter than six, but sharp, you hear me son? I mean razor sharp." He leans forward from his wheelchair to me, crouched in front of him, our heads together like conspirators in the middle of the night in this bright hospital corridor.

"Why do you need a knife?" I ask, careful to keep the alarm out of my voice.

Dad squeezes my arm, his face two inches from mine, his clear eyes locked on mine. "Why do you think?" he says and letting go of my arm and stabbing the air between us with an imaginary blade. "To kill these people," he whispers, "gut them, get the hell out of here and go home." He grins at me, his eyes sparkling with energy and purpose. I can't help but smile back. Dad seems so happy. He's stronger and much more alive than he was just two days ago. This would be great news if he weren't also spouting vicious, bloodthirsty nonsense and physically attacking the nursing staff.

"Dad," I plead, my voice low and urgent, "could you just take the pills they want you to take?"

Dad's eyes narrow. "No," he says. "No way, no how."

"But then they'll have to use a needle..."

"Let them try," he says, his grin flashing, "They've got to get past you and me first. And together we're one hell of a tough nut."

Thomas steps up behind Dad, catching my eye. Dad senses the movement and grabs my arm again. "Don't look at them!" he shouts. "They'll trick you!"

I gather resolve in my shaking body and ignore Dad's protests as Thomas steps forward with the hypodermic of Ativan. I lean forward, holding my father's arms and restraining him with my weight. I tell him to stay calm, that it'll be all right. But as the needle pierces his thigh and the plunger pushes the tranquillizer into his body, he can only stare at me with shocked disbelief. That spark I saw dancing in his eyes just minutes before flickers and dies with the realization that his own son has betrayed him. And then, as the drug takes hold, he understands that now he is completely alone.

Dad's condition since his brain injury has rocked him and our whole family, especially my mother, who at eighty-eight can't help but mourn the emotional -- if not physical -- loss of her one true love even as he sits dozing beside her. Putting all of that into words, trying to understand what I can from the event, is often like reliving each moment all over again in slow motion.

But what's been most unsettling is a sense that in my heart the dad of the injury, confusion, and anger had pushed out the dad whose courage, depth, and insight flat-out blew me away for sixty years. Somewhere in the middle of these difficult few months, what happened to my dad and the family crisis it brought on threatened the definition of this extraordinary man's life.

A couple of days after I'd helped forcibly tranquilize him, I am on my way to visit Dad at the rehab center to prepare him for transfer to a facility that can handle dementia, in the hope that with the right meds, he can eventually improve enough to go home. I know that his impairment will only let him see this as another prison sentence, so I've spent the past night preparing a bribe of sorts -- a cobbler I made with Georgia peaches.

I find Dad in the physical therapy room, depressed, medicated, and unwilling to do his next set of exercises. He nods and gives me a half smile as I sit next to his wheelchair. He eyes the plastic container and spoon I've brought.

"What do you have there?" he asks. "More bad news?"

"No," I say, opening the container lid. "It's peach cobbler."

"Is it poisoned?"

"No," I say again. I pull out a spoonful for him, guiding it to his hand. "I made it myself."

"So?" he asks. "What does that prove? You taste it first."

"Sure." I pop the bite of cobbler in my mouth, swallow, and smile, licking my lips. "I gotta say, I'm one hell of a cook when I want to be. Here, your turn." I load up the spoon and put his fingers around it. His eyes are on me as he brings the spoon to his mouth. But his hand suddenly shakes and he drops it.

"Damn," Dad says. His eyes well up with tears. "Damn it to hell." I tell him that it doesn't matter, that I've got plenty. But he shakes his head and says that's not it. "You didn't know I was joking," he says. "You think I meant it about the poison."

"No, no, Dad, I knew."

But he can see the lie in my eyes and a huge sob breaks out of his chest. "I don't think I can stand this, being this..." he says. And then we're both crying, leaning against each other, my arms around him. Holding him there I am taken back to Christmas 1957.

I am eight-years-old and have discovered my present isn't under the tree. It's on a table next to the wall, covered by a white sheet. As happy as I've ever seen him, my father lifts the sheet to reveal an enormous castle made of grey metal painted to look like stones. It's got a working chain drawbridge, towers, catwalks, little cloth flags, and a king, a queen, knights, and horses made of plastic.

I can't speak. I look at him and back at the castle and I know Santa has had nothing to do with this. In 1957, and in the future in 2010, it is the most stunning, meaningful gift I have ever gotten and my dad made it for me. (Later I'll find out he'd stayed up all night putting tabs A into slots B and placing everything just so.) I look over again at him and my mother holding hands and smiling at each other. I want to jump over and hug him, but the moment is too good, and I don't want any of this to change, ever.

I've often railed against those who would define me or my children by our ADHD instead of seeing the whole person, yet here I found myself doing the same thing; allowing the disability to become who my father is. When we think of quality of life, I think what we're talking about is meaningful connection between people. The challenge facing family, friends, and caregivers of those with any type of disability or chronic ailment is to keep the whole person center stage -- the rest is secondary. The problems, strategies, and medications are important, sure, but the human being comes first.

In the corner of the rehab center, my father and I finally stop sobbing. And wordlessly the two of us get down to the business of eating cobbler, sharing bites, touching hands. The rehab center speech therapist steps up to us as Dad and I, our faces still wet from tears, finish the last of the cobbler. "Are you two all right?" she asks, touching my father's shoulder.

"Oh, fine," Dad says. "Couldn't be better."

"We could use a tissue or two," I say.

Dad nods. "This one has always been a crybaby," he says. He winks at me, a tiny bit of peach drops off his chin, and we both break out laughing so hard we nearly fall out of our chairs.

Though I'll be with my family in Georgia this holiday season, my thoughts will also be with Mom and Dad. And I'll wish a Merry Christmas to the dad who built a castle for me and filled it with loyal knights fighting for honor and true love.

CAR WRECK

One-thirty in the morning. I'm sitting downstairs in the living room of our new house on the old couch that I brought back from my parents' house in the minivan on this last trip.

An hour and a half ago I told my wife, Margaret, that I needed to read a little bit before going to sleep. But I'm really up waiting for our 22-year-old son, Harry to get home safe from work. He's finally gotten his license and he's proudly driving back and forth to work in a well-preserved '98 Jeep Cherokee we found for him. He's also been tooling around town with friends and staying out late, spending more on gas and fun than he makes flipping burgers. After I fronted him gas money to get to work, he promised tonight that he'd drive straight home after he clocked out.

His shift at the fast-food joint ended an hour ago. It's a 10-minute drive away. He's not answering his cell.

Of course, I've been through this before with him. The first time I picked him up from preschool, he was not anywhere any of the other kids were, inside or out. Frantic, I was sure he'd been kidnapped or somehow wandered off into traffic when a teacher pointed him out sitting in the fork of a tree. "He's different, calm," she said. "He stays up there and looks at things."

These days, just as I get frantic, he shows up, still the calm one, and tells me he forgot he'd promised to give the assistant manager a ride home or that he pulled over to talk on the cell with friends and lost track of time. He and Margaret both say he's old enough now and responsible enough to keep his own hours. Fine --

but I'm not calm. And when he walks in the front door tonight, he and I are going to have a serious discussion about responsibility. He better not be drinking or getting high after what we went through with him last year. If he is, I swear I'll kill him.

I notice that I'm up from the couch and pacing in circles around the coffee table. I stretch out on the couch again. I try to refocus on my book, but the fictional, plot-driven violence on the page can't keep the "bleeding son in mangled wreckage calling for his dad on a lonely road" loop from playing in my head.

I've jumped back into family life here in Georgia with a vengeance after returning from my latest trip -- the third in a series of two-week visits -- to Delaware to help my mom and dad handle the ongoing saga of my dad's brain injury. It is something that all of us, especially Dad, are having trouble understanding or accepting. After stints in a hospital and two treatment facilities, Dad's back home with Mom and we'll hope for the best. But my fix-it energy still burns even though I'm back home.

Margaret's hoping that within a few days I'll wind down and stop driving everyone -- her, our two kids, her mother, and our dog -- nuts. I want to, believe me, and I will, but right now I can't shake the feeling that I've got to stay active and vigilant -- whip things into shape, get the kids to do their chores, and most of all, do everything I can to keep everyone in this family safe. I know I'm probably taking it to extremes, but I've learned to trust what I feel.

The weeks and months since we moved from Hawaii have all tumbled together, and sometimes I'm not sure what happened when or what caused what in the recent tumultuous events our family has been going through. It's as if everything we know about ourselves -- our parents, kids, business, health -- is being plowed under and turned upside down over and over again before anything has had a chance to grow. Before, this kind of murky emotional confusion used to make me miserable and anxious. I'd feel powerless, frozen in its grip. But then I learned to take conscious advantage of the power of the ADHD perspective. It's more than using hyperfocus -- it's trusting where your hyperfocus takes you.

Think about it. If every day of your life you wake up already engulfed in a roaring overwhelming flood of extremely urgent but completely confused and unrelated information hitting you non-stop, all at once, all the time, then the crushing cascade of events in a family crisis or any other calamity shouldn't be overwhelming -- it should feel like old home week.

I think that most ADHD veterans know that no matter how much rains down, their attention is held only by what really interests them. They accept that despite their nods to others, nothing else has even registered except for that one project or problem that's caught their interest and they've focused on like a laser. Especially in stressful situations, they've learned to trust that they're doing the right thing and that they'll see whatever it is through to completion ... or until they're not interested anymore. Then, sometimes, it can get messy.

But everybody makes mistakes and I'd rather do that than do nothing. So I say, "Bring it on." I sit up on the couch and realize I just said that out loud. Talking in my sleep -- great. But I wasn't asleep really. I was eye-rest-thinking. Who's playing music? It's my phone. I flip it open.

"Dad? Dad?" It's Harry. He's freaked. My turn to be way calm, tell him it's okay.

"Talk to me, Harry. Where are you? What's going on?"

"We're near Perry, I think ... Oh man, Dad, oh man, this effing huge truck ran us off the road. I can't believe it. Me and Jamaal and Del, we were just..."

"Are you hurt? Is anyone hurt?"

"What? No, I don't think so ... But Dad, this effing guy ran us into a ditch and then we hit this wall ... I don't know what to do." Harry's voice is cracking.

"Hang up and call 911 -- now," I tell him, "then call me right back." Harry clicks off. I get up, put on shoes, get my jacket and keys, and stay focused.

* * * *

Margaret, wakes as I throw on clothes. I give her the basics of the call and she lies back down with a groan, covering her head with the blankets. When I go downstairs to get my jacket and keys, I realize Harry hasn't called me back yet. I try calling him. No answer.

That's weird. God, I hope that speeding trucker didn't come back and ... do something to him. I start to head out the door to the car but stop when I remember I don't really know where he is. I call him again. Now it's busy. He'd seemed reluctant to call the cops; he's probably just getting to it now. I walk out to the driveway and start the car. I turn the radio on and off. Still full-on in my problem-solving mode, I decide I'll try him one more time and if I don't get him, I'll call the cops myself. This time Harry answers.

"Uh, yeah. Hi, Dad," he says, all the righteous anger gone from his voice. "Look, you don't have to come down here, really." He sounds much more subdued; is he in shock? I hear what sounds like police radios in the background.

"Just tell me where you are, Harry. I'll be right there."

"No, really, don't," he says, growing adamant. "The Highway Patrol is here."

"Good, that's good," I say. "Did you tell them what happened?"

"Yeah, well, they've kind of figured that out," he says.

"Figured what out?" I ask.

"I gotta go, Dad..."

What's going on? Why is he being so evasive? The whine of a winch splits the air on his side of the phone. Some guy is yelling, "Whoa, whoa, that's got it!" in the background. Then Harry's hand muffles the phone and I hear him saying "Yeah, okay" to somebody, and then he's back. He doesn't sound good.

"One of the troopers will bring me home later," he says.

"Did you give them a description of the truck that ran you off the road?"

"Dad, stop." Harry's impatient and irritated now. "That's just it. I lied to you about that, okay? There was no truck."

"What?" I shriek. I'm outside pacing back and forth in our driveway in the middle of the night, yelling at the top of my lungs. At the moment, I'm stopped at the curb next to the mailbox facing across the street. I'd better pull it together before the neighbors call the cops on me. We're new here, and with my long trips out of town to take care of my parents, I'm less well known than the rest of my family. Plus, I'm more excitable and irrational than the rest of my family, which I guess is obvious in my present situation. Here's one of the drawbacks to hyperfocus -- transitioning out is like being splashed with a bucket of ice water. You're confused and prone to getting pissed off.

My heart is accelerating in pre-panic attack mode, so I stand still and take a couple of deep, slow intakes and releases. To move things along, I let my left brain cross-examine my right brain during this calming exercise. Splitting my personality in two opposing camps is a good way to burn out all my circuits in one final pop and fizzle. In less than a minute, I'll have centered myself and gained enough self-knowledge and control to not lose my mind screaming at my son over the phone outside at two in the morning. It's a scene we'd all like to avoid. But the argument in my head bangs on. Hey no one else is talking to me.

So there was no speeding truck running Harry off the road -- why do you care? He lied to me. Of course he lied, you idiot, Harry lies like he breathes. But why won't he tell me what really happened? That's simple: because there's no immediate upside for him. But lying never works in the long run. Come on, he's ADHD on top of being in his early twenties. The long run doesn't exist for him; tomorrow doesn't exist. Even the next minute is barely real. It's all about the present moment. It's all that really matters to him -- kind of Zen-like if you want to give it a positive spin. What can be positive about my son only telling the truth when a Georgia State trooper is in his face? How, in just a couple of years, has my honest, good-hearted boy turned into this stubborn, secretive man who lies to me all the time about everything? I don't know; ask him. And stop being so nice and touchy-feely about everything.

Harry's voice filters in from the phone: "Dad? You there?"

"Harry, tell me what's going on. Right now."

"Later," Harry says. "I gotta go." He clicks off.

* * * *

The more I think about this the angrier I get. He'll pay for lying to me, I tell myself, And for being so damn rude. What, does he think because I've got the disability too, I'll let this slide when he plays the ADHD card? Why shouldn't he? I've identified with him on that level before and let compassion weaken my resolve as a parent.

Well, not this time, buddy boy. This time I'm going to bring the hammer down. Whether due to my years in the overheated world of television and movies, or just my sleep-deprived parental mania, during the next hour I rehearse and revise Harry's punishment with an intensity that obliterates reason. I pace, hiss, spit, and wave my arms around as I play out scenes of retribution the likes of which my son will not soon forget.

Now at three in the morning, he walks in the door and sits next to me on the living room couch where, trembling with grim righteousness, I wait. The look on my face startles him. It should, for I am no longer his understanding dad. I am Samuel L. Jackson bringing death and destruction in *Pulp Fiction*. "You will know my name is The Lord when I lay my vengeance upon thee!" The big gun spits hot lead. Ka-blooey.

"Dad, are you all right?"

Well, no. I'm not. In the middle of a rage fueled by a hopelessly confused mess of concern, hurt pride, love, betrayal, and exhaustion, I've lost some connection to reality. Looking at my twenty-one year-old son, nervous and wide-eyed, sitting next to me on the couch, I'm reminded of myself when I was in my early 20s.

The Vietnam War was raging, and I was a conscientious objector assigned to serve as an orderly for two years in a Kansas City hospital. On most weekends during that time, I also drank and did drugs and dealt a little pot from the back of my motorcycle. Obviously, I didn't share my dangerous and illegal weekend activities with my parents. From everything I told them, they believed I was a good conscientious objector kid seven days a week.

I lied so they would have no idea I was a whacked-out Easy Rider on Saturday and Sunday, not because of any punishment they could dole out, but because I cared what my mom and dad thought of me. Because of that, and their influence by example, I eventually changed that behavior myself. It also took me having a minor nervous breakdown and my bike throwing a rod, but I did change.

So now in the living room, instead of letting my confused fury out at Harry, I ask him as calmly as I can to tell me what happened tonight. Turns out he lied to protect his friend who Harry was letting drive his car for practice before taking a driver's test. The friend lost control somehow; the car went over a ditch and into an abandoned building. The car's totaled but no one was hurt.

He'd tried lying to the state troopers, telling them that he was driving, but they didn't buy it for a second. Luckily no one was charged. It was dumb and wrong-headed, I mean, come on -- driving lessons at 1 a.m. on a dark country road? But although I'm not going to bring down some huge punishment on him, we're not helping him get another car either.

Over the next few weeks, I stay calm and all of us keep talking. His mother and I tell him that we're looking out for a number of people in our family who really need it. He's twenty-two and healthy and all we ask is for him to take care of one person -- himself. He says he figures that's fair and he's decided that it's time for him to move out on his own.

I'm still impatient with introspection and other self-moderating stuff. I'm not built to be rational and reasonable; I'm wired to be impulsive and emotional. But that's not often what's needed in a dad. It's like the seemingly nonsensical flight attendants' instructions to put on your oxygen mask first before helping others.

For me, even though riding in on an emotional rage and bringing down the hammer feels true to myself and justified, taking the time to turn off my own noise and listen to my kids first has always turned out to be more truthful and in the end, causes less damage to all concerned, and is much more gratifying.

ACME'S ANVIL

Harry's moving out on his own, a decision everyone in our family participated in and we all agree is the right one for him and for all of us, too.

But as the time shortens before Harry leaves, my anxiety grows, and Margaret, picks up on it. "He'll be fine, Frank," she says. "He needs to go out on his own to grow into a man."

It's in our nature, for Wile E. Coyote and me to always be standing under the falling anvil, but we can still learn something from the together ones. I know she's right. I've said the same thing myself. But lately my commitment to Harry's adulthood has been clouded by memories of his childhood. As he was growing up in California, our house had a tiny basement that had just enough room for a TV and a small couch, which became a mini man cave for Harry and me. We played video games and watched cartoon videotapes and rooted for Wile E. Coyote to one day get something from ACME that worked. And we went on fishing weekends together up at Big Bear Lake, just the two of us.

Harry's quiet by nature and withdraws even more when overwhelmed or upset. The first trip, floating on the lake with our fishing lines out, I started worrying and kept asking if he was all right until Harry said, "Stop, Dad. I'm fine."

Now, at the end of the month, he'll be packing up and moving back to Hawaii where, before moving here to Georgia, we'd spent the last ten years and where he has a bunch of supportive friends who are at a similar point in their lives. He plans to get another fast-food job, get a place with a couple of roommates, go to community college part time, and God willing, begin to find out what he wants to do with his life. After making sure he packs enough underwear and socks, we'll have a family good-bye tamale dinner party with all of us -- his cousin, uncle, aunt, nana, sister, and parents. Then we'll blink back tears, hug him, and slip him twenties.

The morning after the party, because she's concerned that she'll cry and be clingy at the Atlanta airport, which would upset her and embarrass Harry, Margaret wants to say good-bye to her son at the house. I'll drive him and his two sixty pound suitcases to the plane without her. It seems odd that Margaret, the only even-keel type in our immediate family, is opting out of the airport trip to avoid an emotional display. After all, she's the together one. I'm the adult prone to panic attacks and other basket-case behaviors that in cases like these verge on the perversely sentimental and corny.

Of the two of us, I'm much more likely to be caught emotionally flat-footed when we watch him walking away from us at the airport to take his first uncertain solo steps into adulthood. I'm also sure that Margaret is aware that I'm much more likely than she is to break into sobs, dash across the waiting area, and tackle him as he checks his bags. My arms wrapped around his neck, I'll beg to him through my tears, "Be careful, Harry. Don't talk to strangers, take your meds, and find a nice strong-willed girl to whip you into shape, someone who knows what she wants from a man and won't settle for less from you." Finally, Margaret would be forced to pry me loose, free our son, and drag me kicking and keening back to our minivan.

Wait, that's why she's not going with us to the airport -- it's a together person's trick. Like Wile E. Coyote, I somehow manage to be shocked every time an anvil falls out of the sky and smashes down on my head just like it has done countless times before. But people, who have it together, like my wife, remember things like cause and effect. They can sense when life is going to get messy ahead of time. They know what to do to avoid being flattened by the sight of either their son walking off into an uncertain future or their husband scrambling after him, baying like a wounded beast. "When we smell trouble coming down," they chant at their secret, Road Runner-only, smarty-pants meetings, "we get out of town."

One family member who won't be nearly so upset by Harry's departure as me or her mother is our 15-year-old daughter, Coco. The other day when I was driving her back home from school she said, "I'd like to sit down and watch Hornblower with you again sometime."

"Sure," I said. "That'd be fun for all of us."

"No," she said. "I mean just you and me."

She loves her brother and all, and she's had some empathy for him and his struggles. But her form of the disability is closer to mine; she's easily overwhelmed and prone to bursts of panic. I can only imagine the relief she must feel at the prospect of simply not sharing a bathroom with Harry anymore. In terms of privacy and sanitation, that will be a brand-new world. She'll also have undivided attention from her mother and me.

But as her days as a newly minted only child begin to accumulate, it might become too much to take. With her thoughts no longer interrupted, contradicted, and ridiculed by a guy seven years older and twice her size, Coco could become delirious and need private time with her dad and to be sedated with vanilla ice cream and her Horatio Hornblower DVDs. Let's hope I'll evolve enough in the next few years to not freak out completely when Coco announces it's her time to leave the nest.

How I handle her brother's exit should be one step in the right direction. Having picked up clues from both Margaret and Harry, I'm pretty sure the airport trip should go off without a hitch. It's in our nature, for Wile E. Coyote and me, to always be standing under the falling anvil, but we can still learn something from the together ones. I've looked ahead, seen what's coming and made a plan. I already bought the Harry Chapin song, burned it on a CD, and preset it in the minivan.

Harry and I will talk about the benefits of Hawaiian living on the drive up to Atlanta. Curbside at the airport, we'll do our manly hugs and shoulder whacks, and I'll wish him luck, slip him another twenty, turn away before getting weepy and embarrassing him, and head to the parking garage. When I'm on the I-75 heading home, I'll play the CD and do a loud, long sing and sob.

COCO HITS THE WALL

This fall Coco started high school in Georgia. She had a hard time in Special Ed in Hawaii. We knew Coco had a great, compassionate spirit, as well as talent and a sharp intelligence, but it seemed that few teachers and even fewer of her classmates recognized those qualities in her. Her frustration with her ADHD, dyslexia, memory issues, and resulting low self-esteem would build up until she'd lash out with explosive bursts of temper, which resulted in her feeling even more isolated.

So in her individualized education plan (IEP) meeting at the high school here in Georgia, Coco, the counselors and social worker, and Margaret and I all decided that when she started ninth grade this fall, Coco would transition out of Special Ed and begin mainstreaming into the regular high school curriculum This is what Coco wanted but it also presented more chances to fail.

Margaret and I were prepared and ready to be there for her in any way she needed. After all, we had experience and the use of the resources we have developed over the years of being parents of two ADHD children.

Sure, Coco's twenty-two year-old brother, Harry, dropped out of college and at that time was still living at home, halfheartedly looking for a minimum-wage job, rarely leaving his rat's nest room, but so what? Every child is different, and besides, we'd learned from our mistakes. We'd keep communication open with the teachers and be supportive and understanding but firm with our daughter. So

Coco, Margaret and I all felt confident about her prospects and told each other so as she stepped out of our car and walked to class on her first day of high school.

Now here's the thing: When the three of us were telling each other how confident we all were of success -- I was lying through my teeth. I was terrified. I had no confidence that Coco would do well in this school. How could I? She and I are wired in nearly the same way -- easily overwhelmed, quick-tempered, and strapped to an emotional roller coaster that in an instant rockets feelings of shaky pride to profound self-loathing without the slightest warning. Imagine a brain with synapses that already misfire, putting you out of sync with normal folks in the best of times, now pressed nearly flat under suffocating adolescent anxiety that guarantees failure in front of hundreds of strangers who, I guarantee you, are desperately looking for a new geek to humiliate and dismember when their scopes focus in on her. When they do, you can bet all of her internal alarms begin screeching, "This is not a drill! This is not a drill!" Good God, if I were in Coco's shoes, you couldn't drag me into that school with chains and a three-quarter ton pickup.

This is my daughter, who I love and treasure beyond reason. How could I allow her to be subjected to the ignorance and judgment of strangers who don't value her as I do? I went to high school; I know what happens in there to people like Coco and me. If it hadn't been for my oblivious geek fog, I never would have survived. But Coco's more social, fogless and vulnerable. I wanted to yell, "Turn back! Homeschool!" But I kept my feelings hidden pretty well. As Coco disappeared through the front entrance of that soul-killing. spirit-crushing hell hole, Margaret gave me a sidelong glance and asked, "Are you all right, Frank?"

"Oh, yeah. Mmm-hmm," I said, my eyes wide over a fake smile and nodding like a bobble head. "Good. Great. She'll do great."

Margaret shook her head, and drove us back home. By the time we turned into the driveway, I'd calmed down a bit and half convinced myself that Coco was strong, she's be fine and whatever happened, Margaret and I would be able to handle it. Now that we'd moved, we'd be able to focus more on Coco, so we'd be able to catch signs of any trouble and give her the help she needed.

This was last August. About this time my parents in Delaware had a crisis and I had to go there for a couple of weeks to help. In Georgia, Margaret had to deal with several issues on her own. Her mother had moved in with us and our son, Harry, had spent $1,500 of the money we'd given him to buy a car on rap music and online porn and still needed rides back and forth to the part-time job he'd finally gotten at Taco Bell.

By the last week of September, I was back at home and after a long search we'd just found Harry a cheap serviceable car. I asked Coco to help me set the table for dinner, to which she replied, "I hate it here! I hate it! I hate this school. I don't have any friends. I want to go home to Hawaii!"

So much for being prepared to handle anything, Coco's eruption caught us completely by surprise. My first thought was that this was a false alarm. Coco really wanted more emotional attention from us and this was her way of getting it. So I apologized for her mother and me being so preoccupied by the other dramas going on in the family that we'd missed some distress signals from her. But Coco said no, we hadn't.

Still, tears were running down my daughter's face. And with a "duh" smack to the side of my head with our similar emotional structure, I should have guessed what was going on. Coco had given no sign that anything was wrong at school because she, as I do, wants at all costs to appear normal and competent. So we saw what she wanted: a well-organized student who did her homework after school and didn't want help. Because if she did want help or looked like she did, she would appear as stupid as she was already convinced she was and hated herself for it, that she wouldn't have been able to stand the embarrassment.

Though she had missed a recent one, Margaret's early status meetings with teachers seemed positive because Coco did as I have done at school and in jobs my entire life: She put up a good front, but it was wearing her out.

* * * *

I follow Coco upstairs as my wife, Margaret, finishes setting the table and getting dinner ready because our new roommate, Margaret's mother Nana, has to eat by five p.m. or she gets cranky.

Upstairs, I supply Kleenex and hugs while I listen to Coco vent her misery for a while longer. Her new teachers don't help her, and she feels trapped in this huge new school that feels so different from her one back in Hawaii.

Then from her pocket, she pulls out a slip from her math teacher that has to be signed by a parent and returned. This apparently was the straw that broke my daughter's back.

At midterm, she was failing math. The curriculum was new this year, and a whole lot of the kids were also failing and barring a miracle, would have to take it over. But Coco only saw this grade as her personal failure and proof of not being smart enough. On top of that, she admitted her biology, geography, English lit, and health grades all looked to be teetering toward low Cs, at best. The only bright spot was music appreciation, where she was getting an A. But Coco said you had to murder someone to not get an A in that class.

When she starts cycling back to blaming and degrading herself, making herself even more miserable, I interrupt to ask her if she's told her teachers when she needs help.

"If I ask for help, everybody knows how stupid I am," Coco, cries. "And nobody will ever be my friend. I know what those other girls are thinking. They know I'm really Special Ed, and I'm sick of being looked at that way. I'm sick of being judged. And don't say I should just ignore them, because I can't, okay? But never mind, you just don't get it."

"I do get it," I say.

"Why? Because you have ADHD too? No you don't." She says, her crying now pushed back by anger. "It's not the same for you. I'm a high school girl! You're ... you're, like ... an old man."

She's got a point there. But still, my pronounced multi-decade immaturity has to count for something.

"Maybe it's not the same, Coco," I say, "but you've told me yourself that I act like a kid."

She smiles. "Yeah, but Dad, I didn't mean, like in a good way," she says.

I smile back at her, glad to feel her sense of despair lighten some. And then, without intending to, I begin telling her about a humiliating experience I had on a job about three years ago.

I was directing a local reality TV show in Hawaii. A lot had to be done all in a matter of hours. It was a tense day, and because either a location wasn't ready or somebody was late, I went outside to switch assignments for one of the cameras. As I tried to explain what I wanted in front of the camera crew, my ADD/ADHD brain got ahead of itself trying to plan the rest of the day. It took me all the way into the next day, when I'd be at home reading or writing, which would certainly be much more fun than being here talking with these people.

Shaking my head, I tried to backtrack to the present and got stuck in the reasons why I get so anxious over a simple job that I give myself a headache. I then realized I'd been standing in front of these guys mute for, I don't know, maybe a couple of minutes, so I tried to parachute back into the here and now, which triggered my stammer, and suddenly, I was in full, wide-eyed stupid in front of these guys.

"Yu ... yu ... yu ... yu ..." I said as a couple of them traded smirks. I took a breath and tried again, "Ju ... ju ... ju ..." I said.

"Yu ... yu ... ju ... ju ... what? Spit it out, for Christ's sake," one of the cameramen said. And the crew burst out laughing. And, as Coco would say, not in a good way.

"Omigod. Did you want to kill them?" Coco asks.

"Yeah," I say. "Or run away and hide."

"Not very good options, I guess," she says. We trade smiles and I shake my head.

"No, not on that job," I say. "Or in high school either."

"You don't have to be obvious, Dad. I get the point," she says. "So, what did you do?"

I tell Coco that even though I was embarrassed and angry, I stayed standing where I was and took a minute to do some breathing, get calm, and think. Then I looked up and told the crew what to do. Later, the cameraman apologized; he'd just been trying to break the tension in a weird situation. I said no worries, and we all got on with the job.

I also tell her that even though I'd told myself I was a grown man and I knew it shouldn't, the embarrassment stayed with me the rest of the day. But, as I replayed the incident over in my head the following week, I discovered I hadn't really been embarrassed in front of the crew. I'd been embarrassed in front of myself. I was angry because I didn't live up to my idea of myself as the boss on the job. By far the harshest judges of those of us with any impairment are inside ourselves. Left unrecognized and unchecked, those unforgiving interior judges can do more harm than our original condition ever could.

Coco nods. "I guess that's right," she says with a sigh.

"Anyway," I say, standing up, "let's have some dinner and then bring your mom in on this discussion."

"Okay. But see Dad, I don't want to be like those kids who don't care at all," Coco says. "And it seems like that's who I get stuck with, even though I put extra time in to really study. Math, biology -- you remember how much time I spent on the biome project. I work so hard to get it right and learn things, but the next day, I can't remember, and it makes me think it's hopeless. Like, maybe I should just give up."

"We'll see what Mom has to say about all of this, but I don't see you giving up, Coco," I say. "With you, I'm more worried about spontaneous combustion."

"You should talk," she says.

As we headed down to dinner, I knew that her mother's perspective and input would be crucial for her to put this new panic aside and hopefully let her natural confidence blossom in this new environment.

At dinner, Margaret asked Coco if she felt she was being bullied or if there was someone at school she felt threatened by. Coco said no. Then Margaret asked about individual classes and teachers. Coco wouldn't answer some of these questions with Harry, Nana, and me sitting at the table with them. But Margaret didn't push. Instead, Margaret moderated the conversation and said "No, thanks" to a couple of suggestions along the lines of "Spit in their eye" (Nana) and "Call in sick" (Harry). I kept busy passing plates around and eating mashed potatoes to keep from butting in.

After dinner, I did the dishes while Margaret and Coco went into the living room to dig into Coco's backpack and into the specifics of what was going on at school. Margaret is a genius at organizing, and I knew that she and Coco would be digging into more than academics. I was an ADHD teenager like Coco, but Margaret was a teenage girl. Unlike Coco, Margaret didn't struggle with learning disabilities in high school, but very much like Coco, Margaret was and is free-thinking, rebellious, and sensitive to the realities of the female adolescent emotional jungle, whether it shows itself as bullying (it didn't) or as feelings of intense new-girl social pressure and uncertainty over attention from boys. Coco couldn't have a better sensei for any of those challenges.

So, that it mind Coco, Margaret and I came up with some informal ideas that could be altered when necessary by any of the three of us. No Nana or Harry suggestions included.

1. We consciously tried to meet every aspect of our daughter's needs (not just the academic ones). We not only provided homework help but also offered encouragement and made ourselves available for hangout and venting time.

2. We developed a flexible but structured routine. After that first night, we developed a pattern -- Coco would come home from school to cool her jets by herself or to vent to a member of family until after dinner, at which point Margaret and she would dig into the homework plan for the night, coming to me for occasional help or encouragement. For months, this was what we all did every day, hoping it would help Coco succeed and feel less frustrated.

3. We relied on our parenting strengths: I gave moral support and some ADHD insight, Margaret gave homework and high school politics help. As a father, I'm the empathetic sort, which is good up to a point. That point is reached pretty quickly by a 15-year-old girl when she becomes convinced she's going to smother to death under her overprotective dad's heavy blanket of understanding stitched through with seemingly endless instructive life stories.

That's when it's good to have a mother who is as practical and task-oriented as Margaret to break you out into the unsentimental daylight.

4. We did our best to avoid family conflicts, to make sure not to add to the pressure our daughter was already coping with. Not that there weren't some disagreements, with slamming doors, accusations, and crying from Coco and, much to Coco's frustration, a nearly always calm, cool response from Margaret and when very rarely needed, mediations from me.

5. As parents, Margaret and I followed what we call the "Parental Divide and Conquer Prevention Protocol," which has one directive: "No parent will take the side of a child against the other parent in an argument, unless said argument is serious enough to call the police." Margaret and I constantly discuss both our kids and discuss and sometimes argue about what's best for them in different situations. But that's our private parent business; it's never done in front of those who will suffer the outcome. We're old-fashioned here. Experience has taught us that without a united front, the young barbarians, wielding iPhone apps and Rice Krispies Treats, break through the gates and lay waste to civilization.

Through conflict and drama we kept at it, especially Margaret, though I provided moral support, entertainment, sporadic factoids, as well as rice pudding and brownies. We dedicated all the attention, time, and patience Coco needed, along with a moderately flexible home routine to provide support for her as she dug in and did her best. In trying to keep her raging self-criticism at bay, we continued to tell her that doing her best was all that mattered. (And it is.)

Other stuff kept happening in the family, of course: As mentioned previously, Harry totaled his car (bad), then we hosted a big family Thanksgiving at our house (good/bad -- the turkey was fine, but I didn't do the sweet potatoes the way Nana likes them), we did our Christmas shopping (good/bad -- we limited our spending but still ended up maxing out our credit cards), Harry decided to move back to Hawaii (good), and then one day near the end of the semester, a junior boy in Coco's high school who had been showing polite, respectful interest in her (always walking with her between classes) took off running when I drove up to pick Coco up after school.

Coco had been in a better mood lately and got in the car laughing. "What was that about?" I asked.

"He just knows what an overprotective dad you are," she said.

The next day, Margaret picked Coco up after school and they walked into my office together with the end of semester report card. They didn't look happy.

It was a fake-out. The big news for Coco was that she passed math and that was her only C. She got a B in English lit, an A in biology, a B in geography, a B in health, and because she didn't murder anyone and also because according to her teacher, she works hard and contributes enthusiastically, she got an A in music appreciation.

So our Christmas was happy. But more importantly, since then, Coco has been happy and much more confident as we stick to our flexible routines and she makes her way through her second semester. But strictly from a dad's point of view, that polite boy better keep on running.

MUTANT AND PROUD

Coco and I are in the kitchen. It's a nice morning; school's finally out, which takes some of the pressure off both Coco and her mom.

Margaret has been substituting at a local middle school lately and had been gone a lot. Which one of the three of us is stressed out more by her absence and having to work depends on your point of view, I'd guess. Margaret is the one sleeping in this morning, however. And I did promise that after Nana goes to bed after dinner tonight, I'd take Coco to see the New X-Men movie, leaving Margaret alone to watch *Oprah Behind the Scenes,* and maybe a little *Real Housewives of New Jersey* in peace, which means without Coco and me hanging around making rude cracks about her shows every two seconds.

So, the sun's shining, Nana's taken her Rice Krispies and coffee into the living room to read the paper, I'm putting dishes in the dishwasher and Coco's making Ramen noodles. She glances out the kitchen window that faces our backyard.

"Those squirrels are never going to give up on that birdfeeder," she says.

I glance out the window as a gray squirrel jumps from the trunk of a pine tree trying to reach the feeder hanging from one of its branches. He misses wide. Coco laughs. The jays, cardinals and finches chowing down on the new seed we just put in, ignore the frustrated squirrel chattering and jumping around. Our freakishly oversized standard poodle, Danny doesn't though, and he whines desperately until Coco lets him outside and he chases the squirrel up another tree barking in outrage, scattering the birds. Then Danny checks the perimeter for any other squirrels skulking about, and then satisfied he's put things right, settles down on the patio to guard the birds, now fluttering back to the feeder.

"That dog is nuts," Coco says.

"He thinks he's protecting the birds," I say.

"From squirrels?"

"Yup, just like he protects us from UPS guys." I say, closing up the dishwasher. "Oh, did you give Amy a call yet to see about getting together over summer break?"

I don't know why I brought it up, the thought just popped in my head, like a million thoughts do every second of everyday, but obviously I should have kept this one to myself. Coco's face flushes red and she slams the spoon she was stirring the Ramen noodles with onto the counter, shattering the pleasant morning mood.

"No!" she yells, "I didn't, okay? And I don't know if I'm going to, so just drop it!"

But thinking I can fix things because that's what dads do, (or at least the dads on Lifetime movies when they're not plotting murder or sleeping with babysitters,) and because I love my daughter beyond measure (blah blah blah, as she would say) but mostly because I want to get back that pleasant morning mood I was so enjoying just seconds ago, I do the wrong thing and don't drop it. Coco had just this last semester started breaking out of her shell and having the beginning of a social life. I was sure there was something I could do to help. Nobody in the world has less of a clue than a father with good intentions.

"I thought you guys were friends," I said.

"We are." She says through gritted teeth and stirring the noodles so they're slopping all over the stove, hissing on the burner.

"Did something happen, Coco? Somebody say something or something?" I ask, getting lamer by the second as Coco's ramen was beginning to look like it was in a blender with the top off. When "something" starts sprouting in their sentences like this, smart parents shut up, but not me. "Looks like your noodles are done, honey. Maybe you should turn off the burner..."

"I know! I will!" she yells, turning to me with tears in her eyes. "Amy's got tons of friends. <u>Tons!</u> See? Get it?" And with that she turns off the burner, pours what's left of her noodles into a bowl, grabs a spoon and stomps off to her room.

My daughter's nerves, like mine, are often on edge. We are both cheerful, high energy types, but can swing into dark and distrustful moods without warning. We also share short term memory issues, often forgetting familiar names of people, places and things in the middle of sentences, which can make one feel like an idiot. Because she's an adolescent dealing with a new and intense social world, feeling like an idiot is more of an issue for Coco. I've gotten used to it, except when I forget how it felt when I was undiagnosed but still very much ADHD in high school myself, and had the same problems with fitting in and self-worth that Coco does now.

Later that night, Coco and I were sipping sodas and sharing popcorn, engrossed in the X-Men First Class movie. The two of us have seen all of this series and we've loved them all. The stories of people ostracized and misunderstood because of differences in their genetic makeup they couldn't control, not surprisingly resonated with us.

But this particular movie, with all the heroes young, new to their gifts and confused resonated with Coco especially. At one point, a young heroine who finally accepted what she was completely, yelled out, "Mutant and proud!" And Coco and I turned and smiled at each other. She gave my hand a squeeze and we turned back to the screen, both of us still learning to live mutant and proud.

SON FATHER SON

"Let go of me!"

It must be near midnight, but I have no idea what day it is. I do know that the man in front of me is very angry and very drunk. I try to keep a grip on his wrist, but it's slick with blood and sweat.

"Stop it!" he says. "Leave me alone!"

As my mother and I finally get the man, my 87-year-old father, to stand, he pulls free of my hand, but the sudden momentum throws him off balance, he bumps against the edge of the bed, and still flailing at me and my mother, falls toward the floor again. Even at his age, he's still a big man, but throwing all my 220 pounds into it, I half catch and half body block him back up and onto the top of the bed, where he lands with an angry grunt and immediately tries to get up again. My mother puts her hand to his chest and tries to calm him as I get one of his tranquilizers.

"Frank, you cut up your arm when you fell," she says to him (he's Frank Sr. to my junior) as she reaches back and I drop a Lorazepam into her palm. "We have to fix it. But first, darling, take your night pill."

"Nonsense, I'm fine!" Dad bellows, pushing her away, nearly toppling her back into the dresser. I reach out, and she grabs onto my arm to steady herself. Trembling, Mom stares at her husband in fear and disbelief. She turns and hands the pill to me.

"I can't," she says. "You try."

Over the years I've seen my mother when she was unhappy or depressed, even furious or confused. But she has always been a steel magnolia of the first order, a determined farm girl -- indomitable in the face of any disaster. The pain and bald defeat I see in her eyes tonight is new to me -- and terrifying.

Protective fury sweeps over me and I again grab my father's flailing arm, this time smacking my hand against the bloody wound from his fall. He cries out, shocked.

"Dad, look at us! Look at this mess!" I yell. "You have got to stop drinking! You can't do this to yourself anymore. You can't do it to Mom."

"The hell you say!" Dad bellows. "It's not your business!"

I yell back at him, swearing -- then stop, suddenly dumbstruck by the awful absurdity of this moment. I'm standing in my parents' bedroom in the middle of the night yelling at the top of my lungs. Their sheltie, Toby, barks at me as if I'm an intruder.

Right now, I think the dog's right, but I really don't have a choice. I bear part of the blame for this mess. I came to their home in Delaware from my home in Georgia to help my mother get home from the hospital and recover from stress-induced severe dehydration and exhaustion. She'd been home maybe a week and was just beginning to get some of her strength back when my father -- still adjusting to life after the traumatic brain injury and stroke he suffered last year, which left him and the rest of us to deal with his new unsettling memory problems, diminished capacity, and anger issues -- started drinking like he was on a mission of self-destruction. Earlier, against his doctor's orders, because one of his best friends had just died, I'd reluctantly gone along with Mom and Dad's new plan of letting Dad have a martini or two instead of the agreed-upon one glass of wine a day. Over the last few days, the plan has blown up in our faces, with my father making less and less sense earlier and earlier every day and the nights filled with fights, falls, and tears.

But how could I have stopped him? I hate myself for failing -- but come on, I had too much else to think about. I was trying to concentrate on my mother's needs, but of course, my dad couldn't stand that and had to manufacture his own emergency. Then I think, No, it's not him, it's the altered personality and narcissism of his injured brain. No, it's not, it's me and my stupid, incompetent, overwhelmed disordered brain. As my thoughts begin to spiral, an alarm goes off inside my head, and all the therapists I've ever had band together and shout in unison: "STOP IT!" (The voice is always Judge Judy's. I don't know why.)

"I'm trying, I am, I am " I sputter. "But I'm in an ADHD stressalanche! Everything is my fault."

"ADHD is never an excuse," Judge Judy says. "Finding fault is useless. Breathe. Calm yourself and accept your situation. Look at what's bothering you about it and then do what you can that's positive to make things better. That's all anyone can do."

I take a long, slow breath and look around. Mom leans against the wall with her eyes closed, catching her breath. Dad continues to yell at me, but I don't listen. I focus on reigning in the storm of rage, anxiety, guilt, and sick, hopeless dread that's blowing apart my chaotic brain. As I breathe, I remind myself that I do not want to lash out at my father and make things worse. Dad suffered a debilitating brain injury last year. His drinking is out of control, but above all, this is a man I love and respect. This is the man I was named after and whose stubborn hot temper I inherited. I make myself continue to breathe slowly and deeply. I let go of his arm and, shielding Mom, I step closer to my dad with the pill and some water. I speak with what I hope is the voice of quiet authority.

"Dad, listen," I say. "You need to take your Lorazepam. Then I'm going to put a bandage on your arm, all right?" He looks me in the eye. I look back. "Here," I say, holding out the pill. "Please." I'm trying for Clint Eastwood in Unforgiven, but considering my interior chaos and the effect my war hero professor father still has on me, I'm sure I come off more like Jerry Lewis in The Bellhop.

Nonetheless, Dad takes the pill and, still staring daggers at me, swallows it. I begin to fashion a makeshift bandage on his arm to hold him until morning when he'll be slowed by his hangover and I can properly clean and dress the deep gash he somehow gave himself. "Presumptuous little snot," he mumbles.

He's joking, I think, but I don't respond. Taking advantage of the calm in the storm, I roll tape around the bandage on his arm.

"There's nothing wrong with having a drink once in a while," Dad says.

I stay quiet, remaining focused on the job in front of me. I think the ADHD brain breaks everyday experience into pieces and makes it into sort of a cubist painting. It distorts and refigures your perspective of what's important and, especially under stress, puts a huge amount of importance on minute details and "fixing" activities. In my case, this sometimes happens at the expense of the larger picture -- but not this time.

Now that the collective voice of therapists past has calmed me down, I realize that right now, there is not a thing I can say that will have any effect on my father's drinking. I could remind him that his doctor told him that due to all the damage from the fall and previous hard living, alcohol was poison to his brain and body and that any more drinking would kill him. I could tell him again that the stress of his continued drinking has been hurting Mom and was partly responsible for putting her in the hospital. But he'd just shout me down. I'm a recovering alcoholic. I've been where my father is, and in that place, the bottle is all you listen to. Besides, I've already decided what I'm going to do to fix the problem.

His tranquilizer has taken effect, and Dad's lying back with his eyes closed, mumbling to himself. I tell my mother my plan, and she agrees -- though, as exhausted as she is, she'd probably agree if I told her I was taking Dad off with me to join the circus. I kiss Mom goodnight, then gather up the first aid stuff as she tucks Dad's legs under the covers. Toby stops barking, wags his tail, and follows me into the kitchen. I give him a dog biscuit, straighten up the living room, clean up the kitchen, start the dishwasher and a load of laundry, and then get to work.

By 3 a.m., I've gotten every drop of alcohol out of their house. Gin, bourbon, brandy, red and white wine, champagne, and a bunch of little chocolate bottles of liqueurs, all either poured out and tossed or sealed up in a duct-taped box and stacked on a high garage shelf, along with two wine mini-fridges, ready to be disposed of with the rest of the neighborhood's trash pickup tomorrow.

As presumptuous as it is, I feel it was the only thing to do. And I know it's just the beginning. I'll have to call Margaret and tell her

I'll have to stay here for another couple of weeks. Who knows what my father's going to do when he discovers what I've done. But he's going to do something.

* * * *

I blame a lot of what happened on my parents' cat, Clifford. I know you shouldn't speak ill of the dead, but I'm going to anyway.

I know alcoholism can't be scrubbed away; once it's there, it's permanent. When I woke up the next morning, I had to face the unpleasant truth that maybe all the self-righteous rage I'd taken out on my father and his booze supply was really rage at the powerlessness I feel as an alcoholic myself.

I haven't had a drink for 10 years, but still, the dismay I felt these recent nights with my father lurching around the house with his walker, gin-blasted and giggling, was partnered with envy. Even when he fell by the back door and later in their bedroom, ripping a gash in his arm, I was as jealous of his oblivion as I was concerned about his and my mother's safety.

But Clifford, the black cat is responsible for this mess. Last January, right before I came up for a visit, my brother, Rob, and sister-in-law, Sharon, gave Clifford to my parents. A veterinarian friend had rescued Clifford, full-grown and long-haired, from beside the highway. Mom, Dad and their Sheltie, Toby, were happy to take him in. I, however, am super-allergic to cats (allergy pills barely work), and honestly, I just don't like cats that much. But Rob and Sharon live near my parents; they do the day-to-day checking-in and assisting. I, as an occasional visitor and helpmate, really had no grounds to object. The first day of my January visit, I sat on the couch with my eyes running and sneezed. I looked up. Yellow-eyed Clifford was two feet away, sitting in front of me on the coffee table, smirking.

During those two weeks in January as we tolerated each other, he became the kitty apple of my parents' eyes. They loved to chuckle and complain as they let Toby and Clifford in and out of the house and gently scolded the cat for jumping on the kitchen counter but objected when I pushed him off. Neatly lined up spice containers clattered into the sink when I turned my back. Long black cat hairs began appearing in the butter. "That crazy cat," was all my mother would say.

Maybe it's because cats show no regard to my lifelong attempt to bring order to my scattered brain by bringing disorder to my immediate surroundings. Maybe it's the hungry yowl and sudden appearance of a jumping cat that undoes all of my careful concentration. Maybe it's my constant sneezing in their presence. I just don't get along with pets of the feline type. Dogs, I love. I have a dog brain, they have dog brains, and we understand each other. Toby, their Sheltie, and I have always gotten along. Then toward the end of the January visit, I found empty boxes of doggie treats on the floor that had been pushed off the top of the refrigerator. The dog and cat were working together.

So when I showed up in March to help out and give Rob and Sharon a break, Mom was in the hospital suffering from extreme dehydration and exhaustion, Dad was drinking gin and eating bratwurst with the TV blaring CNN, and Clifford ruled the roost with Toby as co-conspirator. I popped allergy pills, went to the hospital to see when I could get Mom home, went to the grocery store, and reluctantly -- at my father's insistence -- went to the liquor store to get a couple of gargantuan bottles of Bombay Sapphire.

Since Dad's head injury, my brother, Dad's doctor, and I already considered dad's drinking a problem. But Dad and Mom had worked out an agreement where he'd (supposedly) drink in moderation. So I bought the stuff (along with healthy ingredients for homemade rice pudding and chicken soup). After bringing everything home, I watched and worried as Dad poured his monster martinis. A couple of nights later during dinner, I told him that Mom could be home from the hospital within a few days. After he put his plate down for the animals to finish, he let them both outside. He shook his head and smiled as Clifford jumped up on the ledge outside the living room window and yowled before taking off across the snowy yard. "That crazy cat," he said. Later, Toby came back but not Clifford. Dad was still up and told me to go on to bed.

He'd let the cat in when he showed up. "Clifford always shows up eventually," he said as he poured himself another martini.

The next morning, I had to go to the corner drugstore for allergy pills and meds for Mom and decided to walk to get some exercise. It was still wet and icy from the night's storm. When I turned the corner around the front hedge, lying on the sidewalk in front of me was Clifford. He'd been dead for some hours. He was covered with a sheet of ice crystals, blood from being hit by a car in a frozen pool by his head. I stood over him, stunned. I felt pity for this headstrong animal but even more for my parents. They'd formed such an immediate bond with Clifford, the crazy cat.

I went back to the house and told my dad what I'd found. It was decided I should bury Clifford in the back yard under a tree between the shed and the woodpile. Later, I'd tell Mom when I visited her at the hospital. Dad, Toby by his feet, had a morning martini and stoically watched CNN as I dug the hole.

But what I really wanted was to be able to drown out the confusion and conflicting voices in my head, like Dad was doing. I was pissed that I wanted my dad's easy abandon of pouring martini after martini, thumbing his nose at responsibility and fear. When you're drunk, you don't care. And more than anything, I wanted to not care. But I'm sober, so I kept digging. As I covered Clifford with the last of the dirt, I cried and blamed that cat for shoving death in my face, for showing me that no matter how I feared it, I couldn't ignore my mom and dad's looming mortality.

Lying here in bed days later, on the morning after I went off the rails, yelled at my father and threw away all his liquor, I wonder if in my confused and desperate attempt to save him and my mother, to protect them from what I'm powerless to stop, I just made things worse for them. I can hear Dad's rolling walker go by my door as he heads for the kitchen. It's time for me to get up, make some coffee, and find out.

* * * *

"Your move," he says.

I look up at my father, and he nods at the chessboard between us on the dining room table. Mom's in my parent's bedroom taking an afternoon nap. Dad sips his coffee and takes a bite of the liverwurst sandwich I made for him. "Well," Dad says. "Are you going to do something or just give up?"

Good question. When I got up this morning, I knew I couldn't have actual face-to-face communication in this new day I'd created until I'd showered, shaved, and take my morning meds,.

The thing is, when I got myself together and went out to the kitchen that morning, neither Dad or Mom were acting any differently. We had breakfast and coffee, shared the paper, and Dad flipped through morning TV news shows. Everything was eerily Twilight Zone normal. Not even my fine-tuned WASP radar could pick up a trace of buried emotions or hidden meanings until my mother asked me to help her to bed for a nap. As I tucked her in and gave her a vitamin drink and pain meds, she told me that Dad had noticed the empty cabinet and hadn't said anything. "But I think he's fine with it," she said. "I think he understands."

Sitting across the dining room table from me now, waiting for me to move a chess piece, chewing liverwurst and drinking black coffee, my father doesn't look fine. His eyes search mine. To me, he looks like he's setting a trap. I know for sure he is on the chessboard. Ever since he first taught me to play chess, our games reflected our personalities. I bludgeon straight down the middle of the board, heatedly chopping through game pieces, reigning terror. Dad lays back, cool and calculated, drifting to the sides and then springs his calm logical trap, destroying my desperate emotional attack.

I know that this chess game and what I did after the fight last night are all tied up together somehow, but I'm too caught up in all the emotional tendrils of that to know what to do. I'm so completely bound by the strained cabling of love, anger, respect, fear, and adoration wrapped through my history with my father for me to be able to make any sense of it at all. And now I'm back to bottling things up. I bring my queen forward on the attack. My father smiles.

God Almighty, I'm a complete wreck. As my father studies the board for the most diabolical way to destroy me, I think about my own son, Harry. Unlike me, Harry's a guy who just doesn't let things get to him.

Last March, a week before I went up to Delaware to help out with my parents, my wife, Margaret, and I threw a little good-bye party for our 23-year-old son. In a couple of days, Harry was going off on his own and moving back to Hawaii where he has longtime friends from the 10 years we lived there before we moved to Georgia. Harry's favorite food is chicken tamales, so we ordered a couple of trays of them from the best local Mexican restaurant. Margaret made guacamole, and we cooked rice and black beans and stocked up on beer and soda.

All the while Margaret and I were running around gussying up the house, Harry just watched, looking bemused. I asked him when his new friends from work were coming over, and he said, "They're not, Dad. We hung out last night."

"Oh," I said. "Why, because the dingbat bozos are embarrassed of their part in wrecking your car? Hey, that was a few months ago. I don't hold a grudge, Harry."

"Uh, yeah, you kind of do, Dad," Harry said. "But that's not it. They've got work or other stuff. It's probably better that it's just family."

I took a minute and looked at him. He really wasn't upset that his friends weren't coming or that I hold a grudge, nor was he the least bit hesitant in telling me so. If there's a perfect example of a guy who takes things as they are, who doesn't get his feelings hurt or become emotionally confused and says what he thinks, it's my son. As maddening as his basic disengagement with day-to-day emotional life is, I admire his detached "no worries" shrug. Standing there in the living room with him, I knew I'd miss it.

I sure as hell could use some of Harry's emotional detachment right now, I thought as I watched my father contemplate his next move on the chessboard. Dad wasn't saying anything, settled back in his chair, sipping his coffee, and stared at me across the chessboard again. And once again, it was my move. Even though he had opened and closed the now-empty liquor cabinet, Dad wasn't saying anything about it. He was just eating the sandwich I'd made him, sipping his coffee, and staring at the chessboard and then at me.

It was my move I guess, but really, it was his move. I'd moved like a maniac the night before, and now I wanted to know what he thought about all his missing gin, wine, and whisky. I had done it to try to save him. But I didn't want to mention it first because I'd be stepping into the trap he'd successfully used on me since I was a kid -- the presumptuous emotional boy blows his cool and then is firmly put in his place by the wise, logical dad. But I wasn't falling for it this time. This time, I realized, was too important to get caught up in the old games. "Your move," Dad said.

Maybe that's it, though -- I should stop bottling up everything until it gets confused and explodes. Maybe the only way to fix this mess between my father and me is to be more like my son, Harry.

My dad had moved his chess piece, and he was staring at me, chewing his liverwurst on rye. It was my move. I was pretty much terrified of his as yet unvoiced reaction to my throwing out all his liquor. But if I'm calm and non-judgmental like Harry, it doesn't bother me. If he wanted to use the chess game to play out this conflict, fine. I could do that. But when I looked at the chessboard, I saw that he'd moved my knight. "You're white," I told him. "I'm black." I moved my piece back.

"Right, right. Of course," he said. "Sorry." He studied the chessboard again, and then he smiled to himself and carefully picked up my knight again.

"Dad," I said. "That's my knight. You're white, remember?"

"What?" he asked. "Oh, did I do that again?" He snapped his hand away and sat back from the board like he'd touched a hot stove. For a second, I thought he was messing around, trying to lure me into the old trap, but when I looked at his face, all I saw was muddled embarrassment.

That's when everything finally clicked into place. He wasn't laying a trap on the chessboard or in our argument. He was really trying to figure out which was his chess piece. And he was trying to figure out what happened to all his bottles of gin, and he was afraid to ask. This was no game. He was just trying to remember. And that's what I have to do, too.

I have to remember that my father is 86 years old, that he suffered a brain injury a year ago that he has yet to really recover from. I have to remember that our history of lessons, arguments, conflicts, and butting heads is just that -- our history as father and son, not what's going on now. There's no time for right and wrong anymore. Because I feel I know what's right -- that my father's an alcoholic just like me -- and because I love him, I want to save my father from harm by cutting off his liquor supply and fighting with him as I have.

But the real harm I can do is to his dignity. And as I looked at him that day, trying to cover his confusion and shame with the face of the tough soldier and scientist he at his core would always be, I realized that at this time in his life his dignity is more vital to him than his next breath. By trying to do right for this man I love so much, had I instead taken what is most valuable to him? I don't know.

By my next visit in June, Dad and Mom had decided he should have his liquor back, and I stayed out of it. Dad didn't show any interest in playing chess. I made dinners, did laundry, and worked in the garden, and we talked. I was careful to show no disapproval about the liquor. Though to help sponge up the alcohol, I did bring him a snack every time he made himself a drink. That's a lot of snacks.

On my next visit, I hope he'll feel comfortable enough to come back to the chessboard. I still don't know if letting him make all the tough choices in his life is the right thing to do for my dad in his condition, I think, as I'm sure Harry would, it's enough that it feels right for him.

Go Home

"**M**om says to tell you that now I have the most expensive hair in the house," Coco, tells me over the phone from our home in Georgia.

Coco called me as soon as Margaret brought her back from the salon where Coco apparently got a major, life-changing, going-back-to-school, radical cut and dye job. For the last ten days, Coco and Margaret have waited patiently for me to get back from my latest trip to my parents' place in Delaware to help my mother take care of my father.

But Coco starts her sophomore year in high school in three days, Margaret starts teaching middle school part time the same week, the carpet in my mother-in-law's room in our house needs to be shampooed, the dog needs to go to the groomer, new furniture needs to be assembled, the yard's a mess, and they needed me back home yesterday.

I tell Coco that I thought her long blond hair looked great already. I ask her what it looks like now, but she won't say. "OK, then are you even more beautiful than you were before?" I ask her.

"What? I don't know. It's cool, though. But I'm not telling you anything about it until you get back and see for yourself," Coco says. "And Mom isn't telling you either!" she yells to Margaret who's with her in our living room. Coco's now 15 years old and, like me, still has a bit of a problem with her temper.

"Watch your tone, sweetie," I say from my parent's house in Delaware. I've got the phone cradled on my shoulder as I clear dinner dishes from their dining room table.

"I'm just kidding around, Dad," Coco says.

My 87-year-old father glares at me as I take away his dinner plate. I smile back at him. He shakes his head and looks away. He's been even more confused and irritable lately. My mother thinks the recurring pain from yet another fall he took recently has intensified his spells of dementia. Whatever the cause, all we can do at this point is stay as cheerful and calm as possible so that he doesn't get more agitated and hurt himself again.

"OK," I say to Coco. "But still that's your mother you're talk--..." The cell phone begins to slip away from my ear, and I press my shoulder and head together harder to keep it from falling as I head to the kitchen with the dirty dishes. For some reason this causes my lower back, which I strained this afternoon pulling weeds in my parents' yard, to spasm.

"Ow."

"Dad?" Coco asks. "Are you all right?"

"I'm fine, honey," I tell her.

"For God's sake!" my father yells. "Stop all this, right now!" He tries to lurch up from the dining room table but he's stuck halfway, one hand on the table and the other on his wheeled walker.

"Darling, sit back down," my mother says from the kitchen, where she's getting ice cream. "Just for a second, okay?"

"No, damn it, it's not okay at all! Why won't you listen?" my father yells, his voice straining. And ignoring her and me, as he ignores everyone these days, he continues struggling to stand, bending over, teetering dangerously on unsteady legs.

None of this is my father's fault. He's suffered a traumatic brain injury, and as a result, he has recurring headaches and back pain, has bouts of dementia and depression, and copes by drinking. But a rush of irrational anger surges through me. I'm in emotional overload. I can feel my heart racing and my breath quickening, but I don't care. I should take a minute, do my deep-breathing exercises, and let the storm settle in my brain. But I don't want it to settle. Though part of me fights to stay calm, the truth is, I want to explode.

My cell phone squeezed between my ear and my shoulder, the dirty plates and silver rattling in my hands, I snap. "Stop acting up," I yell at my father. "And sit back down!"

My mother looks over at me, startled. The only bright spot in all of stress-filled lunacy is that my 89-year-old mother, who continues to be strong and lucid, seems determined to plow on with good cheer through her 90s. But doing what? Being a permanent caretaker for this irritable, demanding man who, lost in his own pain and confusion, lashes out at those, especially my mother, who just want to try to help? Why does she let herself be used like this? Because she loves him. It's a terrible, dark, heartbreaking trap that I suddenly have no patience for, and here I am taking it out on my defenseless father.

Over the phone, real concern in her voice, Coco asks, "What's going on, Dad?" And I realize, as I told Coco a minute ago, that I had at least better watch my tone. I tell Coco everything's fine and that I'll call her right back. I let the phone fall to the carpet, place the plates back on the table, and help my dad get up. But my mother is quickly by me. "It's all right," she says with a pat on my shoulder. "Talk to Coco. I've got him." As she holds out a steadying hand for Dad, she tells him, "You should listen to your son, you know. He's trying to help you."

"Nonsense," my father says.

I pick up the phone and take the dishes into the kitchen. After the kitchen's clean, dishwasher cycling, and Mom's managed to get Dad in his chair peacefully eating mocha java ice cream with a martini on the side, I go to the guest bedroom and call Coco back. I assure her that everybody's fine in Delaware and that I'll be getting on the plane home tomorrow.

"I can't wait for you to come home," Coco says. "There's a centipede in the garage you've got to get rid of and a huge dead cockroach in the living room behind the couch. And oh yeah, my new bed was delivered. You're going to put it together as soon as you're back, right?"

I tell Coco I'll take care of all that. I tell her I love her, that I'll see her tomorrow, and to put her mother on. I lie down on the bed. As Margaret and I talk, my breathing and heart rate slow, my back spasm eases, and I feel calmer and a little more human. Margaret says she knows how much my mother and father have needed me. They're okay now, I tell her; things have settled down. She says she's sorry to put more pressure on me, I tell her she isn't. She's sorry that they need me so much at home too. "Thank God you do," I tell her.

As Margaret and I talk, joking and comforting each other, I realize how much I treasure the sound of her voice. And suddenly I understand that my mother isn't being used. She knows she's needed by her husband, a man she loves and vowed to have and hold in sickness and in health over 60 years ago, and that means the world to her. Then my anger at my father and the pain his injury and disease have brought us begins to ebb under the influence of my mother, my daughter, and my wife's gentle voice.

As I'm flying home to Georgia the next day, I begin to see that family is a messy proposition, full of conflicting needs, and maybe my family is a little messier and more conflicted than most, I don't know. But I do know that the world can be a dangerous and uncaring place. And I know that to need those you love, and to be needed by them in return, is a profound gift. When you have that, you have proof that no matter how tough the times, Bob Marley's right, every little thing will be all right.

When I walk into the house from the airport, Coco runs down the stairs and jumps into my arms nearly knocking me over and wraps me in a hug. Then she steps back and says, "What do you think?"

Her hair is a little shorter. And deep black. In the middle front, a purple stripe down each side. It's not what I would have picked out as a look for her. It's not anything really that I could imagine. I miss her blonde hair. But as she stands there smiling expectantly at me, I can see that she loves it and that when you give it a chance, the black frames her face dramatically and the purple brings out the sparkling blue in her eyes.

"It's gorgeous," I say.

SIXTEEN

"**D**o you ever feel like something bad is going to happen, but you know if it does everything will still be all right because you know everything's really basically good but you still feel really bad anyway?" Coco, asks me on the way home from school.

She rests her red and black Keds straight in front of her on the dashboard and leans back in her seat, all casual. This is new. If I were a mature, safety conscious dad (For God's sake, if we get hit by a truck the airbag will snap your sneakers smack through all that expensive orthodontic work) or a dad who cared about car upkeep (Hey, you're scuffing up my freshly Armor All'd dash), I'd tell her to put her feet down. But I'm not. I think my daughter looks as cool as she thinks she does with her feet up, musing about life. Back in 1984, I thought it was extremely cool when Margaret crossed her bare feet up on our new Mustang's dash during our first road trip together. Sometimes being cool trumps it all, so I just shut up and drive.

"I mean," Coco continues, "I went through the whole day today at school mad at everybody and keeping it in, so that by lunch I was exhausted and just wanted to go to sleep. My eyes kept closing, I was so tired. You ever have that with your eyes? But wait - see, at the same time I know I've had a great Sweet 16 birthday weekend at home and all my friends at school liked the cupcakes I brought today and Arianne even brought brownies for me. And I love the Kindle Aunt Liz got me, you can even get Manga on it, I'll show you when we get home, and I got an 85 on my math test, and not much homework tonight, so I've got nothing to be mad about, and I even know that really, I'm happy, but I'm still feeling really sad. Do you ever feel like that?"

I park in the driveway, turn off the car, put the keys in my pocket, and pick up Coco's backpack. She looks me in the eye as I hand her the empty cupcake container and her class binder.

"Do you know what I'm talking about?" she asks.

I can see this isn't an idle question from Coco. And I know what exactly what she's talking about. I've constantly felt simultaneous multiple contradictory emotions most of my life. Aside from the ADHD, she and I share other mental quirks like dyslexia (hers way worse), short-term memory issues (mine worse), name-retrieval problems (tie), and trouble controlling our tempers (depends on who you ask). So my daughter expects a little insight or at least some understanding from me.

But right now, in this split-second, I'm stuck back when she mentioned her birthday. Obliterating everything else, wailing through my head like an air-raid siren is, "Coco is sixteen years old?"

So that's why she's been talking about getting a driver's license. But wait – this is happening way too fast, I feel like I'm lost in some boozy lounge ballad about turning around and my little girl's not in pigtails in the autumn of my years.

But why shouldn't I blubber – in two and a half years she'll graduate high school and then she'll leave for college, which is sad and scary because I know she's anxious to get out into the world, but my wife Margaret and I haven't had enough time to prepare her, to make her safe.

We did private, public, and home-school for both of our kids, always looking for the best for them, though a lot of time we all just goofed off and had fun. But we thought we had years to get them ready to deal with the real world.

I swear to you it was just last week that Coco was a six-year-old camping out in the back yard with her mom and their Brownie troop. A couple of days ago she was twelve, and she and I spent three days non-stop watching the complete *Horatio Hornblower* series on DVD, repeating the mutiny episodes a couple of times.

She's sixteen? We need to stop goofing around and give her more guidance and attention in the time we have left to get her prepared for the real world, but there's no time. And it's our fault, or my fault or whatever – we wasted time, we're obviously terrible parents for special needs kids or any kids. We shouldn't even be allowed to have plants.

"Dad," Coco says, "Hello? You all right?"

I snap out of it to see my daughter cocking her head at me.

"Hmm? Yeah, Coco, I'm fine." I say, as she and I walk to the front door lugging her school stuff. "I was just thinking about what you said. And yeah, I know exactly what you mean. I get that sad thing shooting through good feelings a lot these days myself."

"You mean about Grandpa and Aunt Liz being sick and stuff?" Coco says. A bright cool wind snaps through the trees. Fall's here.

"Yeah," I say, "And other stuff."

Coco gets to the porch and turns back with a smile, waiting for me to catch up. "Hurry up, mister," she says, "I haven't got all day."

No Thanks

Most of my memories of childhood Christmas mornings have blended together into a pleasant haze of torn wrapping paper revealing box after box of just what I always wanted and one holding a dopy sweater from Great Aunt Jean.

But Christmas 1955 stands out. Santa gave me a "Family Doctor" play set. I was six, and despite early behavior alarms from Montessori teachers, Santa apparently still held out hopes for a stable professional future for me. Maybe on one told him I was, according to my early teachers, a cheerful individual but also "distracted," "unruly," and a "trouble-maker." As a matter of fact all my teachers, until I dropped out of college, said approximately the same thing.

But Santa believed in my medical career. And he was right; I loved the play set and the whole doctor idea. I literally shook with excitement opening the plastic doctor bag. This was the most amazing present ever. I would do things, great things, and everyone would call me "Doctor," like they called my dad. But he was a scientist, not a real doctor. I'd be the real deal, smiling wisely and patting heads.

But once I put the stethoscope around my neck, opened up all the individual tongue depressor and little Kleenex packs, ate all the sugar pills, and blew air into both sides of my nose at the same time with the two plastic syringes, I was bored with medicine. I'd put my cap pistol in my doctor bag and decided to turn to a life of crime as a train robber, when my best friend Doreen came over with her dolls, Maria and Marsha, and saved the day by turning all my scattered doctor junk into a story.

"First," she said, "We have to save Maria's life." Then, pointing with her paper fan at the yellow plastic doctor specs on the floor, she said, "Hurry up, Doctor, put on the doctor glasses."

I pushed the glasses onto my nose and got to work. Under Doreen's direction, my boredom flew out the window. Maria needed a shot and a heart operation, but before we could do that we had to fix Marsha's broken leg, which we did but she kept running out of the doctor's office and breaking it again so Doreen had to use my cap pistol to hold Marsha captive at gunpoint, for her own good, as we tried everything we could to keep Maria alive, which was no longer necessary when we discovered that Marsha and Maria were long-lost sisters.

It was touch and go at the start, but with Doreen and I working together that Christmas day flew by, filled with life and death drama, touching reunions and miracle cures. And because of Doreen, I ended up that night feeling like I'd done great things.

This last November I went to Delaware to help my 89 year-old mother make Thanksgiving dinner for my dementia-saddled dad, on a day trip to their house from the nursing home where he lives. Margaret and Coco stayed home for Thanksgiving in Georgia with Margaret's mother, Nana. Margaret teaches middle school with her sister Liz, who was diagnosed with ALS last year and is retiring to fight the dark, unrelenting disease full-time, and she and Margaret planned to get together a few times over the holiday. Coco is completing school projects and studying like a dervish for upcoming tests, determined to prove to her teachers and everyone else, especially herself, that she can get straight A's, except for math, but she wants a B there and I'm worried that she's going to burn herself out.

So, I'm up in Delaware, and on Thanksgiving day I'm so worried about my dad getting up out of his wheelchair and falling while he and my mom watch an "Above the Chesapeake" video that I keep running out into the living room to check, and burn the half the dinner.

That night, after I got Dad back to his nursing home, and mom went to bed, I called home and told Margaret how I'd messed up my parents' Thanksgiving, and how sick I was of constantly forgetting what I was doing, and being frantic and turning something nice I was trying to do for them into a trial for everybody.

"First," she says, "Did your mom or dad care at all about the overcooked ham and yams?"

I told her no, it didn't seem so. I made plenty of mashed potatoes and the middle of the ham was still good.

"Did your dad fall?"

"No," I said, "but I had to stop him from getting out of his wheelchair a few times." After continued unrelenting cross examination from my wife I had to admit that I'd looked after my father well, transported him back and forth from the nursing home with care, helped keep Dad safe and his dignity intact during the visit and that both my parents were happy, grateful, and tucked in their beds.

"So you did a good thing and it turned out well, yes?" Margaret said, "So stop your bitching."

I gave up, laughed and asked how she was, and Coco, Nana, and Liz. "Everybody is doing well enough," she said, "And we'll be fine as long you get home at the end of the week. We need you here too, you know." I thanked her for talking me off the ledge, she said she was happy to and always would, but she suggested I talk to my therapist to see why I keep climbing up there, sticking my toes over the abyss. I said I would. We traded I love you back and forth and finally hung up. And because of Margaret, I ended up that night feeling like I'd done great things.

LUMBERJACK

I can't exactly see where I'm going while carrying this seven-foot pine tree, but I keep moving ahead to the Christmas tree check-out shack with our prize.

Coco is behind me carrying extra decorating loot we've picked up. My daughter and I are an edgy couple of nuts but over the years we've developed an understanding and patience with each other.

Although lately, as my daughter's growing up and handling herself, and developing her own coping skills with resulting increased confidence and success in her world, I sense that she's looking at her dad and seeing some cracks in the foundation. But she's wrong, I have no cracks.

This holiday season, our whole family, extended and just in our home, is dealing with more combinations of life-changing challenges than we ever have before. We'll get through it together and be fine, but I've become convinced that this is no time for Dad to expose any chinks in his armor. I am father, hear me roar.

"Dad, look out, you're going to hit those people in front of us," she says, "You should have let that guy help you."

"Have you got the snow blanket thingie for the base?" I ask, ignoring Coco's warning. I'm focusing only on my two immediate goals: 1) Show my daughter how strong and competent a father I still am. 2) Pay and get out of here.

And we're so close to the finish line, but stalled.

"Yeah, I've got it," Coco says. "If we need another one we can come back, right?"

"Sure," I say, "Of course." Ever the positive, steady, reassuring father-figure a girl can count on.

"And Dad," she says, "The thingie is called a tree skirt."

"Yeah, you're right," I say. Like she doesn't forget just as many words and names of things as I do. Hey, cool it you're the dad, calm, unruffled, thick-skinned and wise. Never mind I'm notoriously thin-skinned, jittery, and quick tempered. But not this holiday season, this season my face cracks in the knowing smile of the grizzled older guy in the Mexican beer commercials, except I'm an alcoholic, so I don't drink.

My arms ache from carrying the tree, but right now I've convinced myself that putting it down, resting it on its trunk even for a second, before we get to the check-out stand, would show lack of resolve and diminish me in my daughter's eyes. The over-stimulating claustrophobic-inducing, anxiety-ramping crowd in this place with their incessant yammering about the comparable festiveness of colored or white lights or if the LED ones look like Christmas lights at all, doesn't help.

And if the sweet and sickeningly calm and chuckling elderly couple with matching red and green reindeer scarves and two apple-cheeked grandkids in front of me doesn't get their attendant to roll their giant cart filled with three huge red bowed wreaths and a Rockefeller Center sized Noble Fir, the press of the crowd mixed with the tinny, distorted never-ending loop of "Little Drummer Boy" blaring from broken speakers tacked up on light poles is guaranteed to bah-rump-a-pum-pum me into a humiliating uncontrollable raving insult-filled fight-or-flight freak out. God knows what Coco would think of me then.

But then a little Christmas miracle, we're at the check-out shack. Coco pulls the wallet out of my jacket pocket and swipes the credit card, and I rest the tree trunk on the ground. Coco holds up the tree as I sign, my hand shaking only a little.

"Would you like us to bag your tree and trim the trunk?" the lady in the shack asks. I tell her no thanks. "I'll trim it at home myself with my chain-saw." What, I'm a lumberjack now? My face flushes.

I grab up the tree by the middle of the trunk, carrying it like a briefcase and stride out toward our mini-van ahead of Coco. Why did I mention my chain saw, for god's sake? I'm caught in some embarrassing panic-induced manliness proving ground that doesn't mean anything to me or my daughter or anyone else. Besides, I have the smallest chain saw ever made. It's electric, makes a little humming noise. My wife says it's cute.

Coco says, "Dad, you are so crazy."

"Yes," I say, "But I'm such a tough and together guy, nobody else notices."

Behind me, Coco laughs.

PIECE OF MY HEART

I never knew what comfort was before.

I am worry and debt-free. I sit on the sun-dappled back patio of my paid-off house, smiling as I scroll on my tablet through zero balance credit card statements and pull up a fat savings account. It strikes me that my mind isn't racing and I'm not confused for the first time I can remember. Margaret's hand is on my shoulder - god, how I love her touch. She's gripping harder, now she's shaking me, and I turn to tell her to stop it. Snap –

It's the middle of the night, I'm awake, confused, mind racing, up to my ears in debt, and Margaret's shaking me awake to hand me the phone. She says it's Harry. He says it's important; he needs to talk to you. I take the phone, barely conscious. Harry moved to Hawaii a year ago. He wrecked his car before he left, this can't be about that. I manage a grunt into the phone.

"Hey, Dad? Sorry to wake you, but I didn't want to worry Mom, and I thought you might know about this," he says.

"What? About what?" I mumble.

"Um, well what do you think it is when your arm hurts bad and kind of swells up, like a pimple but bigger?" he asks. "Plus I think I've got a fever."

I tell him to get to an ER; he's got an infection. Probably from that stupid tattoo he never should have gotten. He says thanks for the advice but, he's at a friend's house -- too far to go to a hospital tonight and, besides, he's tired. Maybe he'll go tomorrow.

"That's a brilliant idea, Harry," I say, "If you want to lose your freaking arm! What the hell is wrong with you?"

At this point, my wife Margaret takes the phone back from me before I go into a rant about the pure insanity of Harry having his friend try out his new tattoo gun on him the week before, which we discovered via photos on Facebook of Harry's two huge tattoos, one on each shoulder. After some low-intensity conversation, while I sit on the bed holding my head and mumbling darkly to myself, Margaret convinces Harry to get to the ER tonight and to call us back when he sees the doctor.

But Harry's call has me rolling in worry of blood infection, amputation, and tearful prosthetic fittings. He works the night shift full time at a McDonalds, and stays with friends as he works out a more permanent place to live – and just maybe even figures out what he's going to do with his life. Either that or he's just sitting there in the middle of the Pacific smoking pot and playing video games. So what if he is? He's a sweet guy and he seems happy, and I admire his non-judgmental calm outlook. But that's no way to lead your life in a dangerous world, is it? And that's when I remember 1968.

I'm nineteen and stretched out across a mattress on the floor of my rented room, way-deep-down drunk with my hand around an almost-empty fifth of J&B scotch I got Wino Will to buy for me last night. Except for my bare feet, I'm still in the greasy work clothes from my night shift in the restaurant kitchen up the block. I've got my stereo turned up to the max, my head sandwiched between the speakers, and Janis Joplin wailing "Piece of My Heart."

That's why I don't hear the knocking on my door. I finally realize that someone wants my attention when a hand on my shoulder shakes my eyes open and I'm looking at my mother and father leaning over me. They look scared and horrified. Dad's real upset, turns off the stereo, and pulls me up on my feet. Mom is looking around my little rental with her hand over her mouth. I can't figure out why they're here. They live way on the other side of town. "Hey guys," I say, "What's up?"

"We haven't heard from you in weeks," Dad says.

I say I've been doing extra shifts at the Ivanhoe, been kind of busy.

"And we couldn't get ahold of you when we got the notice from the college that you dropped out," Mom says.

"Because your phone's disconnected," Dad says.

I try to explain that I'm working more hours so I can get my phone turned back on and that I just couldn't take all the stupid regimentation of college anymore – a German class at 7:40 AM is just stupid and none of it was worth the trouble. But I'm having trouble getting my point across because my professor parents can't even conceive of college being boring. And also I'm drunk and high and want to lie back down and listen to Janis - which is why I sit back down on my mattress. I lean over to re-set one of the speakers back up that got knocked over when my guests arrived.

"You're drunk at ten in the morning and living in filth," Dad says.

I tell him I work nights, so cocktail hour is sort of, you know, switched around. Patience with thick-headed parents doesn't come easy to a 19-year-old drunk pot-head, but I'm doing my best. I check to see that the Janis LP didn't get scratched in all the excitement.

Dad throws up his hands. "Don't you care about anything? What the hell is wrong with you?"

I look at him, not sure what he wants me to say to that. I tell him it'd be good if he stopped yelling. I think he's upsetting Mom.

"Maybe you're getting sick," Mom says, "Do you think you need a doctor?"

"Really, I don't know what you guys' problem is," I say, "I'm cool. Everything's cool." I crank the stereo up as Mom and Dad walk out, closing the door. Sorry, but I'm glad they split; they were bringing me down. I lie back between the speakers again and Janis screams to come on, come on, take it - take another little piece of her heart now, baby.

Years later, my mother told me that on the way home, after she and my father left my room in the flophouse, they pulled the car over to the side of the road, held each other, and he wept in despair. "I'd never seen your father so bereft. He was certain that his son was lost to him forever." She said she told him to be patient and not be so hard on me -- or himself.

Like my father did with me, I have trouble accepting the stubborn carelessness that seems to have become my son's guiding force since adolescence. And as my father did, I work at being more like my wife, who listens more and judges far less than I do.

No School for You

It's 7:30 Sunday night when I tap on Coco's bedroom door.

She looks up from the laptop on her desk, her forehead still furrowed in concentration from working on a PowerPoint project that's due tomorrow and the thumb of her right hand twitching over her rollerball mouse.

"What?" she asks, her blue eyes under black- and purple-streaked hair darting from me to her screen and back again.

"Going okay?" I ask.

"Yep," her eyes are now firmly back on the screen. She clicks something with the mouse, nods to herself, thinking.

"Did you finish the take-home, open-book test for science?" I ask her.

She looks up, startled. "What test are you... Oh my god!"

She leaps up from her desk and bolts past me toward the stairs to get her school backpack, mumbling curses to herself. At the top of the stairs she turns to me and says, "Dad, thanks for reminding me." That was a shock. I'd fully expected her fury to spill over onto me, her mother, and anything else within striking distance. Only a few months ago, it would have. Coco, like me, has a hot temper. But as she's told us, she's working on all that -- her temper, her impatience, and understanding how her sometime whirling dervish behavior affects others.

Coco's also been working on another problem we share, procrastination. Her mid-semester progress report of four A's and three B's suggests she working pretty damn hard, too. But tonight, when she opens her backpack, she discovers that she's forgotten to finish a project for Art as well, and there's reading she has to do for Lit Class and World History, and oh no, oh no, no, no - Math.

Tomorrow is the first day back from winter break at Coco's high school. It's a week off around President's Day every year, and the break is filled with projects and papers to finish, so it's more of a home-study time than any kind of mini-vacation.

One day in, I asked her about the schoolwork she'd mentioned when I'd picked her up the day before. "Don't worry," she said, "I've got it all scheduled." Now, I knew that was the viewpoint of a teenager on the first day of break, but I decided to believe she had it under control. And now the week has disappeared and only disaster looms.

Life's challenges are not easy to navigate for any adolescent, especially when we've brought them on ourselves. But I think they can be especially difficult for an adolescent girl with ADHD, and even more so for an intensely self-critical perfectionist like Coco.

Now looking back from this Sunday night, I'm afraid that I let her down. That I might have chosen to believe Coco had it under control because it was easier for me not to worry about it - father and daughter, tag-team procrastinating.

Not that I don't have my excuses. Coincidentally, Coco's break week has been a particularly stressful time for the family. It's been the week before Coco's Aunt Liz, my wife Margaret's sister, went in for experimental surgery for her ALS. Also, Margaret's night class homework spiked this week at the same time her new full-time middle-school teaching job is demanding more from her. So Margaret's tried to be available to Coco, but she's often exhausted, overwhelmed and needing to do more work or sleep when she gets home.

Also this week, our other house-mate, my 83-year-old mother-in-law, Nana began a cycle of being actively irritable with all of us in the house, yelling and slamming her door. Maybe it's the anxiety of her daughter Liz's upcoming surgery. Or maybe she doesn't realize she's yelling and slamming her door because her hearing's getting so bad.

Also, last Tuesday, Thursday, and Friday our dog threw up on the carpet. Coco said it's because I gave Danny too many dog treats. She's probably right. At any rate, on my knees Friday, scrubbing the stain with rug cleaner, I resolved that I'll die before Danny gets another biscuit from me.

Like Coco, I've been working on how my behavior affects others, but this week I've been a cyclone of barely subdued panic. With my office stereo blasting soul music, I've worked night and day to finish compiling the 110 individual 12-page "Words About Me" books by second graders that finishes a months-long project we started with a neighboring elementary school thanks to a grant.

Then at the end of every day I ran around doing shopping, housework, and a slap-dash dinner before calling my 89-year-old mother in Delaware and talking her down from another day dealing with my dad's dementia. I'm usually in a dark mood for about an hour after I hang up, and not someone you'd want to chat to about homework or school. Considering all of this, you can understand why Coco spent her break week avoiding all the family craziness, zoned out in her room watching videos. Don't get me wrong, we're a cheerful bunch; we laugh and kid around. But still, I'd say from Coco's perspective, this week reeked.

So at midnight Sunday night, I sit on the edge of Coco's bed as she stews about tomorrow and all the work she's only half-done. I tell her she's so upset she's made herself sick and she should stay home from school tomorrow. We argue. Coco honestly wants to go in and take her lumps, but I insist that take the day, do her work and get organized. I also tell her how I feel that I let her down the last few days. She says no, it was her fault alone; she just didn't care enough until it was too late. We decide on equal blame, I give her a kiss goodnight. As I turn out her light, step out into the hall, and pull the door closed, she says, "Wait — are you just letting me stay home out of guilt?"

"No. Yes. None of your business," I say. "Go to sleep." And close the door.

KEEP DIGGING

Thunk – rip, thunk – rip. I swing the pick down harder than I need to and the head buries itself into the hard-packed red dirt.

I get a dark gratification from this. It's like I'm stabbing some beast in its thick, vital gut. I came out here to plant a dogwood sapling. But now, sweat pouring off my face; I'm digging desperately for a fossil from a past life: peace of mind.

Swing it down, thunk. Pull it up, and the rip of the roots being torn from their home makes it sweeter. Down and up again, and again, the pick handle sliding easily in my leather work gloves. I hear myself grunting and chuckling with each blow. Must be why my mother-in-law has gathered up her Better Homes and Gardens magazine from the picnic table and bustled back inside. Even my dog is keeping his distance, sitting back up on the deck and watching me with his head cocked in concern.

I couldn't care less what either of them thinks. I came out here in our back yard to plant a dogwood sapling for Margaret. But now, sweat pouring off my face; I'm digging desperately for a fossil from a past life: peace of mind.

Thunk – rip, thunk – rip. I'm a middle-aged ADHD parent of ADHD kids, and I have a responsibility to model problem-solving behavior, but right now I don't care. I've had all I can take so now all I want is a minute like the ones I remember: iced tea by the pool with nothing but calm on my mind, nothing constantly gnawing at my sanity and self-worth.

To be honest, those minutes could be from TV commercials. They may not be my minutes at all. But that doesn't make me yearn for them any less. For the short time we had a pool, I stayed up nights fretting about fencing, filters, the heating bill, and what having a pool said about us: nothing good. And I never drank iced tea. When I wasn't tossing back martinis, I drank diet sodas by the gallon and had terrible acid reflux.

Thunk - rip, thunk - rip. Stop; look at what's good now. I love my wife. She's jumped into teaching middle-school full time, racing through night school courses to take over for her ailing sister. My son lives in Hawaii with his pals and has a steady job moving up the McDonald's ladder. My daughter, Coco, is doing great in high school and we're getting along better than ever.

Thunk - rip, thunk - rip. Sure, but the stress is keeping us all up nights and now, for the second time in as many years, I've got to go to my parents' house to help my mom move my dad back home from the nursing home, just when Margaret and Coco are getting off for spring break. So I won't see them again until we're back in the school-day roles of busy teacher, student, and stay-at-home cook/launderer/mother-in-law caretaker. Oh, boo-hoo, right? Everybody's got problems. Next I'll be complaining about taxes.

Thunk - rip, thunk - rip. I also want to take the worry off the shoulders of my wife and daughter, but I know that most of it is theirs to carry and deal with themselves. And damn it, with the state of his dementia and physical limitations, my dad shouldn't be going home at all. Even with part-time nursing help, it's dangerous for him and my mom. But it's what he wants, and Mom is determined to let him have his way.

"All he wants is a little peace of mind," Mom says, "and looking after him gives me a little, too."

Yeah, no shit. I'd like some of that too, Mom.

Thunk - rip, better stop. There's dirt all over the yard and this hole is way deeper than necessary for a dogwood sapling. I pour soil into the hole, place the tree on top, fill in around it, pat it down, and give it some water. I stand back a few feet. It looks good, though it does seem to be sinking a little. My dog barks and drops his ball at my feet. I throw the ball down the hill, away from the new tree and he lopes after it, not a care in the world.

* * * *

It's Saturday, the morning I get to sleep in, but I ruined that by staying up most of the night reading, so even though it's 10 AM, I've only gotten my normal four hours of sleep. I sit on the edge of the bed looking over at the dark, yawning hole and feel its gentle pull. I know depression; I've lost too much time, terrified and numb, curled up inside depression's poison comfort not to know what I'm looking at.

This isn't the cute little hole of depression with googly eyes that follows that woman around in the cartoon anti-depressant commercial. This is a real depression hole. It is not little or cute, and it's not a metaphor. It's as real as dead birds, burnt dinner, and migraines. It has no edge; it's a growing shadow across the floor, an ever darkening smudge on the wall and bedroom closet door, which carries a familiar old sick-sweet smell. It tugs at the sleeve of my T-shirt like a childhood friend. Come look, it whispers, you like this.

My own tired voice comes out of the dark center of the widening hole, "Be honest for once, you know you're already here," it sighs. "You don't have the strength to push back anymore, so accept it." So even though I know I shouldn't, that's exactly what I do. And once I'm there I tell myself that it's no wonder I'm depressed; I've got a lot to be depressed about.

But that, of course, is complete crap. No matter what the voice in the black hole says, I'm not depressed about my life, my weight, or six more months of election year coverage. Yes, our family is facing emotionally tough stuff these days. But my wife and I have a solid, deep marriage. We're good partners. We talk and listen to one another. We've weathered challenging times before, and we've always come out the better for it. There is no "about" or "why" for depression — it's just screwy wiring and mixed-up brain chemicals. I know that's true, but the problem is, when I'm in the hole, I don't believe it. Down there I don't look for ways to get out. I look for all the reasons I deserve to feel like the worthless toad I clearly see I am. It takes a whole lot of time and energy to keep my mind constantly ticking off the countless times I've failed others and myself, and what each failure illustrates about my lack of human decency or worth. Luckily, I don't sleep much.

My therapist told me that my insomnia and bouts of depression were linked. If I concentrated on strategies to get more sleep, he thought, I could break the cycle and my outlook would improve. Now, I could have given him a lot of crap for pointing out the obvious, or I could have been honest with him. But I rarely do either with therapists. In my experience, most of them prefer short, entertaining stories with simply solved problems attached. So do I. It saves a lot of frustration and confusion on both sides. So I accept the advice and my monthly ADHD and anxiety scrips with a smile, load my dark heart into my old Dodge Caravan and head over to the Walgreens drive-thru on my way to pick up my daughter from high school.

The frustrating truth I didn't mention to my therapist is that when I'm in this depression hole, I treat the sandman like he's a suicide bomber. I do the sleep strategies: I exercise during the day; I do my breathing, take my pill, and read quietly in bed at night — all to calm myself so I can fall asleep. But when I start to doze, I rebel. I know this is when I should turn off the light and lay down my weary head, but I don't. I jerk the book off my chest, and flip back a page to catch what I've missed, and push my attention back to the story. In this latest bout of depression I was reading a series of novels set in the misery of WWII Europe, which fit well with my ongoing self-loathing.

If necessary, I'll go down to the kitchen, get some granola bars and a diet soda, and sit up reading in the living room while everybody else in the house sleeps. If that doesn't keep me up, I'll go hard core into sandwiches and Haagen-Dazs. (Added plus: the fat fits the toad image.) To fight off sleep, I've gone as far as rolling up my sleeves at one in the morning and doing the laundry, mopping the kitchen floor, cleaning and waxing the kitchen table, and setting it for breakfast, all the time reliving shameful scenes of weakness and dishonesty from my past. Hey, I'm an alcoholic. I know how to have a good time.

* * * *

If nothing else, I'm a family man, so I didn't stay holed up in my bed with my dark hopeless thoughts brooding by myself. Heck, no. I brought them downstairs with me when I made breakfast for Margaret, Nana and Coco. Like your oatmeal with a sprinkle of brown sugar and ground ash-grey despair? How about coffee brewed dark enough to roast that smile off your face forever? Welcome to Frank's happy morning kitchen.

Understand, I wasn't greeting my wife, mother-in-law, and daughter with frowns and bitter warnings of defeat facing them when they left for work, bridge club, and school. Though I was pretty sure that setbacks and shame were all that was waiting for them outside our front door, I kept my brave smile on, and a strained cheerful optimism in my conversation. This only increased my personal desolation because it intensified my awareness that I could do nothing to protect my loved ones.

I over-bought groceries, stocking pantry, fridge, and freezer as if there were a war coming. I obsessed over my daughter's grades, checking every assignment and test on the school computer. I cleared dead trees from the forested area of our yard, ripped and rooted out predatory vines, planted day lilies and morning-glories. Then sometimes, exhausted, I'd stop everything and just sit, quietly freaking out — one time forgetting to pick my daughter up from school. "What happened to you, Mr. OCD?" she joked when I drove up to the high school, "You never forget this stuff."

"Nothing happened," I said, "I just, you know...forgot." And then I shrugged as I pulled into traffic. My daughter nodded, said uh huh, put her feet on the dashboard and looked out the window.

So now I was completely weirding out my family. My wife and daughter were finishing breakfast in record time and deciding they'd like to get to work/school/anywhere but here earlier every day. When my mother-in-law didn't have church, bridge, or knitting club to escape to, she stayed in her room with the door closed. Our dog followed me everywhere I went in the house or yard with an unchanging look of concern on his face. When I'd lie down, he'd put his head on the bed and stare at me, one eyebrow up, his dog brain-waves saying, "Just tell me what to do, I'll fix it, dog's honor."

But by now, there wasn't anything he or anyone else could do. I told my therapist again that I couldn't tolerate anti-depressants. He said we'd talk about it again next time. I didn't answer. I was so deep in the hole that I'd lost sight of sunlight at the top.

ADHD and depression don't always go hand in hand — they're not necessarily co-morbid conditions. They live in similar neighborhoods in your brain, but they don't live in the same house. I don't think so, anyway, but maybe they do, I don't know. I'm not an expert or a medical professional of any sort. Really I'm just laying out what I think based on what I understand from my own experience or from what my various therapists have told me, and I could have easily gotten that mixed up.

That said, I think dealing with any permanent mental or physical impairment day in, day out, can be incredibly frustrating and can help bring on rampaging defeatism of the "Why try at all, I'll just mess it up anyway? Just wake me after the big one drops and we're all dead anyway" variety. And depression can make you forget what you're supposed to be doing, and distract you from appointments and other necessary life duties because all you can think about is whether there is anything anywhere in the universe that makes life worth the effort of living at all.

So I was in complete emotional darkness, feeling about as useful as laundry lint, when my brother called from Delaware saying he was following the ambulance that was taking our 90-year-old mother to the hospital again. She's been there before due to gastric problems brought on by the stress of being the primary caretaker for my father who struggles with dementia.

"Maybe this time will convince her to let us bring regular nursing care into their house," my brother said.

"We can hope," I said, not mentioning that I didn't put too much stock in that stuff lately. Due to my obligations to family here in Georgia, I couldn't get up there to help until my wife and daughter were out of school in a couple of weeks. Then I'd come up and do what I could. But since I was seeing myself as some combination of Eeyore and the plague, I couldn't imagine me doing anything but making things worse.

A day later my mother called from her bed in the hospital. Her voice was weak and breathy, but the steel determination of her personality came through the phone as clear as always. "I know you want to come and help, but I don't want you ignoring your family for us. I mean it — you do so much when you come, but this time I can take care of your father without you and your brother moving heaven and earth. I can handle this fine," she said, "It's my job."

When she said that, something profound snapped, and depression began to lose its hold on me. I don't know if it was her sense of duty or pride or just that steel determination in her voice, but a light filtered down from the top again and I could see small footholds on the side of the hole, leading up toward the sun. They looked like they'd fit my mother's feet, and I remembered that she'd fought depression herself in her life. It seemed like a good idea to follow in my mother's footsteps. And step by slow step, that's what I did; first, by not taking her advice. As soon as school was out, I went up to Delaware and spent time with my parents, getting mom back home and helping my brother with setting up home care for them.

But the slow steps up the side of the hole of depression were founded on something more fundamental than responding to a family emergency. What my mom said about the impossibly heartbreaking task of taking care of my dementia stricken father was, "That's my job."

As I've kept on making progress pulling myself out of depression and other holes I've dug for myself in this life, one step at a time, I've begun to understand why those words broke me free. At any moment, when you look outside yourself and focus on what someone else needs, you can begin to see what you can do to help. Fulfilling that need gets your mind off yourself, gives you a job, and not too far behind that comes some self-worth and maybe a little bit of meaning. For me, my job's my family. But to whomever or wherever you extend outside yourself, bit by bit your strength builds, and instead of a hole, you've got yourself a mountain. And the view's a heck of a lot better from up there.

CAREER DAY

It's Career Day at the middle school where my wife, Margaret, teaches. I'm here to tell these sixth, seventh, and eighth graders what it's like being a writer for a living. I'm standing at a lectern in an empty classroom waiting for the first group of students to file in and I feel the sweat soaking through the back of my shirt. I fiddle with the remote control for the video projector — on and off — making sure it works. It's hard to tell with the lights on.

I don't know which clips from the TV shows I wrote I should show. I probably shouldn't show any of them. The shows were all produced before these kids were born. The material doesn't relate to their lives, they'll be bored sick, and I'll look like I'm bragging about working in Hollywood and setting up impossible and worthless goals. Besides, I've only got fifteen minutes, and I can't possibly explain how conflicted I feel about my past TV writing career and that I'm conflicted now, that I'm always conflicted and unsure, constantly confused, and that the only way that I can find even a hint about what's going on in or outside my head is by writing.

That's why I'm a writer. To survive. To beat the random overwhelming noise into a shape I can start to understand, before I get overwhelmed and burrow into a corner of a dark closet. Stop it. You are not at your therapist's office.

It's Career Day. Today the students at your wife's school are hearing from a flight attendant, a couple of EMTs, a vet, a real-estate entrepreneur, and me, whoever or whatever that is.

I look up as two teachers corral the first group of 30 into chairs facing me and tell the kids to be quiet and listen to the presentation. My blazer is sticking to the back of my wet shirt. What can I possibly say that will be of any use to these young people?

"My name is Frank South, and..." I have no idea what I'd planned to say. The notes in my hand are gibberish. I can feel the rolling heartbeat of a panic attack coming on, so all I can do is keep talking and try to be honest somehow. "Like I said, I'm Frank South and I am a writer. And I have ADHD. That's attention deficit hyperactivity disorder, and I think that ADHD helps me write. And writing helps me understand."

From there I went on with a rapid-fire description of my daily househusband routine, squeezing in writing after laundry and shopping and before picking my daughter up from school, who also has ADHD and how we both struggle with procrastination and being overwhelmed, and how writing helps me understand the life I'm living a little better, which is a more important a job than the TV jobs I used to have. And I do show a short video clip from Melrose Place that I wrote and the kids love, and that I'm surprised to hear from the kids, relates to peer pressure and bullying.

But it was when I said out loud in the classroom how much I needed writing in my life day to day that I realized what I was saying was true and important for any career. And driving home afterword, I understood why I was so uncomfortable at first talking about being a writer on Career Day; it was because I wasn't writing.

About a year ago, with my family and me facing some difficult life transitions on the horizon, I decided to take some time off from writing. I put aside a blog and other projects as well. Without the distraction of trying to write about my life, I thought, I could focus on the others in our family who might need help when the troubles we all knew were looming, finally hit.

And hit they did. My wife Margaret's younger sister, Lizzie, who had been diagnosed with ALS the previous year, went into a serious decline over the summer and died last September. We live close by, so I was able to assist her husband, Earl, with hospice and caretaking. But the unrelenting nature of the disease and the family's heartbreak was terrifying. And somehow, sometimes it seemed so impossible and ridiculous we once or twice laughed at the sheer unreality and horror of this disease, but never stopped to cry until the end.

In February of this year my father, who has struggled with dementia due to a brain injury a couple of years ago, began deteriorating physically and emotionally and I went up to Delaware again for a few days to help. I was back home in Georgia for a week, feeling pretty confident that things with my dad were stable, when I got the phone call that he'd died.

The next morning, driving back up to Delaware, recent events banged around in my head, Lizzie, Dad, suffering, loss, death, love. I couldn't make sense of any of it. I couldn't attach it to real life.

These are trials we all face in one way or another. Our family is getting through, providing help and strength to one another, and avoiding self-pity like the plague. My weird brain wiring actually helps in emergencies, there's nothing like a hyperactive clean freak for organizing med schedules and keeping things spotless. But I was coming unmoored and detached from others. I was missing something, an understanding of my place in all of this. I didn't think I had a real sense of what others were going through. I need to write to find that. Though honestly, that seems a little scary. It could wait.

This weekend, Margaret brought home thank-you notes from some of the kids who saw my Career Day presentation. One of them, a seventh-grader named Ashley, wrote "I enjoyed the story of how you began to write. I feel the same way about forgetting things, because I have ADHD, too. I have enough imagination for about ten people. So I think I'll pursue being a writer."

Okay, Ashley. I will too.

Push Here

On Memorial Day weekend I'm at the bottom of our hilly Georgia backyard, raking up piles of dead leaves, pulled weeds, tree-killer vines, and trimmed branches and piling them into the wheelbarrow.

Full load, so now back up the hill to add to the mountain of dead vegetation at the front curb. Hope to God I pulled the gate closed after the last load or Danny Boy, our oversized standard poodle, will have escaped and the rest of the day will be spent running him down through our neighbors' yards. According to Danny Boy, obedience training doesn't apply if you break out into the front yard, it's all free range dog and wind flying through your floppy ears.

Halfway up, I pause beside the only large tree that I have to cut down this week. It lost a major branch in a storm a couple of years ago and is down doing the slow old tree lean — looking for support from its younger brothers, who want nothing to do with him and his old greedy sun-grabbing leaves. I'll get the chain saw on the way back down and get it over with. When I grab the handles of the wheel barrow and start back up the hill, my heart starts racing like a bastard and I'm short of breath. I set the wheelbarrow down again. There's no real cardiac issue here; it's just another panic attack. This isn't all that scary, but it's extremely irritating.

I had these handled. I hardly had any during the terrifying months leading up to and after my sister-in law's death last fall. Maybe it was because people needed me and I was distracted from my favorite subject: me. But now this spring, panic attacks come in unpredictable flurries. There's no rhyme or tension to the onset; you could be peacefully reading a fulfilling book, or watching a classic movie on TV with growing irritation as it's chopped into non-sensical scenes by erectile dysfunction and reverse-mortgage commercials. The solution is the same: deep breathing, conscious calm. Or last resort, Xanax; not a good choice if you've got pressing lumberjacking plans.

Which are plans I know I could just decide not to do. I could reschedule, take a break, but I really can't. I have to accomplish this today. I have to push through my own bullshit and accomplish something worthwhile and visible. And I forgot - Danny Boy might be out the front gate I left open. He could be hit by a car all because I'm wasting time with my self-obsession.

So ignoring my racing pulse, I dash up the hill pushing the wheelbarrow, ready to face whatever disaster I've caused. But the gate is safely closed and latched. Danny Boy raises his head from the warm sunlit bricks on the other side of the patio, checking if it's anything important. But it's just crazy Frank, panting and wild-eyed, so he sighs and lays his head back down. I unlatch, go out with the wheelbarrow, push the gate closed with my foot, and roll toward the curb with the branches, leaves, and weeds.

My wife Margaret and my therapist Dr. Ellis say the flurry of panic is part of the grief I'm feeling since the death of my father a couple of months ago. I guess that makes sense, but though I love him still and spent my life with his overpowering intellect, courage, and strength as a frame to model and build what I could out of my life, I'd recently seen a whole other side of him. And because of that, I felt myself pulling away even as I helped care for him. His constant drinking clashed with my sobriety. His increasing dementia scared me witless.

I am anxiety ridden, scattered, attention and memory-challenged continually, and trying to help my mother and my dad navigate his own mental and emotional wilderness made me feel like I was stumbling into a dark passage of confusion, blame, and regret that was destined to be mine as well, dragging my own wife and children down with me.

Doesn't sound like grief to me. At both of his funerals — the one at the local church and the military service at Arlington National Cemetery — I felt my grief was for my mother and brother's loss, not mine.

I realize I'm standing, staring vacantly at the street, like Boo Radley. I shake my head clear. My heart rate is back to normal, but all this obsessing about my dad isn't helping me get the wheelbarrow unloaded. Focus on getting the load on top of the pile, so I have room for the next. Pull up, and good. "Nice job, son," my dad says. I can feel that big hand that patted my shoulder after stacking two cords of firewood behind the garage when I was twelve.

As I roll the empty wheelbarrow back toward the gate, I think that what I have isn't like dementia. It's not like my dad where your focus arbitrarily shifts and you completely lose track of time and place. He'd have to constantly regroup, popping from the present to an ocean liner docked in France after World War II to a train taking him home to Nebraska to see his grandmother when he was eight.

Pushing the wheelbarrow onto the driveway, I stop to look back across the front lawn at the mountain of yard debris at the curb to make sure it hasn't fallen over into the street, and I think that the problem with ADHD isn't necessarily being distracted away from your focus.

The problem is maintaining your focus on what's happening now, instead of being distracted by the insights it sparks about what has happened before, what might happen in the future, and what all that might mean to others or you.

But once you do hold focus it's hard get free when it pulls you under the surface into deeper perceptions and emotional traps and you concentrate so hard to either shake free or dive deeper that you forget everything else, like rent or flight times or you get blind lucky and slam into a memory that's perfectly preserved every sight, sound, smell, and touch of when last year on Memorial Day, I was with my Dad in Delaware, and we took a picture for his few surviving WWII Ranger war buddies. Oh, great. Now I'm Boo Radley in the front yard staring at the street crying.

Wait, what's that five-foot-long branch doing in the middle of the lawn? I didn't drop anything. I'm crazy as a bed bug but I keep my landscaping neat, damn it. Besides, well, branches don't move. That's when I notice the birds screeching and swooping down, and the black head of the big snake rears up, flicking its tongue in my direction. I stand still, not sure what to do.

My first thought is to ask Dad.

ROAD WORK

About a month ago, I had it nailed.

Margaret, Coco and I were driving up to Delaware for a two-week vacation. We were going to stay with my now 91-year-old mother and help her clear out my dad's study and closets that she hadn't touched since his death last March, so it wasn't exactly a carefree poolside resort holiday. My brother Rob, his wife Sharon, and their young kids live in the same town as my mom, and Rob was going in for a back operation during our visit, so it was more of an intense family reunion after a recent tragedy and during major surgery kind of holiday.

Despite that, I was confident it was going to be a great time, a meaningful time, anyway. Margaret and Coco were up for it, excited even. I had planned the whole trip carefully. I'd built in travel time for changes, emergencies, or just relaxing. The route I laid out from our home in Georgia to Mom's house was a new one, along the Blue Ridge Mountains, up through Virginia and the Shenandoah Valley, places neither of them had ever seen. So, to make it a leisurely tour, I booked two overnight stops, making sure they each had free breakfast buffets, which I thought was silly, but my wife and daughter didn't. It turns out they were right, it's nice, slows things down. It slows me down some, anyway. And you get to make waffles.

At the first free breakfast buffet of the trip I gulp my coffee and try to scoot Margaret and Coco along a bit by pulling out one of the two trip plans I spent weeks researching and preparing, the final versions of which I finally printed and stapled together the morning we left. Trip Plan One is to get us to my mother's house in three days in order to relax and see the sights, and Trip Plan Two is to get us back home in two days. I point to the second page of Trip Plan One. "See, today is Leg Two of Trip Plan One, and it's way longer than it looks 'cause of the, uh, Appalachians, which we wanna see...and have enough time to really relax and, uh, well, appreciate the beauty of the drive, which means the sooner we get movin' on, the more time we have, for that relaxin'...and the, um, uh, beauty spreadin' out around us."

"Dad, come on. Put down your maps and legs and eat something," Coco says, "And you should, you know, breathe." My daughter stands and pats me on the shoulder. She's seventeen, now, still as obsessive, short-tempered, and jumpy as I am, and now she's handing me back the advice I've given her since she was too small to even fidget properly.

"Don't you worry about me, young lady," I say, "You just hop on over there and get some chow." Coco shrugs, and then punches in a number on her cell phone as she walks over to the buffet to get her waffles and tea. I take in a deep breath and slowly let it out, silently counting to twenty before taking another. Margaret smiles at me from across the table.

"Are you all right?" Margaret asks.

I glance up from studying Leg Two, "I'm okey-dokey, darlin' why?"

"Well," she says, "your stammer has picked up a whole lot, which you know means you're stressed. But I have no idea why you're talking like a demented cowboy all of a sudden."

I'm sure I'm carrying off the big, calm, seen-it-all sheriff persona I pasted together from the heroes of *Longmire* and *Justified*, a couple of westerns I've been watching religiously, and I mean on-air, DVD's, Amazon buys, the whole full-tilt addict immersion. I'm not lean and leathery. I'm a little over six foot and two hundred pounds with big teeth. But still, I think it's a natural fit for me. So what if it's all made up?

For a few months now I've felt like small chunks of me were falling off like cracked glass and spreading out on the ground as I walk and I don't know where I can go and not step on them. I had to have those TV heroes' sure-footed toughness. I needed their thick skin and strength. The day before we left on this trip I was trying on boots at the western store. I'm an inch away from going off the deep end and getting myself a cowboy hat, when Margaret smelled something fishy at the free breakfast buffet.

So, I spill all of it. Embarrassing and stupid as it was, I have to. It's Margaret. That's our deal with each other.

Margaret leans forward and looks me in the eye. "You are stronger than any guy on TV or anywhere else." she says. "You always have been." I'm heartened by this, and deeply touched, but my tears and snuffling probably undercut her point.

Fortunately, Coco's waffle is done and she sits down with news from her cell phone. Margaret's mom, Nana, who stayed home in Georgia to take care of our dog, Danny Boy, told Coco that Danny Boy hasn't eaten since we left. Margaret and Coco are a little worried, but I'm sure he's just ticked off that we left without him. He's seven years old and a big, healthy, wonderful dog. At this point in our trip, I'm positive that in a day or two, everything will be back to normal. As it happened, it would be quite a while before anything got back to normal.

* * * *

Back in my early road days, before I blew out a piston that I couldn't afford to repair and had to fall back on hitchhiking, I tore over the highways on a sleek and powerful black and chrome motorcycle. I didn't like VW buses and I wouldn't have been caught dead in any of the minivans I left in my dust on I-70. They were the bloated, underpowered symbol of America's complacent middle class: people that a rebel-artist-writer like I was would have nothing in common with, ever.

Now, driving our Town and Country along the crest of a hill in West Virginia with my wife and daughter safely tucked inside with me, the minivan feels like a sleek and powerful family-protection machine. And a few years ago when we were scrambling to keep from going under financially, I realized that it takes years of unrelenting effort and anxiety to hold on to a spot in the middle class. Complacency has no place in the world of work and worry.

So now that my wife Margaret has a full-time job teaching, and our life is on a steady course, I can devote every waking minute of my life to worrying about what could go wrong. Worry is my calling, what I was built to do. But it has to be clandestine so I don't undermine the confidence of those I love. I keep all of it locked up in a dark hole in the Centralized Internal Apprehension section in my brain. Safely hidden away, my private CIA gathers information on all real and imaginary threats to family peace and well-being and keeps them front and center so I can worry them to death.

It's our third morning on the road and we've settled into a nice companionable family rhythm. One of my four travel mix CDs plays, Margaret's in the seat next to me flipping through a magazine, and Coco's in the far back with her feet up watching the Appalachian country roll by. Leg three of my trip plan has us getting to my mom's house early afternoon, arriving in time for a late lunch. But I'm not pushing it. I'm working hard on my calming breath work, enjoying the present with my family and trying my damnedest to let the future take care of itself. But that's hard, because the future doesn't follow instructions.

"Look at that pretty little town," Coco says as we crest the hill on a two-lane blacktop in West Virginia. "From a distance, it's so perfect, it looks made up." I slow down, Margaret looks and I manage a glance to our left. The small group of red and white buildings, one with a steeple cluster around a river in the valley below us. The early morning sun freezes them with backdrop shadow next to the shining water.

"You're right," Margaret says, "It is perfect." We roll down into the valley, closing in on an outlying farm. "And that is one pretty cow, even close up," Margaret says.

"You don't have to make fun of me, Mom," Coco says.

Margaret turns around in her seat to face her. "I'm not, Coco," she says, "I'm agreeing with you." Coco doesn't say anything, just stares out the window. Margaret sighs and goes back to her magazine.

One of my many long term self-improvement projects is to stop acting on the belief that the attempt to control the behavior of others is a part of demonstrating your love for them. This is an odd belief for someone who has rarely had any success controlling his own behavior. But even though from experience I know being the know-it-all peacemaker is a sure way to confuse things and make it worse for everyone, normally this is where I'd jump in. Worried that they were hurting each other's feelings, I'd try to get Coco to accept her mother's good intentions and also make sure that Margaret understood that it was just Coco's ADHD frustration flaring and she didn't mean to be so defensive.

But I don't because over the last year they've each told me to butt out. "We're fine," Coco told me last winter after one noisy kitchen confrontation with Margaret that I got in the middle of — pissing them both off. "Mom and I are working things out our way." And she reminded me that I always told her she couldn't use ADHD as an excuse. Then she asked if she could start seeing a therapist again, so she could work on her anger and stuff. Sure, I thought, be more mature and together than your father. See if I care.

So I keep my mouth zipped and drive on. I focus on the road in front of me, and enjoy the shift of light in the passing trees as the morning moves on. Keb Mo's "Just Like You" comes up on the CD. I smile, but that dark, anxious hole in my head wipes the moment of peace away with an image of our big, beautiful dog Danny Boy back home in Georgia with Nana. This morning when we called, Nana said that Danny still hadn't eaten since we left. Earlier I convinced Margaret and Coco that there was no cause for alarm, he's a stubborn dog. He's just upset that we left. I tell them it's a normal thing for his breed, and my wife and daughter seem to feel better.

But I don't believe a word I've said and I'm sick with worry. Danny is my best friend back home. The only other guy in the house, he follows me around while I do housework, shaking his head at the mess created by female humans. Last March, during the days after my father died and I couldn't get out of bed for more than an hour at a time, he stayed next to me, his big head resting on my chest.

Danny has to be fine. "He's not and it's your fault" booms out of the mean, dark hole in my head. Stop it, you're overreacting. But what if I'm not? I can't go back home to Danny now; my mom and brother need me. Breathe. When we get to Mom's house I'll call our vet, see what she says. Nana doesn't drive. Maybe I can get my brother-in-law Earl to take Danny in to see the vet. I'll call him too.

As a recovering alcoholic, I'm familiar with the serenity prayer, but that part where you accept the things you can't change never took hold, which is another thing to worry about.

My mind in self-inflicted, outwardly silent turmoil, I turn into my mother's driveway in Delaware and pull to a stop. Coco's out of the minivan like a shot and runs in to see her grandmother. Margaret gives me a squeeze on the hand and a smile before she's out and on her way inside the house too. I sit, hands still on the steering wheel, winding my brain down. I tell myself I have to learn to let go, focus on what's in front of me and trust in the future. Maybe stop worrying so much and show a little courage.

"What are you doing still sitting in the car?" A happy grin lighting her face, my mother stands in her doorway, shouting at me. "Get in here," she says, "before your family eats all the sandwiches and oatmeal cookies." I smile back. Standing there leaning on her cane, carrying not an ounce of self-pity but only deep grateful love for her family, my mother once again shows me what real courage looks like. I get out of the car, step to the door and fall into her embrace.

*****

For a couple of days Mom and Margaret talk and have martinis, Coco sleeps and visits with her cousins and I read books and eat cookies. My mother always stocks two bags of grocery store bakery oatmeal raisin cookies before I show up. On the third morning my mom and I waved goodbye to Margaret and Coco as they left for a few days at a summer camp with my brother's wife and kids — Margaret subbing for my brother due to his back problems and so he could prepare for the surgery to fix it.

As the packed van took off down the street my mom turned to me and said, "Let's finish breakfast and get this closet thing done, shall we?" She was up in the morning wearing a chore-ready sweatshirt and jeans; she hurried me through our yogurt and coffee.

That done, she led me back to their bedroom, without a glance to Dad's office, where a hospital bed had once been set up and he, my Mom's one true love, had quietly died in the middle of a March night with my mother holding his hand.

In their, now her, bedroom she opened the closet doors. "Thanks for agreeing to do this with me," she said. "I need the space and it's too ghostie like this anyway. Now, some of these shirts you or your brother might want, but most of this should go to Salvation Army." Mom put the first load of Dad's clothes in my arms, and that's when the rogue wave hit, nearly drowning her in grief. I dropped the clothes and held her.

"We can't, it's not right...," my 91-year-old mother wailed between sobs. I held her in my arms as this harsh rogue wave of grief rolled through her heart, splintering the careful defenses she'd built up stick by stick since my father died last March after the three years of his mental and physical deterioration that nearly killed her too.

Still sobbing against my chest, her wails began to transform in tone. "He was my love, my one true love," Mom said, her words underpinned with the steel of moral certainty that steered our family through every crisis we faced when I was growing up. She looked up at me, her deceptively frail body still in my arms, her face soaked with tears. "It's wrong," she said, her voice ringing with that old unbending conviction. "We can't throw your father away like this. I won't do it." Then her gorgeous compassionate face fell against my chest again, the courageous steel washed off its foundation by another ferocious wave of grief. Between sobs she choked out, "It's wrong, everything's all wrong."

Standing in my mother's bedroom, my mind should be in step with my heart and focused only on comforting her in her moment of need as she had done for me since the first time I skinned my knee. But my mind traveled, looking for reasons, clues to her conflicted feelings..

This was happening in July. It had been four months since Dad's death, and two months since his burial in Arlington National Cemetery, so her anguish made sense.

Our sympathetic Arlington rep told me, after the guns and ceremony and the honor guard had marched off to the next burial, that Dad actually had a pretty quick turnaround, considering the combined number of eligible military dead from WWII, Korea, Vietnam, and ongoing wars converging on the National Cemetery these days.

When the rep turned to my brother and mother to finalize details of the headstone, I closed my eyes and saw an impossibly long, dark train reaching across the country filled with families, each needing to tell the story of their loss, constantly rolling toward this sacred place and these kind people.

So now I was holding my mother in my arms and crying along with her because of course it was too early to move Dad's clothes out and clear out his office. I can't remember, but I'm beginning to think that doing this clear out might have been my idea, some solution to help her grief that I came up with in one of our nightly phone calls. If this was something I had forced on my mother, my clean up solution for everything had turned me into some kind of monster.

But my mother patted my shoulder and pulled away, wiped her eyes, blew her nose, straightened her glasses, and pulled a smile out of somewhere. "I'm sorry, Trey. It's just well, I know when we spoke about this before you said you thought it was too soon, But really, your father is already always with me, so I have to clear all this out now I'll be crushed by it. I need your help to do it, and I knew you'd understand."

So it wasn't about me. That keeps happening. My mother was grieving. And also blaming herself for betraying her husband by still being alive, and after years of caregiving for him, beginning to look after herself.

That's why I was here in all my obsessive, distracted weirdness. I was here to stuff and cart boxes, yes, but more to help her fight that blame and defeat. So, with whatever steel I inherited from her, my first task was to get my mother into a comfortable chair, so she could direct the obsessions with order and neatness that will help her begin to build the new life she needs to survive.

DOG IS MY CO-PILOT

Going on midnight on a Tuesday night in the middle of last December, I'm rubbing my eyes, scratching my head, and doing that neck-rolling stretching thing to try to stay awake and focused.

Sitting next to me in our living room, one foot propped on the edge of the coffee table, Coco, now eighteen, flips through her textbook on the cushion beside her, checks something on her laptop on the arm of the couch, and writes another answer in the AP Environmental Science worksheet on her lap. Like me, Coco wrestles with ADHD, but tonight, unlike me, she has the wandering daydream distraction part of it whipped. She's got the hyperfocus part of our shared condition dialed up to ten and is powering through her homework and studying for finals like a fiend.

I dropped my writing yellow pad under the coffee table a couple of hours ago and after reading some, I've degenerated into playing FreeCell and Blackjack on my Kindle. But I don't even have the gas to keep my mind on that.

Back in the fifties and sixties, when ADHD symptoms just meant you were a vacant, lying, retarded troublemaker, the school systems in Illinois, Colorado, and Missouri, each tried their best to bang some sense and basic life information into my out-of-sync, sidetracked, moving-target head. We moved a lot, but not because of me. Though right before we left Chicago I was drummed out of Boy Scouts for being a thief and a liar (true). And the month before we followed the moving truck out of Fort Collins, Colorado, I was

getting in fist fights and threw the school into an uproar with my
letter to the school paper's editor that the Principal called pro-
communist (a misinterpreted stand for free speech, I thought, but I
did get carried away a little, so... true).

The point is, back then homework was something you got to
right after dinner, in your room, alone. This was how a kid,
especially one like me, was supposed to develop a sense of
responsibility, self-motivation skills, and learn that there were
consequences for what you did or didn't do. Instead in my room, I
developed greatly advanced procrastination and day-dreaming skills
along with the practiced wide-eyed deceit to avoid any and all
consequences for as long as possible.

By now, though, many of those vacant, lying, retarded
troublemakers have grown up to be doctors and researchers, and
discovered what was really going on. So today we know that some
brains are wired differently and parents have tools to help their
attention-challenged kids. At our house I often "co-pilot" homework
time with Coco, which means keeping her company while she does
the work. I help if I'm asked, but most of her work is way beyond
me. I'm just there to help her keep calm and focused.

I stop at the end of a neck-roll, and look at her as she puts
away the science stuff and picks up her Spanish textbook. This is the
third night in a row we've been down here from after-dinner to late
night. Plus she has tutoring after school. Man, I envy her energy and
concentration. She's completed mountains of worksheets, class
projects, study guides and book reports and tucked them neatly into
her backpack every night.

I, however, got maybe half a paragraph scratched onto my pad
Sunday night and have since only made signpost and arrow doodles
in the margins before giving up in favor of detective novels and
video card games. Then those get too hard and I get back to my
primary skillset: daydreaming. I yawn, sigh, and scratch the back of
my neck. I'm tired; maybe I can beg off early tonight. I know this co-
pilot thing works for her, Coco says it does — but part of me says,
Oh, come on, how can having me, the worst student that ever was sit
next to you and stare into space like a big empty-headed dog

possibly help you at all? Then the ghost of my big dog licks my face and takes me back to last July.

"The X-rays don't show any kidney stones, Mr. South," Marcia, our veterinarian says, "or anything lodged in his stomach, but Danny Boy has lost another ten pounds since you left. His blood work doesn't look encouraging, and even after the I.V. and hydration treatment, he still shows no interest in food. This is more serious than a dog missing his family, I'm afraid."

I'm afraid, too. Coco, Margaret, and I are in the middle of our family summer vacation up in Delaware to help my mom sort things out after my dad's death in March, and I'm on the phone with the vet back home in Georgia. My best friend — a big standard poodle only seven years old — is most likely dying with canine hepatitis and I'm stuck seven hundred miles away, unable to help. We won't be back in Georgia for another two weeks. There's no way I can go back early, so Marcia and my brother-in-law, Earl, will do their best to keep him comfortable until we get back.

I hang up and pretend it's nothing that serious with Danny Boy so we can focus on helping the family we're with in Delaware. But as I put another load of my father's clothes into the car to take to Salvation Army, all I can think about is that dog. He's with me when I work in the backyard; he's right behind me room to room as I pick up, do dishes, laundry, and make dinner. I talk to him all the while and he mostly he agrees with me, unless he thinks it's time to take a break and throw the ball. I bounce ideas off him when I write. I do my best work when Danny Boy is in the room with me.

"Dad?" Coco says, "You all right?"

I blink at my daughter sitting on the couch next to me. "Who, me? I'm fine," I say, "just stretching my neck."

"I'm almost done," she says, you can go up to bed if you want."

"Nah, I'm good," I say, grinning at her the way Danny Boy used to grin at me, except my tongue isn't hanging out. She shrugs, then bores back into the Spanish textbook. I lean back into the couch. I'm not going anywhere. Because Danny Boy, my co-pilot, taught me that just being there is the biggest help of all.

THE PALE KID BY THE COKE MACHINE

I keep forgetting that we're all a work in progress.

It's easy for me to see myself as a wreck. I accept it and try to learn from it day by day. But I often forget to appreciate, or see, the nittty-gritty struggle of others to grow and learn, even when an ADHD fellow-traveler like my daughter is desperately struggling with an avalanche of self-doubt and fear.

Last January, the first day of the last semester of her high school senior year, Coco jumps into the passenger seat of my beat-up old Dodge Caravan in her stocking feet, boots in one hand, backpack in the other. She drops the pack between the seats, slams the door, and yells, "Go, hurry, I'm going to be late!"

Being the patient, perfect parent I am, I don't mention that I've been ready to go for a half-hour while she ran up and down the stairs in a hyperventilating tornado of remembering and forgetting, losing and finding pens, clips, clothes, hand-sanitizer, and hair bands for her hair. She need hair bands for her wrist to help her remember to breathe and calm down, so she can remember stuff without all this insanity. I also don't mention that I told her last night to get ready ahead of time. I will bring it up at dinner though, count on it.

Though our shared ADHD can be great for understanding and helping her, as well as her helping me, it makes her panic very contagious. I hate panic. As I get older, I also hate conflict, loud noises, surprises, and any conversation that begins with "We have to talk."

As Coco pulls on her boots and looks through the zippered pockets of her backpack, I stay mum and wrestle with the van's dying power steering to get us out of the driveway. I put it in drive, get ten feet down the street, when she yells, "Oh, no, my calculator!" I pull over to the curb and remind Coco to tie her boot laces before she runs back to the house. "I'm sorry, Dad. I really I thought I had it."

"It's fine," I say, and it is, as long as I keep my breathing calm and in control. I could use a couple of those hair bands Coco's hair bands on my wrist, too. "Hurry, and double check, this is the last stop."

She jumps out, slams the car door, and runs back to the house. The passenger side window rattles and slides down a little. I worry that Coco is wound tighter than usual. She has been like this the whole week, since we got back from the family Christmas trip to Delaware. That trip nearly did the whole family in. Plus we're waiting on college applications, Federal Student Aid Application, and still haven't gotten her ACT scores back. It's a tense time.

I focus on the falling car window instead. The electric windows on the right side haven't worked for a couple years. They'll stay that way until she's got a college diploma in her hand. I'll press my hands on either side of the glass and push it back up when I get back from Walmart after dropping Coco off. It usually holds for a week. I push the CD player on and turn Lyle Lovett's version of "Stand by Your Man" up loud. Coco gets back with her calculator, snaps on her seatbelt, and we head off. She doesn't make any objection to the music. She just turns the volume down a bit. It's gratifying and a little weird to have a teenage daughter who shares your taste in music.

"You know," I say as we stop and then turn on to Green Street, "you can change the words around on this song for any member of a family and it works, I mean if the family works." She shrugs. "I know you say that, but no, it's really old-fashioned sexist. Good song, though."

I decide to let it ride, think about what a noble, patient, nonreactive parent I'm being this morning, enjoy the music and drive. A block from a stoplight, I'm thinking that my therapist will be happy to hear how, in stressful situations, I've been working on staying calm and listening to everything being said, instead of flash reacting. But wait, I'm not doing all this to make my therapist happy. I've got to stop making everything in my life about pleasing others. Why do I keep looking for his nod of approval during our sessions, like a dog doing tricks for treats, for god's sake?

So what if I react oddly to some kinds of stress? It's not like the FBI is hunting me down on Criminal Minds: "We've identified his stressor as driving his daughter to school January 7th. But we still don't know why he always bites his nails on the way home." Because I'm nervous and confused, you Fed fools. I've always been nervous and confused. I'll always be nervous and confused. But now I'm learning how to hide it better. I don't bite my nails in front of my daughter. "Hide and listen," my new motto.

"Wait, Dad, stop!"

"No! I'm not stopping and not going back!" The patient, perfect parent just went out the broken window. "Whatever you forgot, you'll just have to do without..."

"No, listen," Coco says. "It's the car. It's making that noise." There's genuine terror in her eyes. "Pull over, Dad. It's a blowout!" Her fear is bone-chilling and based on reality: last month's Christmas trip. What was I thinking back then? We could have all been killed.

I pull over, punch the hazard lights, and breathe before I talk. It isn't a blowout, I explain. That hollow grinding thumping is just the sound the brakes make in the rain. I need to get new brake pads. This doesn't calm her down much, even after I get wet walking around the car checking the tires. The rest of the way to school she trots out bloody scenarios involving innocent lives destroyed due to failed brakes in the rain. I have to promise that I'll get the brakes fixed today before she'll get out and go to class. And I do go to the auto repair shop, biting my nails on the way.

At the repair shop, I sit in the waiting room, with foam plugs stuffed in my ears to drown out the negative television news network they have on all the time, and stare at the floor. Coco's not wrong; it's good to keep your brakes fixed. But she was so frightened. She's always been pretty easily spooked, but ever since the Christmas trip, she's acting as if she expects the world to collapse on us any second. I pick up on her panic phases, and it feeds all my barely hidden tiny panic buttons.

I start going off about how nobody in the house except me loads the dishwasher right. And who left clothes in the dryer? Not finishing and folding is not doing the laundry. On and on. If the house weren't built on a slab, Margaret would have shot me and Coco with tranquilizer darts and tossed us in the basement.

But look at it. Maybe Coco's freshly compounded fear is my fault. The Christmas trip did get frightening. If things had gone a little differently, we could have all been killed. Wait, no, we were just a little too ambitious and, like the guy at the tire place said, pulling our shredded tire out of the back of the minivan, "Now right there, that's just plain unlucky."

Now, over a month later, I stare at the black and white tile between my feet, the murmur of angry newscasters fading into the background beyond my plugged-up ears as I replay Christmas Trip 2013, and look for what I did wrong. My newer motto: "Hide, don't listen, and blame yourself." This I can do.

* * * *

Christmas presents, luggage, travel snacks, drinks, pillows and blankets, seating arrangements for me, Margaret, Coco (eighteen years-old) and Margaret's mom, Nana (eighty-seven years-old) and we have guaranteed interpersonal friction on a road trip with three generations of a family crammed into a confined space for 851 miles—it seems too much to ask of any vehicle, even the 2006 minivan we call the "good car." The 2001 model I normally drive around town—with the dodgy brakes, no a/c or heat or power for the passenger windows—we call "the other one." I'm saving up for a pick-up. But that's not until Coco's college fund is solid. We don't even know how Coco did on the ACT yet, and she and I are so nervous about whether she'll get into the college she wants, we can't even talk to each other about it. Coco talks to Margaret. I talk to myself. Mostly about how I'll never get all of this crap into the car. Something's got to go.

Somehow on the exact December morning we had planned to leave, I'm behind the wheel of our 2006 minivan and we roll out of our Georgia driveway fully packed and head toward the freeway with Coco in the far back, Nana in the middle, and Margaret and me in front. I keep checking the rear-view mirror to make sure no one has stuck anything up in the back to block my view. Packing a car is like packing a dishwasher; nobody knows how to do it but me. It's all clear.

Over-packed with luggage, presents, pillows, blankets, trip food, and beverages going seventy miles per hour on I-75 North somewhere south of Atlanta, I notice that at this point, forty-five minutes into the two day drive, I'm actually kind of feeling a quasi-relaxed sort of maybe good mood coming on.

This 2013 Christmas trip that is seared in my memory is the prime example of everything warm and life affirming about family, and, at the same time, of the personal misery and terror barely under the surface of life, fate, and relatives during the holidays.

Not just the holidays—any day: because fear is especially contagious to an ADHD brain at any time of year. I think it is, anyway. There's no proof of this that I know of. Maybe it's me, again, finding an excuse for a set of confused and frightened reactions to the world around me. But maybe not. Chicken Little seems like a prime ADHD candidate. As a kid, I empathized with that guy. He didn't demand that Clucky Lucky, or whoever, jump into his terrified life. But they did, which spooked him even more and, in the end, he got blamed for everything. So there's some scientific proof right there. Also, closer and dearer to my life, I've often seen Coco catch and ride the panic wave, sometimes we're on the same one, not sure who started it. So there are at least two of us. And we're crammed into this small heated space on wheels with Margaret.

And then there's Nana. A resilient woman who raised her five kids on her own in New Jersey and still keeps her Irish immigration photo ID as a one year old in her purse. She's also prone to anxiety attacks and is so worried over her long-awaited visit with her sisters that she's been frantic and hyperventilating since we left the house, her breaths coming out in angry little yips.

I've just relaxed enough to settle into the left lane and put on cruise control when we hit critical mass.

"Where's my purse?" Nana calls out from the back, her voice rising past yip into screech, "I forgot my purse! We have to go back!"

I glance at Nana in the rearview mirror, nod with no comment and a sigh of defeat, slow down, turn on the blinker, and head toward an exit. At that point, Margaret catches my eye and quietly says, "Don't you dare turn this car around." Then turning to her mother explains in a similar quiet authoritative tone, that we can't turn back, we're already over an hour into trip and it would take too much time. But Nana only becomes more agitated and insistent.

She needs her ID, money, she says, and cards when she gets to her sister's house in North Carolina. She knows exactly where she left it, right in the middle of the pillow on her bed. She wouldn't have forgotten it if Margaret hadn't been pushing and rushing her to get out of the house this morning. "This is all your fault, Margaret," she tells her daughter.

I've been married to Margaret for close to thirty years and, in all that time, I've never ever said to her, "This is all your fault." You'll have to take it on faith that it's not due to any fear on my part. It has more to do with respect and our commitment to do our best to keep each other whole. Besides, ask my therapist, I blame myself for everything. And I don't like to share.

But I've noticed that Nana sometimes finds that blaming her eldest daughter Margaret to be an emotionally freeing exercise and calming to her nerves. And Margaret most times doesn't argue or fight back, choosing instead to keep the peace and go along. This was not one of those times.

So, off goes the blinker and we're back up to seventy mph in a flash. I tuck into driving mode, conscious to avoid panic waves rising anywhere near me, as Margaret, keeping her tone of calm, compassionate, but unbending reason, gets into it with her mother.

We're not turning around. She's sure Nana's purse is here somewhere. If it's not, Nana will have to do without. Nana could sense there was no winning here, and got more worked up, saying that she couldn't believe how Margaret has treated her. After all she did for her. What have I ever done to deserve this? You see how she treats me? Do you?

Which would have probably have been the precursor to a grumbling armistice, but for Coco, paddling up to catch the panic wave in her Nana's voice and taking it to heart. Nothing I can say here, just keep the car between the lines.

"Mom, Nana, really it's all right, we'll find the purse! Don't argue about it, please!" Coco says, leaning forward from the far back seat.

"There's nothing to get upset about, Coco," Margaret says. "We were just talking it out. It's settled now."

"For you, maybe," Nana mumbles "Not for me."

"I have to pee anyway, so can't we just stop someplace and then we can look for the wallet. I'm sure I can find it. Please?" Coco pleads.

My ears poke up out of driving mode, hearing the touch of alarm growing in Coco's speech. Margaret and I share a married-mind-meld glance, and I slow down and hit the blinker again, angling for the next exit with services.

"Okay, we're stopping, and we'll look in the car, but understand, Mom, we're not going back," Margaret says.

"I understand perfectly, Margaret," Nana said. She then turns to the far back where her granddaughter is sitting up wide-eyed and concerned like a meerkat, and says, "Thank you, Coco."

We stop at a McDonald's and everyone pees. Later while we search through the luggage, Coco cries out, "I found it!" Her voice filled with the victory of resolving a family crisis, she hands Nana her missing purse. "It was right under your seat, Nana, isn't that funny? Now you don't have to worry."

Nana nods and takes the wallet, but she's still worried. In the process of looking through her luggage for the wallet, Nana has noticed that she's left something else behind. "It's blue, a blue nylon bag. You remember I handed it to you, Frank?"

I did remember a blue nylon bag; I just didn't know what I did with it.

"I have to have that bag, Frank," Nana says, her voice rising. "It has my underwear in it, and my toiletry items, and a couple of little presents for my sisters. Really it's the only bag I care about."

Then I remember. I must have left it in the garage when I was pulling things out and repacking for the fifth time. I had insisted on controlling the packing, told Nana and everybody to calm down, and that I knew what I was doing. Leave me alone, I've got this. Trust me. I confess I might have left the blue bag at home.

"I'm sorry, Nana," I say. "We'll fix it somehow."

Nana nods, shrugs and sighs in one full-body gesture, a signature sign of predictable disappointment. Then with sincere no-baloney tears in her eyes she gets a hand from Coco to get back into the minivan. Coco helps her buckle her seat belt, then gets herself settled in the back. Before I close the sliding back door Nana says she knows we can't go back. It's fine.

Outside the car, I tell Margaret I know we can probably replace all of this for her mother when we get to North Carolina, but still, I should have let her mother or her check behind me. She says, "Come on, it can't be helped. We'll buy her more underwear and presents when we get there, she'll be fine. Let's get going, nobody blames you."

Oh, yeah? I do. In a way, I was glad. It would give me something to chew on all the way to North Carolina. The sky is falling, the sky is falling, and it's all my fault.

* * * *

It's Christmas day and my mother's house in Delaware is packed with family. Margaret and my mother are making martinis in the kitchen and laughing as Margaret lays out the story so far. "Before we could finish getting her settled in Chapel Hill for her Christmas with Aunt Patsy and Aunt Mary and get the hell out of there, my mother had to tell her sisters the whole terrifying story of her near-death experience at the hands of Frank and Coco."

My mother turns to me as I open the oven and reach for the roast. "My god, what did you do?"

"Nothing," I say. "Nothing happened."

I pull the standing rib roast out of the oven. I'm making Christmas dinner, soup to nuts. I insisted. I don't know why, except that it keeps me away from the holiday hubbub. Now the hubbub's in here. My teenage niece, the observer from the vegetarian contingent, keeps a watchful eye from the kitchen door making sure no stray globules of "flesh juice" drop into the salad or mushroom pasta as I move the roast to the carving board.

"Frank's right," Margaret says. "It wasn't that big of a deal, but after he left the magic blue bag behind, Mom was looking for anything more to add to the guilt and drama."

"What, though?" my mom insists, "What happened?"

"Nothing, really," Margaret says, "He drifted into the lane of a car coming up behind us, their horn blared, the van swerved into a skid..."

"A little skid," I say, and I put the roast on the stove next to the carving board.

"Yes," Margaret says. "Teensy, but my mother was dozing so she woke up scared out of her wits, screaming."

"Oh no..." my mother says.

"Not screaming," I say. "Yelps. Little yip-yelps. It was no big deal, really."

"Of course it wasn't," Margaret says. "But it wouldn't have happened at all if you and Coco hadn't been focused on the GPS maps on her phone instead of the road."

"You're right, you're right," I say. "Now please hand me that big sharp carving knife on the table beside you and get out of the kitchen, please."

"Hmmm. Sounds like a threat buried in there," my mother says.

"Not buried, sitting right on top," Margaret says. She kisses me, and then turns to my mother. "Let's go talk with civilized people in the living room."

She scoops our niece from the doorway as they head out and tells her, "Trust me; your vegetables are safe with your uncle."

As I carve the roast I think that after Christmas we'll all be calmer and the drive back home will be less hectic than the trip up. Of course, I'm wrong about that.

* * * *

Thump. Thump thump. Thump thump thump. "Dad, that sound. Hear that? There's something wrong with the car!" yells Coco from the far back seat.

"Don't hear anything, car's fine," I say. "Try not to worry so much." I do hear something, but I'm sure it's a bass run under "Backstabbers" that I'm singing along to with the O'Jays. Coco's anxiety is more easily triggered than mine. She seems to expect disaster with any new sound, sight, or insect bite. In a flash, she can go from mild concern to doomsday certain with no middle zone.

I used to panic right along with her, which was exhausting for us both. Lately, I've been consciously staying calm and over Christmas at my mother's shared my breathing strategy with her in the hope of modeling a more adult, tranquil path through life. Life is hard enough for kids, it's important to help them see the difference between the imagined difficulties and the real ones.

Thinking about this parenting improvement puts me in a good mood. The Christmas trip to my mother's house in Delaware, with all of the fear and anxiety I heaped on it, is nearly over. I'm no slouch at imagining difficulties myself, so these are good teaching moments. Sort of. Anyway, right now, I'm in a good mood.

My wife's napping beside me, daughter's buckled in back, it's thirty minutes to Chapel Hill where I will pick up Nana from her sisters', then we drive straight on through with no unnecessary stops until we all four roll into our gorgeous cracked, overgrown, pine-cone covered driveway in Georgia. I start to pull out from between the two semis that have our minivan sandwiched, headed south on I-85 in North Carolina.

Thump, thump. "There, you have to hear that!" Coco says. "We hit something, I know it!"

"Don't worry, hon, I promise we'll be home safe and sound tonight," I tell her calm as pie. Good parent me. I hit the left blinker, and accelerate into the left lane, singing with the O'Jays, "They smile in your face, all the time they want to take your place..." Thump,

thump, thump, thump. Thumpthumpthump,
THUMPTHUMPTHUMPTHUMP.

"Dad! Omigod!" The minivan lurches to the right, and I tap
the brakes and head back across the right lane toward the shoulder.

"Stay calm, Coco," I say, reciting our mantra, "And breathe."
The semi behind us brakes, then blasts his air horn as he roars past
us. My wife Margaret startles from her nap, the road atlas falls off
her lap.

"What? What is it?" Margaret says, quickly snapping awake,
turning around to keep an eye on traffic coming up behind us and,
her voice calm, saying to Coco, "It's just a flat, honey," she says.
"Your dad is good with this kind of thing." With a bump and a
shudder as the wind from the passing traffic buffets us, I get the van
stopped on the shoulder, push the hazard blinker, set the emergency
brake, and finally breathe. Coco unsnaps her seat belt and clambers
into the middle back seat, closer to Margaret. She's freaked, fighting
tears, but not hyperventilating. I don't know about me.

"I told Dad I heard it, Mom," Coco says. "I told him and told
him, but he wouldn't listen."

I catch Margaret's eye and nod. Yep, that's me all right. Then I
close my eyes, lean back, give myself a second to stay calm, and
breathe before I dig out the spare and change the tire.

It starts to snow while the three of us unpack the back of the
minivan looking for the spare tire. First the good luggage, then totes
with opened Christmas presents, then out comes the yellow duffle
with the broken zipper, the plastic bags with who knows what about
ready to rip through the side, and finally my parents' rusty old gas
grill, that we couldn't say no to. I could sure say no to it now. Finally
it's all out. But there's no spare tire anywhere. "This can't be true." I
stare hard at the open wheel well cover in the now emptied back of
the minivan, trying to make what I see turn into what I imagined I'd
see. The I-85 holiday traffic thunders by a few feet from me,
Margaret, and Coco, and our luggage, presents, bags, and rusted
grill parts perched on the dirt and gravel highway shoulder. Coco is
just this side of frantic imagining us turned into three little white
roadside crosses unless we immediately get back in the van and call
a tow truck.

"She's got a point," Margaret says before she joins Coco inside.

"I know, I know," I say, but I can't let it go. This makes no sense. The jack was there and the tire iron with an odd little square socket on the other end of the lug wrench. "Where the hell is the spare tire?" I haul off and kick the bumper. "I wouldn't have done something as stupid as taking out the spare to make room when I was packing would I?"

"How would I know?" Margaret says. "That's your top-secret private operation."

"Of course, I wouldn't!" I yell. I'm unraveling because it sounds to me exactly like something I'd do. It's so embarrassing that it's beyond my ability to cope. The snow turns into rain.

I'm about to kick the bumper again when Coco calls out, "Stay calm and breathe, Dad!" So I do. And then I start shoving luggage back into the rear of the minivan. I look up expecting to see Margaret ticked off at me, the ill-tempered mental-defective, but no. She's smiling at me, sweetly amused. I'll never figure her out.

"Alright, go ahead and call roadside assistance," I tell her. "Number's in the glove compartment."

A few minutes later, Margaret's digging through the glove compartment and I'm squeezing the last of the luggage into the back, when Coco looks up from her smartphone grinning. "I know where the spare is!"

It hadn't occurred to me to Google the missing spare tire problem, but it had occurred to Coco and there it was pictured on her phone – a teeny spare up front, underneath the minivan. She scrolls the screen and lo, between the front seats under a little rubber plug is a bolt you turn with the odd little square socket on the tire iron to lower the spare.

Saved by our calm, tech-savvy teenager, we set to solving the problem again. Working together against the forces of fate, like the people in those Alaska shows. But the last lug nut won't budge no matter what, so instead of me kicking it, we're about to call the tow truck when an Oldsmobile pulls up and a Good Samaritan steps out. He introduces himself as Mike and says he can help; he's got a hydraulic jack in his trunk and a long handled lug wrench that can lever free the stuck lug nut.

So instead of calling a tow truck, Margaret calls her mom to tell her we're running late, but we'll be there soon.

After Mike and me giving it our all with the long-handled wrench, the lug nut still won't budge. Mike says, well, the only thing is to cut it. He has a saw in his trunk if it's okay with me. Go ahead I say, I'm so cold wet and desperate, I'll agree to anything. The saw and rolling hydraulic jack he pulls out of the trunk of his Oldsmobile make quick work of getting the blown shredded tire switched to the tiny donut spare. Mike won't take the twenty I offer for his trouble. But he does say that donut will never get you home to Georgia. That where you headed? Noticed your plates, he says. Yeah, I know, I say. Know any tire stores around here?

Not many open on a Sunday, but Mike knows one place that could fix us up. He has a friend with a used-tire store just off the next exit, not far, just follow him, and don't worry about trying to get your dirty ripped up old tire in your van, you look pretty packed in there. I'll put it in my trunk, and meet you there.

Fine, sounds fine, and then we're following a stranger's Oldsmobile off the interstate into the woods of North Carolina, shopping for a tire. "Breathe, Dad," Coco says. "You too," I say.

A half-hour later, trailing Mike's Oldsmobile as it turns down one unmarked road after another under lead gray skies, I start to wonder, "What kind of guy drives around with a big old hydraulic jack and a saw in his car?"

Neither my wife nor our daughter is saying a word. And I'm beginning to understand why. Coco and Margaret have realized what I just have. With each turn down these long winding and rain-slicked pine-shrouded roads, I'm driving my family farther into a dark, no escape Stephen King short story. We're the first characters, the ones that don't make it out. We're the ones that suffer horribly because of the sins of the bossy know-it-all dad who had to have a bargain. But there are no bargains where you're heading are there? No, the only things that are cheap here are your lives. And it's your greed, Dad, your self-indulgence and weakness that's doomed you and your innocent family to unspeakable terror and death.

Then the pines recede. The drizzling rain has turned to snow again and we pull into Best Deal Used Tires, a small run-down exgas station on the edge of a closed-up North Carolina town that doesn't look like it's been open for a while. But Best Deal Used Tires is open, and they have a used Dunlop tire our size. So now Mike's back out on the interstate trolling for customers and we're inside waiting for a "guaranteed to get you home safe and sound" used tire to be put on our minivan by a guy who's Mike's best friend. By my watch it's been an hour and seven minutes, not counting the drive here. But I'm not doing that. Other people are waiting too. Be patient. Breathe in and out. Nice and slow.

A pale kid sits by the Coke machine in a T-shirt with food stains on the front, his too-big jeans cinched tight at his waist with a canvas belt. He holds his hands in his lap, pulling on each of his fingers of one hand with his other hand, switching hands when he gets to the thumb of one, then back again with the other, as he squeaks his new black Velcro sneaks on the cracked linoleum. Then he jumps to his feet, and stands staring hard at the eight or nine people in the room, one by one, taking about five seconds per face. Nothing against the kid, but when his gaze falls on me I immediately avert my eyes, nervous and embarrassed for him.

Maybe I'm also irritated at being bothered by him, and maybe I should be more understanding because my kids and I each have our own big bag of neurological snags, but I'm tired and I don't care. He should be taught not to do that thing with his eyes. It's invasive. Margaret's resting with her eyes closed, the woman has a sleep switch that's the envy of all us insomniacs, so the kid passes over her and gets to Coco. My protective father mode surges, no eerie-eyed kid is going to upset my daughter especially with the day we've been having. But before I can stand and do what - I don't know, stand in front of Coco, block his evil eye-beam – I notice that Coco is looking back at the kid and smiling.

"Hi," she says, "I'm Coco. What's your name?" He doesn't answer, doesn't smile back, but he doesn't break eye contact.

"Did you have a good Christmas?" Coco asks. Still no reaction. But his fingers aren't pulling so hard. They've been looking at each other for nearly a full minute.

Then the kid breaks the gaze and goes to the next face. He continues around the room until he eyes a thin, tired-looking woman in jeans and a faded Carolina Tarheels sweatshirt sitting next to him. I think she's probably his mom because, except for the dark circles under her eyes, she's got his same pale skin, and because she hauls off and whacks him on the arm.

"Sit your fidgety ass back down, Eldridge Junior. You're about driving me crazy out of my mind," she says. He sits, fingers still working. He's maybe eight years old and does what he's told. For a couple of minutes. Then the switch goes off in his head, he stands up and the routine starts again. Ignoring him, his mother looks over to a gray-bearded guy in a dirty ball cap squinting at a computer screen and typing on a keyboard behind the counter and asks, "How much longer did you say 'til Eldridge is finished up, Jake?"

"Didn't say, Cassie," Jake says. "He's gotta get the tire on and done for these folks y'alls pal Mike pulled in off the Interstate…"

"He's not my pal," Cassie says, throwing a dirty look at the corner where we're sitting, then looks back up at a family fight on Dr. Phil on the TV hanging on the wood-paneled wall two feet above our heads.

"Don't matter," Jake says to the back of Cassie's head, "Eldridge still has to unload and stack all those truck retreads before he's done here today. Not my fault he takes on some freelance."

"You get your cut," Cassie mutters.

His fingers pulling faster now, Eldridge Junior's eyes have reached his mother again. Cassie whacks him on his arm again. "Eldridge Junior, please!" She pulls him down to the plastic waiting room chair next to her. Then her eyes still on Dr. Phil, she puts her arm around Eldridge Jr., hugs him, and pulls him onto her lap.

Eldridge, lanky, looks kind of like his boy, but without the fidgets and tics, steps in from the garage. "South family? Got your van set," Eldridge says. Margaret's awake in a snap. On our way out, Coco stops near Cassie and Eldridge Jr. "It was nice to meet you, Eldridge Jr." Cassie's looking at the television, Eldridge Jr. looking at other faces.

"We don't put up with people making fun of Eldridge Jr.," Cassie says.

"I wouldn't either," Coco says "And honest, I was just saying hi."

I stop at the door and turn back to my daughter. "Coco, come on, let's leave these people alone. It's time to go."

"Go ahead," Coco says, "I'll just be a minute. Really, we're fine Dad."

Outside, Eldridge shows me the tire, which looks fine for a used tire I guess. We settle up, shake hands, and then join Margaret looking back at Coco, Cassie and Eldridge Jr. inside the Best Deal waiting room. Cassie is talking, Coco nodding. Eldridge Jr. sits and stands a couple of times, quick, like a jack in the box. Cassie and Coco laugh, they shake hands, and Coco comes out, joining us at the minivan.

"What are you two smiling about?" she asks.

As we all pile in to the car, Margaret and I tell our daughter that she's, you know, amazing. She has more compassion and understanding than most people her age, and more than me, for sure. And it took courage to engage like that.

"Well, I'm going to be a special ed teacher, how did you think I'd act?" she says. Margaret squeezes he daughter's hand. Coco begins giving me directions back to the Interstate from the GPS on her phone.

"It's sure lucky we had that flat before we picked up Nana," Coco says, "She would've freaked right out."

Margaret laughs, "Right out of her skin and through the roof, definitely lucky that we were spared that."

"See, Dad?" Coco says, "There's nothing for you to worry about."

She's right, the rain lets up and the drive to Chapel Hill is uneventful, we don't even get a little bit lost on the way. When we get there, Nana is packed – nothing left behind - and ready to go, and not at all bothered that we're late. After happy good-byes with Aunt Patsy and Aunt Mary, we make a change in the seating so Nana can sit up front and talk to Margaret, who's going to drive this leg so I can sit in the back with Coco. The two of us have a quiet chat, she tells me a joke I'm too old to get, but laugh anyway. As Margaret accelerates onto the freeway, Nana telling her all about Christmas with her sisters, I push my seat back, Coco tosses me a blanket and before I doze off I notice I'm smiling.

Thump, thump, thump. "Dad!" No, I don't want to dream about that, something else, please... THUMP THUMP

"Frank, honey? I could use some advice here."

THUMPTHUMPTHUMP "Dad, wake up!"

And I'm up straight and it's the same tire, same side, It's raining like a son of a bitch, we're surrounded by semis blowing their horns as Margaret slows down.

Nana's saying what's happening, what's happening, over and over. Cocos yelling it's a blowout! Another blowout!

Margaret calm, but urgent catches my eye and cutting through the car and people noise, asks, "Right or left shoulder?"

"Right, always right if you can. Cut over after this truck, that SUV is slowing for you."

Margaret nods, and blinker on, the minivan rocking in the wind and limping on a screeching rim, gets us over to the side and stops. I tell her nice job. She nods and we trade a smile and shrug. We both close our eyes and take a breath, and then get to work. At least this time we know where the spare is. Coco grabs the tool and lowers the spare from inside the van.

Cars and trucks roar by, rocking our minivan back and forth, which is already leaning on the edge of the shoulder. I stand in the pouring rain looking at the Dunlop tire we bought from Eldridge a few hours ago. It doesn't even look like a tire anymore, more like a black fronded sombrero framing the wheel rim that's planted in the gravel and mud. Margaret steps up next to me, and puts her arm around my shoulder. "Tow truck?" she asks.

"Tow truck," I say.

We call the insurance company roadside assistance number we should have called a few hundred miles ago, and pretty soon we're all wandering around a Wal-Mart as a guy in the service department puts on a brand new tire. When he saw the sombrero, and heard the story, the guy shook his head and said, "Probably nothing wrong with the used tire, you folks just hit some seriously bad luck is all."

Oh well, that's okay then. But both Nana and Coco like drama, adventure and Wal-Mart. They're off getting some extra supplies while Margaret and I sit together by the car battery display.

"You want to stop at motel up the road a ways?" I ask her.

"No way, uh uh." She says, "I want to go home tonight, I don't care when we get there. I want to sleep in our bed. You okay to drive?"

"Sure," I say.

I don't say it, but I'd do anything, and pay any price to finally pack this trip into a dusty corner of the past. Along with the guilt I feel even over the stress and danger to my family I may logically know I didn't directly cause, but will still be playing in an unforgiving loop in my head for a long time.

The guy tells us the new tire is on, we're good to go. Makes me think I could hold off on the self-punishment until we get home and I can roll my head into my therapist's office, see if he can patch it up, or fix me with a new one.

Storm Watch

After so many years of being so wrong for so long about so many things, ADHD adults don't trust anything their brains say.

This is true if you are undiagnosed and desperate, hunting for a handhold through flying shards of forgotten ideas, names, dates, and blown opportunities. And it's still true if you've been diagnosed for decades, work with your therapist, take meds, meditate, and whether you consider your ADHD a gift, a tool, or a curse.

You have a hurricane brain. You have to learn to stay in the calm eye of the storm, and concentrate to avoid the winds of confusion that surround you, always ready to pull you in and blank out the present, and relive past failures. Then someone asks you something, and you realize that even if you stay stone still, dead center, you can't trust your answer, because you've been so focused on not getting sucked in, you haven't heard much besides the roar in your head. You get better with the balance as time goes on, and you get by, even do well. But the hurricane never goes away. And dealing with it over the long term can wear anyone down. Then again, I might be completely wrong about this, fifty-fifty chance, really. The flip of a coin.

Last week, Margaret and I were streaming the last episode of *11-22-63*, the miniseries based on the Stephen King novel. We both loved the book, and both are into this time-travel love story, but I'm <u>way</u> into it. The early-sixties look is right out of my childhood, the lead character's unmoored mind in a life-or-death battle not only with his past, but the whole entire freaking past, future, and the nature of reality. It's the last eight minutes, both of us rapt, tense, but something onscreen triggers in me what? I'm not sure, an epiphany or connection so strong I have to tell Margaret right now, and I push the pause button on the remote. But it's the wrong button and the screen flips to a talk show. Margaret asks what the hell I was doing for God's sake? For a split second I don't know what she's talking about, and don't know why the remote is in my hand.

"What's wrong? What did I do?" I bleat, completely disoriented. Margaret, married to me for thirty years, says don't worry about it, takes control of the remote. After I go to the bathroom and get a drink of water, we finish the show.

When we go to bed, I try to explain to Margaret why I hit the remote and what I'd wanted to say, but I can't remember, and that's even more upsetting. She says, don't worry. It'll come to you. I have my doubts. We kiss, hold hands, listen to the rain on the window, and fall asleep. At six a.m., the phone rings with an automated voice announcing a tornado warning. The house shakes some, the wind pushing against it with a loud, mean deep guttural roar. Outside our window is nothing but thick gray, can't see two inches. By the time we start downstairs to wake Coco and gather up the dogs and flashlights, the noise lets up. We check the weather report. The tornado touched down a couple of blocks away, then headed east. Feeling lucky, we go back to bed, this time with the dogs and Coco burrowed between us. I whisper to Margaret over dogs and daughter that the tornado reminded me of my brain, but that seems like a trivial comparison. "I mean this tornado was real, did real damage."

"Your brain is just as real," she says, "Write about that."

I still don't remember what I had to tell Margaret when I stopped the TV show. My guess is that it was some bright shock of the love and gratitude I feel for her every day. So maybe there is one thing I do know for sure. Nobody can do this alone. We have to reach out to those close to us. The effort we put out in order to connect with those we love, and that they return, is the one thing that can help us ride out the storm.

DENY IT

My psychologist, Chris, flips through pages of a thick folder on his lap.

I stare outside through his office's white plantation blinds. The morning sun pops off an oak tree's new leaves. Chris finds what he's looking for in the folder. "So, a few months ago, Dr. E notes here in your chart that your depression is in remission..."

Behind the tree, the Georgia sky shines bright blue and cloudless. Hot days already here. Yesterday, our minivan's radiator fried and died. Seven hundred bucks—kablooey. I'll never get my credit cards paid off. You might as well throw me and the cards into recycle crusher with all the rest of the used-up plastic crap.

"Um, Frank?"

I blink, look at Chris. "Yeah, that's right," I say. "I'm good."

"I don't think so," he says. Then we get into this long thing about how back then I'd been off anti-depressants for almost a year and I told Dr. E, who's the psychiatrist and prescribing doc in their practice, that I had my mood swings under control and had stopped digging down into deep holes of incapacitating depression. Maybe I was sincere, but Chris and Dr. E had both noted my repeated dug-in opposition to anti-depressants, which I brought up in sessions with each of them, even when neither of them had suggested the meds. So maybe that was why now, when apparently my depression has returned, I deny it. I'm feeling itchy. I want this session to be over already.

"As you know," he says, "a high percentage of people with ADHD also have depression or anxiety. The right anti-depressant could really help. Dr. E. can prescribe a low dose that could lessen the side effects that trouble you."

Man, I don't want to hear this. "I already take ADHD meds and a bunch of supplements. I don't need any more pills. I meditate. I'm just a little worried. Everybody worries. Or they should. I'm not digging a dark hole. I'm not depressed." We end the session in a truce, me grinning and laughing to prove I'm A-Okay, and Chris concerned.

As I write this post, I can honestly say I'm not digging a dark hole. That metaphor had a little hope. Instead I'm trapped inside a big thick black sack of fear and self-loathing that I make thicker and heavier with every day I deny my depression, resist help, and, eighteen years after my diagnoses of ADHD with comorbid depression, hypomania and anxiety, still refuse to accept the full scope of who I really am. I keep looking at these conditions as something I "have"—like the flu. That view encourages me to disregard symptoms, avoid help, and indulge in self-pity.

Here's the thing, I think. You don't want ADHD to define you, but it does and always will. Because it's not something you have, it's a major part of you, your life experience, and personality. Like it or not, it affects how you see the world and, whether they know it or not, it affects how others see you.

* * * *

Seven a.m. My cell phone starts the doodle-le-do gentle wake-up cycles. I grab it and swipe at the screen over and over to move the circled red X before the alarm goes to circus music and then to the ringing that never ends. Sit up, feet over the bed. So far so good with today's depression double check.

I'm back on antidepressants again after swearing them off some seven years ago. Back then I felt like, look – I haven't had a drink or smoked in years and years. I take Adderall for ADHD and Men's Fifty & Over multi-vitamins every day. I walk a mile with my dog every day, and I haven't bitten anybody's head off in a long time. I'm fine. I'm nice enough to everyone. See? I'm not depressed!

So, since I'd already sneaked off the antidepressants for a month, why not make it official? And, by the way, besides other minor side effects – some of the, um, sexual side effects can try your patience. It's like waiting for a train that's moving right along, but keeps staying just this far from pulling into the station. Who wants to deal with that?

Bigger reason, though, was I was pissed that I had to take another pill to fit in. Even in my own family, I had started to feel like they were making me do something that'd just make it easier for them to live with me. How come I had to do this? Why can't I just be who I am and make my family and friends learn to deal with it, damn it. You know, I'd gone to meetings at my daughter's schools, where they made classroom accommodations for her ADHD. So maybe the world owed me a little accommodation too.

So for a few years, I went without the depression meds. I dealt with and helped others deal with some pretty hairy situations— involving death and taxes— and close family dramas without freaking out that much. That's how I saw it anyway. But I hadn't yet recognized the "How come I had to do this" complaint for what it was.

Recently the family drama died down, and things were looking better. But my cell phone alarm had started constantly going to the never-ending loud ring. My wife, Margaret, had had to swipe it silent after her shower. She'd rest her hand on my curled-up, under-the-covers form and ask, "You all right?"

This was Margaret's and my daughter Coco's tag to most conversations I had with them for the last few months. It was the same with my therapist, except he wanted details. Also with my mechanic, Wiltz, who didn't want details, but was worried about my reaction to the news that my minivan needed a new radiator. I stopped walking the dog. I didn't feel like it. Why should he get special treatment?

It was when Coco was giving me a ride home from the auto repair shop, and Coco asked, "You all right?" and looked concerned and scared, that I took notice. Her father, who she loved, who she depended on to understand and listen to her and give her support and advice, was slowly imploding in front of her.

That's when I realized that "How come I had to do this" was an echo from the old alcoholic voice embedded in me. The voice that says that everybody else gets something that I can't have and that's not fair. I don't want to think about others. I don't want to make others comfortable in my world, I don't want to have to go to the trouble to deal with the reality of who I really am, so that I can see and feel the reality of a world without me at its center.

That voice nearly destroyed me before with booze, and now unless I did something about it, it was leading me down the rabbit hole of depression. So when Coco and I got home, I called my psychiatrist, and went back to the meds. And I'm happy to say, side effects, shmide effects. I say the joy effect is worth it. And so says my whole family. Well, of course they would, they're all on anti-depressants too.

LOST IN THE CITY

"Where the hell am I?"

I stop on the sidewalk and look down at Google Maps on my smartphone. The little pulsing blue dot that's me is all by itself in the middle of a huge grid of white rectangles and gray lines. No thick blue line, no arrow pointing my way. Noise breaks my stunned disbelief that my electronic life-line has failed, and I look up. A tidal wave of Manhattan night washes over me; glaring lights, honking roaring traffic, crowds rushing, heads down. They know where they're going. They won't be late. I will, if I ever get there at all.

I'm not frantic yet. I take deep ten count inhales filled with the smell of the East River wind, truck exhaust, Italian, Chinese, and Mid-Eastern food then let it all out with fifteen count exhales, and repeating a prayer to the Google gods that the blue arrow will come back to my phone, I do it again. But the panic attack weasel is awake and scratching hard to get a handhold in my chest. He hisses that every count sequence is another minute I'm going to be late to the only reason I'm in New York at all.

That reason means the world to me. Tonight I'm invited to a pre-opening dinner at a Chelsea gallery installation honoring The GALA Committee, a collective of artists from Georgia and Los Angeles and all over the country organized by a celebrated conceptual artist Mel Chin who twenty years ago created a nationally televised, ground-breaking secret project creating politically controversial conceptual art pieces that were used as props, set decorations, and costumes from 1995-97 on the television show I ran at the time. In my eighteen years in the business, there's very little that gives me more pride than that two year clandestine art operation on Melrose Place.

My chest weasel bursts out laughing. "Proud of what? What did *you* create? Zero. Nada. So you let them sneak weird junk onto the set of the TV show you ran. So what? You think doormen for soap operas get medals?" By now, he's gnashed into my chest and pulls it tight around him. My heart beats faster and I can see he's right. What am I doing here? I should have stayed home in Georgia with my family who needs me, and the yard that needs raking and the dog that needs walking.

Regret and fear flatten everything in my head to asphalt: memories, plans, ape brain, lizard brain, pea-brain, and all human synapses but the dark impulses bolted back in a dungeon corner straining at the leash with my self-loathing and angry addictions.

Now they slither free and turn consoling, singing in happy harmony with the chest weasel, "Go home, you silly man. But first - get yourself to a bar. A nice one, you deserve that. Sit down, have a few drinks and forget all this, especially your sobriety crap. That sixteen years sober is the reason you, a grown man in his freaking sixties, has nerves so fried he can't even handle getting a little lost. The doc diagnosed ADHD around then too, right? He put you on all those pills. When all you really needed were people to give you some space; some time to think with a couple of shots of quality vodka on the rocks. Make it three shots; you don't want to have to call the bartender back too soon. And three olives free-floating – not pre-skewered with a red cellophaned topped toothpick. A small china dish of cashews on the side would be nice."

"No! Stop it! Get out of there!" I yell out loud and slap at my chest. Desperate, alone, and forgetting that this whole mess started with the question, I don't know or care where I am or that I'm out in public. I repeatedly hit and then push hard against my sternum with the heel of my hand and then down toward my gut, trying to break the weasel's hold. And breathe my twenty-five counts, each silent count in my empty head a prayer to end this particularly vicious panic attack.

Look, I'm not saying that the next time you see some crazy person like me jerking around, yelling at invisible enemies, and hitting himself in the middle of the sidewalk that you should stop and offer help. Just hold a good nonjudgmental thought for him as you walk by. Chances are if he's not a broker having an earpiece cell phone meltdown, he's just someone who has just realized he forgot to take his afternoon meds and is trying to get his bearings. And he'll probably get there. I did.

Still breathing on count I make it back to the F train entrance where I began, and the blue arrow and thick line to the gallery reappear. Fifteen minutes ago I had stepped out from here feeling smart and prepared. Head back and smiling, I had only glanced once at my phone map before I strode off in the completely wrong direction. Now humbled, head bent to the map, I make my way to the Red Bull Studios gallery. When the phone says I've arrived, I look up.

They've recreated the Melrose Place apartment arch and gate at the front of the gallery. And there is a doorman (the weasel's right, no medal). They check my name against a list, and the doorman opens the gate to the gallery filled with cheerful hip, smart people, clinking glasses and oh great, an open bar. I finally made it here, but I'm not sure I can step in.

* * * *

It seems to me that all of us in the mental health community, with our different brain chemistries, spectrums, diagnoses, prescriptions, and coping mechanisms have sometimes wildly different reactions to similar events in our lives. Some folks in our community have found ways to rid themselves of panic attacks completely; others manage them without too much trouble excessive drama, or long-lasting effects.

Not me. Even as an ADHD hypomanic alcoholic with anxiety and depressive tendencies, I've got most of my stuff pretty locked down. Fact is, my coping skills have turned most of my symptoms to my advantage as a hyper-focused writer and hyperactive house cleaner, tree planter and yard raker. I haven't had a drink in fifteen years, and ninety percent of the time I pass as a competent, functioning, if kind of twitchy adult.

But, though I practice mindfulness meditation, go to therapy, exercise, take my meds, watch my diet, and take any solution or guideline for them I come across seriously, I find panic attacks to be the most stubborn, powerful and destructive of the mind games my brain plays on me. So I'm careful, aware of triggers and signs I've catalogued over the years, so as to not let an attack slip in and take over. But all it takes sometimes is missing my afternoon meds before a particularly stressful evening when I should be on guard, but I'm distracted – and bam, my heart's racing and the anxiety weasel is at the wheel.

So, twenty minutes later, calmer but exhausted and wary, I do manage to walk off the New York street and into the gallery. I go to the bar, refuse champagne, but take a power drink. (I know, tons of caffeine and sugar on top of burnt nerves but I can't drink and it's the Red Bull Studios gallery, what am I going to do? Besides, it's orange flavor. Vitamin C is healing.) I eat something-on-a-stick, talk to a couple of nice people and say I'm also looking forward to tomorrow night's big opening.

Trouble is, I can't get comfortable, focus, and be in the moment because I'm still dazed by my panic attack and worried that I might have another one right here in the midst of all the positive, inspiring artists and the stunning work they created. That I couldn't stand. So after about a half hour I head back to Brooklyn, where I'm staying with two of my oldest, best friends, Joe and Debra. Luckily they're coming with me tomorrow night for the opening. I'll be sure to take my meds, and with my friends there for support, what could go wrong?

Tomorrow night comes, with friends in tow and after a bit of walking around, and introducing back and forth, I'm feeling much more relaxed than last night. An hour or so in, unfortunately, a few of us are herded onto a makeshift riser and someone hands me a microphone.

"I just want to say I'm grateful that this happened, not this now, but I'm grateful to be invited here for sure, very grateful to everybody, everybody here, really. But um, what I mean was back then, you know when... uh...”

I try to clear my throat, the microphone is slippery, almost drop it. I switch hands wiping the other on my jeans. This riser that the four of us who are meant to speak are standing on is really part of the installation and not meant to be a stage. I'm just now noticing that it is seriously narrow. The paper slippers they had us wear to not damage the painted surface barely fit over my boots, and sure don't help with the footing.

Stop staring at your feet, idiot. Look up and get this over with. Still clearing my throat like “There was an old lady that swallowed a fly, I don't why she swallowed a fly, I guess she'll die.” Hope that wasn't out loud. I quick glance around the small crowd for Joe and Debra, they were with me a second ago. I could really use a nod-wink- smile lifeline about now. Can't see them.

I can't see much of anything really, because the big gray floaters in my eyes that I've had for the last fifteen years or so have settled front and center blurring out everything. I've told my ophthalmologist that this happens like clockwork when I'm severely stressed. They hear the floater alarm go off in my prefrontal cortex and move in to cut off an incoming threat. Klingon photon torpedoes, shields up. And I can't see. My ophthalmologist says medically that's complete baloney and nothing he could do anything about anyway. And besides, he says, Klingons are Federation allies now. It's Romulans who want to destroy you and blow everything you treasure into oblivion.

This pause is going on way too long. Minutes? Seconds? The crap in my head runs at all speeds. No way to know. Heart rate's up, though. I have to speak, open my mouth and make enough words so I can hand the microphone back and get my paper feet off this unsteady skinny perch that feels like a cop is going to run up and grab me from behind yelling “Don't do it, kid, don't jump!” I've liked cops since I was a kid. Cops have always come through for me. Stop. Stop following every random thought down a rabbit hole. You know better. Focus on here. Focus on now.

Back in charge, I blink, smile, cease with the OCD throat clearing, push down paper slippers, swallowed flies, floaters,

Romulans, cops saving me from suicide, get a handle on my breathing and the slippery microphone. But all the throat clearing has made a huge glob of phlegm that's taken over all the space behind my teeth and I can't spit it out and now my mouth is too dry to swallow, and with all the random thoughts and rabbit hole shut down, all that's left is "Phony, phony, bobony bananaramarony – *Phony.*"

What the hell am I doing up here? The people standing with me on this riser are substantial, respected art people. I'm an ex-TV writer who twenty years ago just said yes. Then they and their whole community of wildly talented artists invaded the show I was running and for two years filled this nighttime soap with original set decoration, props, costumes, all made for the stories and characters, most filled with subtle topical political statements, and all reflecting the depth and care with which they were made.

So that was it. All I did was open the door, and I was rewarded with, by far and away, the two years of programming I am most proud of in all my time in Hollywood.

In the middle of this half second or five minute silent storm, the respected art person standing next to me, Constance Penley catches my eye and seems to know what I was going through. She smiles and hands me a bottle of water, a lifeline. I gulp, wash down the glob of doubt in my throat, and start talking, an avalanche of talking. Thanked Mel Chin, and everyone there, went on and on and on. I don't remember anything I said; just that it was too long. I hope I got in some of what I felt about all of them and their work.

But I don't know. I was too concerned with my own feelings to notice what was going on with the people I was talking to.

That's the troubling thing to me about the interior storms, mind burrowing, self-doubt, fear, anxiety, confusion, self-loathing depression, manic episodes and panic attacks that are pretty much permanent campers inside the wiring of many of us who have mental health issues. Whatever your primary diagnosis, ADHD, Hypomanic, Bipolar, Depression, General Anxiety Disorder, or something else on one spectrum or another, it seems like the other stuff gets hitched to you in a comorbid trailer, ready to jump to the driver's seat whenever you get some control on your primary. And they all want you to go inside, and to go as deep and dark as they can take you. Farther and farther into haunts of regret and shame and away from the light and mystery in other people's eyes, and the music of their stories.

For many years, I bristled at words like "disability," "impairment" and "disorder." I resented the judgement and diminishing nature of those labels. I rejected that mindset, feeling it was limiting. Then sometime in 2007, during a lunch in Hawaii with the quadriplegic writer, performer, and disability activist, Brian Shaughnessy, I began to see things completely differently. We'd been talking about everything from solo shows, books, politics, doctors, and family when out of the blue he said, "Your problem, Frank, is you don't accept your disability"

"What?" I said, "No I don't accept it *as* a disability, I don't accept the label."

Brian laughed and said, "It's not a label, numbnuts, it's a fact. Why the hell waste time denying what's real? I sure as hell don't. And neither does my blind friend Michael. There's great power in acceptance, the power of accepting that you experience the world differently that the regular Joe because your life experience is totally different, and then surprising the hell out of the regulars. Michael and I pretty much advertise our difference with society. But you look pretty normal, you can pass. Until you open your mouth talk like you do, going all over the place and still make great sense if somebody takes the time to listen. But most folks don't. You're pretty nuts, man. You should tell people the truth about it. You might get other people to open up too."

Not too much later I started writing about my ADHD, alcoholism, and my ADHD kids. And, like Brian, trying to tell my stories without complaint, just as messages from a family with disorders and disabilities that brings the world into a different focus for us that some other people might recognize.

This last November after the election I thought about that lunch with Brian as I headed back to the New York gallery for a taped panel discussion about the art in Melrose Place. There was a change in mood because of the election results, a sense of doom. The Romulans had taken over. But as the discussion began, the mood changed. The talk turned to the power of art to challenge simplistic thinking about race, income disparity, health care, the disability community and mental health.

And I participated, talking freely, and listening and learning. And I started seeing the power of artists who had the courage to show the world how they saw it, experienced it, and how they wanted it to change for the better. But that means engaging in the world, shaking off self-obsessions to look forward and outward.

For me, this realization or maybe rebirth of a realization I keep having, I don't know. But this time it felt like a powerful tool to get me out of my own head. We can look outwards with art, writing, self-expression or any kind of engagement with others in the effort to make all of us who are different visible and heard in a world that needs all the difference it can get.

A MARRIAGE OF MESSY MINDS

"**O**h God! Listen to me will you? Just for one stupid second try to understand what I'm feeling! I'm... I'm... I don't know, balled up inside! I can't say what I mean! I'm scared of myself!"

At this point I'm sobbing, and I can't catch my breath - I'm dizzy, hyperventilating – good thing I'm in a fetal position on the bedroom floor of Margaret's and my new duplex apartment in Los Angeles. Don't want to start off our relationship falling down and breaking furniture. Its 1984, we've just moved in together, and this is Margaret's first time with one of my fits.

After a short disagreement with her about nothing, I'm having an extreme panic attack (though I didn't know that then). In my late twenties and early thirties I let my unacknowledged, untreated mental mess take me over head to toe and raise an obscene monstrous ruckus. That way people who cared about me could appreciate how miserable I was, and do what I wanted, whatever it was, which would make things better, which it never did.

In my fits with my two previous wives and multiple previous girlfriends I rode this hot drama hard, spurring the confusion and self-hatred on until it spewed out at my companion in blaring tear-filled chock-full-o-blame chaos. Later, I came to see that all this crap was a futile stab at dodging a ten ton depression I could feel creeping up behind me on little elephant feet. It would wait. Until, drama done, I was safe, spent, and cozy, then stomp me flat. Hence the many failed relationships.

The pattern of all this had a rhythm. My girlfriend/wife would stay in the mess of the moment with me – argue, reason with me and sympathize. We'd make up. I'd get flattened, go dark for a week or two. When I pulled out of that, we'd be fine for three or four months, and then that elephant began to creep up behind me again and I'm off into another fit. Sooner or later, I was on my own again.

But Margaret doesn't fit the pattern. As I writhe on the bedroom floor, I notice that I'm not hearing any reaction from her. I get my breathing under control and sit up to face her where she had been sitting on the bed. She isn't there. I look around. She isn't here at all. I've been playing to an empty room. I call her name but no answer. I get up, wipe the snot and tears off my face and calling her name again, go downstairs to the living room. Margaret's sitting on the couch, arms crossed, looking straight ahead. I sit down next to her and reach out. She pulls away. I say I'm sorry, I say sometimes I can't express myself, I get anxious, my feelings take over... Not a peep from her. She stares at the wall. I shut up. It's quiet for a long time. Cars drive by outside. One car parks, people get out, walk away chatting. Another car goes by. Another. A dog barks.

After a century of this, she takes a breath, turns her head and looks at me. "You were out of control," she says. I start in with my emotions are hard to control, that I'll work on it, and, and...

She holds up her hand. "I need to feel safe, Frank. If I don't, I can't stay here. And right now, I don't feel safe at all."

Always in the past this was my cue to grab my bag and strut on out like Popeye, leaving with "I am what I am and that's all that I am, if you can't accept that, then too bad." I've always protected myself first. I knew somewhere inside there was a part of me that was not all right, and that if exposed, could break the rest of me to pieces. The pattern of my relationships kept me safe. But now for the first time I knew that the safety of the person next to me was more important to me than my own. And I had no idea why until I said it out loud.

"I love you, Margaret," I said, "And I promise I'll do anything you need to keep you safe." She leaned against my shoulder, took my hand.

"No more yelling would be a start," she said.

We got married the following year, and through our ongoing thirty-three years together, with the help of plenty of couples therapy and individual therapy, especially on my side, I never yelled again. At Margaret, anyway. We had a couple of kids and when I began to yell at them, we added family therapy, and that stopped too. We weathered medical, career and financial disasters and rebirths, buy house, sell house, so what? Baby needs open-heart surgery? Let's do it. Margaret was calm at the tiller, keeping a weather eye on my moods, with an occasional sharp "Don't you freak out on me" shot across my bow.

Then both kids and I were all diagnosed with ADHD, I had – for me – a relatively quiet and relatively short breakdown. Margaret was diagnosed as A-Okay neuro-typical, and the rest of us were put on meds immediately. Margaret was to make sure we all took them on schedule. But here's the thing, I knew we were all going to be all right because Margaret is big-hearted and tough. And she's got a clear reality-based vision of life and a weird, edgy sense of humor to prove it.

A couple of months later, everything seems to be working well, calm waters, clear sky. And Margaret had the first of three completely quiet, completely incapacitating severe panic attacks that brought EMT's to our house, hospital stays for her, and a rude awakening for me.

* * * *

"Do you have your wife's ID?"

I stare dumfounded at the RN standing behind the Emergency Room nurses' station. She waits, gives me an encouraging smile

"Oh no. No, I forgot her purse at home, I think. Wait no - the paramedics must have it. That's it, I'm sure they have it."

"They say they don't, but that's all right. I just need some basic information for now. Has your wife been to this hospital before?"

But I don't hear her. I've got my wallet open on the counter between us pulling out cards, money and paper none of which have any use or information I need. I'm stuck on Margaret's missing purse. Think, I can't think. I'm so godawful stupid. Stupid and dense and stupid. I look up, finally registering her last question.

"What? No. First time. Wait a minute, I'm wrong, maybe she has been here. Last year? I don't know. We thought it was a heart thing then, does that help?"

"No, but I can find out. What's her birthday?"

"Uh, June, no July, no June, that's the sixth month right?"

"That's right, sir."

The ER nurse is being patient, kind, trained in how to handle stressed family members who can't keep it together in an emergency, which throws me into a rage – I'm not like that, I can handle things damn it. I can just see the role playing training she went through with some pre-med jerk named Tag she was hot on who acts loony so she could pat his hand and give him a hug, only Tag was never into her because she was so damn condescending that he married her roommate Celine and they've got a glass house in the Palisades with three kids in private school and she lives alone in some dumpy converted garage in South Pasadena that she rents from her aunt...

"Sir? Your wife's birthday? Or maybe her social security number?" The nurse smiles, she's trying to help me.

Asking for more numbers I can't find in my head doesn't help me – what's her name tag? Phyllis Grant RN. It doesn't *help*, Phyllis. My mind is spinning and frozen solid simultaneously at No wonder Celine and Tag never call you, Phyllis. You're always on their case, wanting answers, answers, answers...

"Her social?"

"If you don't have her birthday, I could use that to pull up her records if she's been here before and the doctors will be able to better understand what's going on with your wife and give her better care," she says

I know, Phyllis. I'm not an idiot. Well clearly I am. Flash of dizziness, I grab the counter, take a breath. A number drops out of the sky.

"Nineteen fifty-six, her birthday," I blurt out. She was born in July, nineteen fifty-six. I think that's right. No I know it is."

"I'm sorry, sir, I need the full date," Phyllis says. Her smile is wearing thin. "The day in July."

"Sure, sure," I say, and I grit my teeth, dig in and push my broken, frozen, spinning synapses down inside to find and pull out the one day of the month that I always remember every year to bring flowers, candy, dinner, trips, books, a Sub-Zero side by side, whatever she desires to my wife, girlfriend, lover and the only reason life makes any sense at all. But all I can find is Tag and Celine in their glass house in the Palisades making cruel jokes about Phyllis having to deal with me as they have a dinner of blackened tuna and snow peas with a Napa white zinfandel.

"Stop it! You're not real!" Uh oh, I just yelled that out loud. I must now look dangerously deranged. But because God sometimes hands out a miracle for his own amusement, before anyone can call security, Lettie, a family friend who stayed at home with our kids, comes rushing in with the two of them in their pajamas - and Margaret's purse. She takes over with a relieved Phyllis and I sit down and hold my worried kids close. I don't need a brain for that.

This happened nearly twenty years ago. I was in my late forties, seemingly a successful adult male with some degree of sense and I'd just spent twenty minutes in a Pasadena hospital at the nurses' station stunned and mumbling as I blindly spun down a hyperfocus rabbit hole, focused solely on my failure to find any date, number or name that could help my trembling, sweating wife as she was wheeled past me and disappeared behind the gray curtain of an ER treatment room. Looking back on it now, I think I was so focused on my own failure and shortcomings that I made up some people to take the blame off me.

I'd been tangled up with my disorderly brain since I was a kid, and starting in my late teens, had poured my confused heart out to my share of psychologists, psychiatrists, couple and family therapists, and non-medical folks from priests to psychics. Finally though, I'd been diagnosed with ADHD and a bunch of other junk for maybe a month and a half before that ER visit, and had begun treatment. But partly because I thought my new meds would fix it all for me, I still hadn't started the work to understand how my unorthodox brain wiring and my emotional unpredictability connected, or what triggers to look for and get ahead of, and not the faintest idea how to get some control of my responses to unexpected events barging in from the outside world.

So, that forty-something me back then was relieved when the ER doc came out and told me that Margaret didn't have anything wrong with her heart. But then he said that she'd been having panic attacks of increasing intensity, length, and frequency for months. This was serious, he said, nothing to mess around with. She was prescribed anti-anxiety meds and also referred to a psychiatrist where she started SSRI meds for her clinical depression, which as it turns out, runs through her family. She'd hid all of this from herself and us the best she could with a steel-plated cover of energetic super competency, self-depreciating humor, earlier and earlier bedtimes, sporadic naps, and compulsive shopping.

But she didn't have to work too hard for me not to notice. In our house the structure had a gorgeous simplicity: Margaret was the sane responsible one in charge. I was the nut - with all the privileges of self-absorption and irresponsibility that comes with the designation.

You'd think that the serious nature of Margaret's diagnoses and the discovery of the lengths she took to hide her symptoms from me and the kids might have spurred me into an awakening back then – a realization that even though I obviously had some mental issues, disorders, whatever, those concerns and whether or how well I was dealing with them, didn't always come first. And when I let them get in the way of really seeing and understanding with any depth what the love of my life and best friend had been and was still going through, my problems didn't matter at all.

But no, that realization and the full understanding of what it meant took a lot of work and long time to show up.

In the meantime, the show I was on got canceled. But I got another job, a show in Hawaii. We decided to go all in - sold the house, packed up the kids and moved to paradise. Once we got there, we'd all be fine. I was sure of it. But, what did I know? I was still the nut.

NEVER LET GO

A middle-aged couple walks hand in hand along a rocky beach on a calm late afternoon.

A light autumn breeze blows off the lake. You can see the ease of many shared years between them, their conversation a shorthand of few words, a smile, a gesture or two. They stop when he breaks away, runs ahead to pick up a flat piece of driftwood with a smooth triangular piece of green beach glass wedged into it, then runs back and presents it to her.

"Amazing, huh? It's like a sailboat for big beetles and teensy ants. Who's in charge you think?" She laughs, accepts the gift, and takes back his hand, anchoring his enthusiasms to her, giving them meaning. You can see she's the steady one, the one in charge. Always has been. He's fine with that.

They leave the beach as night falls. The full moon lights a path they follow into the woods. They have flashlights now, they're heading home. They walk closer to each other, her arm wrapped around his. The tops of the pine trees whip in the gusts of an approaching storm. Thick clouds roll in and cover the moon. But neither of them seems afraid. They've been through things like this and worse before. And they're together. So they're fine. She stumbles, recovers, pulls closer to him. She jokes to keep him from worrying, he does the same. But her flashlight fails. No, you have to squeeze it to make it light, over and over. She always been able to do it before, but as hard as she tries, she can't now. Exhaustion seems to rush from her hand and arm swallowing the rest of her, and the light slips out of her fingers.

No bother, he can light their way. And even as everything around them slowly becomes darker, colder and more unfamiliar, they walk on. But she no longer jokes, and doesn't respond to his. She doesn't respond at all – every bit of her surviving energy focused on holding on to him and forcing one stumbling step forward after another as they push through the dense pine forest. They can't afford to stop.

But he does. The path has ended at a small patch of grass just big enough for the two of them to sit huddled together. The wind has stopped but the moon is still hidden and it's still cold and getting colder. Neither of them speaks now. His flashlight is getting dimmer and he hasn't the strength to make it brighter. He has to stop trying for a minute and rest. He'll pick it back up in a second. They wrap their arms around each other and the driftwood boat falls out of her jacket pocket. The embedded green beach glass shines in the fading glow of his flashlight before it winks out.

"Are you all right?" Margaret asks.

"Yeah, I'm fine," I say, and rub my eyes. Our house sits on a hill in Georgia; our bedroom window faces the backyard that slopes down into a small forest within and beyond our back fence. I must have been staring out there for quite a while. "I was just daydreaming," I say and lean over to her side of the bed and kiss her. We spend a lot of time in bed. Not as much as we did a month or two ago, but usually an hour or so after breakfast, the same after lunch. We read, talk some, hold hands, breathe.

"You looked so sad," she says. "I worry that I'm making you miserable."

"You're not. You never could."

She takes my hand. "I mean that this, my depression, fighting it, it's taken over everything, for almost a whole freaking year. It has to be wearing you out. It's wearing me down to the bone."

My wife, Margaret, has been in a long, frightening and deadening marathon struggle with a steel-cored, sticky, mean-spirited gray depression. This is the worst episode of her clinical depression she's ever experienced. It has been bound and determined to exhaust and smother her with twisted intricate self-hatred that at times seemed impossible to untangle before she became completely unraveled and gave up. But she never gave up. And now because of her determination and strength, and with the help of docs and meds, she's pulling free of its ugly grasp. But yeah, it has been a hard year, especially for this ADHD husband who's so used to being the crazy one in the family. And she's always been the one who looked out for me. So I not only love her, I owe her. I tell her no, I'm not worn out, I'm fine.

"I want you to know something." She pulls me over to her and hugs me. We're nose to nose.

"What?" I say.

She kisses me - for a long time. It reminds me of the long romantic fevered kisses when we were first together. Then she pulls back, and looks at me. "I never would have made it through this without you," she says.

She woke up first. The storm had passed. It was still cold, but early morning light was sneaking in through the trees. She leaned over, picked up the driftwood boat and put it back in her pocket. When she leaned back against him, she noticed a bright red cardinal land on a branch above them, flutter its wings, fly back the way they had come, and hang a sharp left through a break in the trees. Another path. She woke him and they were off again, hand in hand, finding their way out of the woods.

ABOUT THE AUTHOR

Off-Broadway playwright, longtime television writer and producer, Frank South has spent the last nine years primarily writing about life as an ADHD adult. He performed his one-man show *Pay Attention* for extended runs in Honolulu and Los Angeles. His stories and articles have been published in ADDitude magazine and in blog posts at ADDitudemag.com and have been reprinted in other magazines and websites.

He's been featured in programs about Adult ADHD on *Second Opinion* for PBS and *Rock Center* for NBC News.

websites: **www.franksouth.net**

www.rattlesnakepublishing.com

facebook: **Rattlesnake Publishing Inc.**

email: franksouth@franksouth.net

Please leave a review of "A Chicken in the Wind and How He Grew" at amazon.

Made in the USA
Las Vegas, NV
16 September 2022

55429554R00152